# OTTAWA

## A COLOURGUIDE

Edited by Carol Martin and Kevin Burns
Photography by David Barbour

FORMAC PUBLISHING COMPANY LIMITED

# CONTENTS

# Contents




Formac Publishing Company Limited
5502 Atlantic Street
Halifax, Nova Scotia
B3H 1G4

Printed and bound in Canada.

Distributed in the United States by:
Seven Hills Book Distributors
49 Central Avenue
Cincinnati, Ohio, 45202

Distributed in the United Kingdom by:
World Leisure Marketing
9 Downing Road
West Meadows Industrial Estate
Derby DE 21 6HA
England

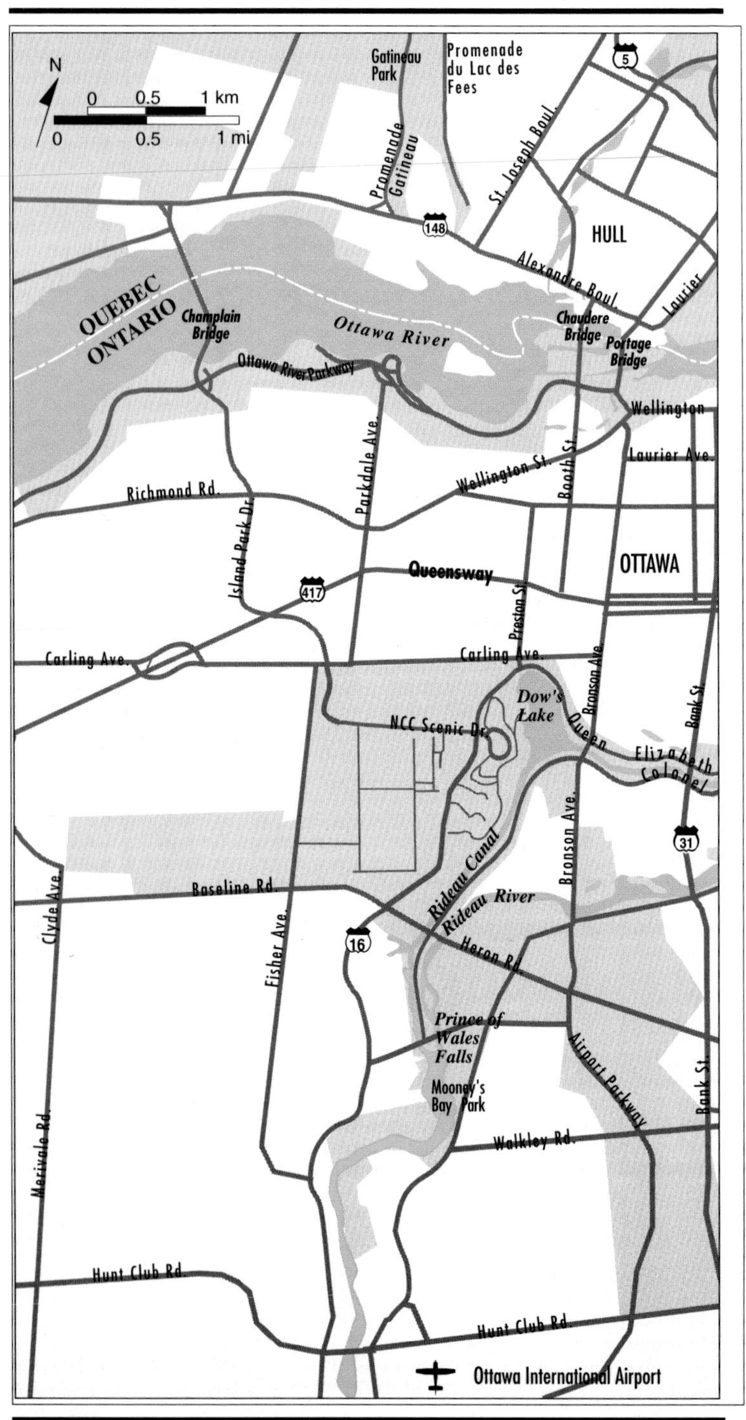
N
0 0.5 1 km
0 0.5 1 mi
Gatineau Park
Promenade du Lac des Fees
Promenade Gatineau
St. Joseph Boul.
5
148
HULL
Alexandre Boul.
Laurier
QUEBEC
ONTARIO
Champlain Bridge
Ottawa River
Chaudere Bridge
Portage Bridge
Ottawa River Parkway
Wellington
Laurier Ave.
Parkdale Ave.
Wellington St.
Booth St.
Richmond Rd.
Island Park Dr.
Queensway
417
OTTAWA
Preston St.
Carling Ave.
Carling Ave.
Bronson Ave.
Dow's Lake
Queen
Elizabeth
Colonel
Bank St.
NCC Scenic Dr.
31
Rideau Canal
Bronson Ave.
Baseline Rd.
Rideau River
Clyde Ave.
Fisher Ave.
16
Heron Rd.
Prince of Wales Falls
Airport Parkway
Mooney's Bay Park
Bank St.
Walkley Rd.
Merivale Rd.
Hunt Club Rd.
Hunt Club Rd.
Ottawa International Airport

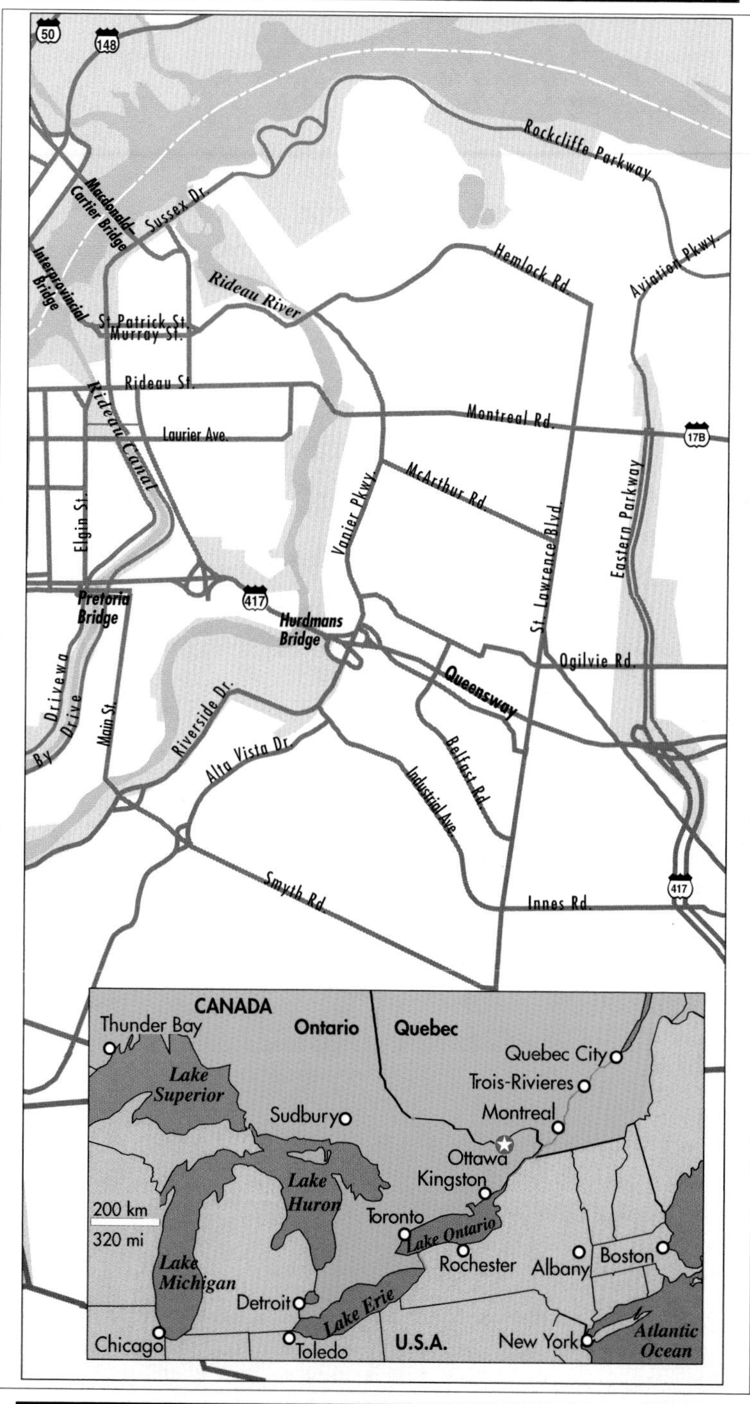
50
148
Rockcliffe Parkway
Macdonald-Cartier Bridge
Sussex Dr.
Interprovincial Bridge
Hemlock Rd.
Aviation Pkwy.
Rideau River
St. Patrick St.
Murray St.
Rideau St.
Rideau Canal
Montreal Rd.
17B
Laurier Ave.
McArthur Rd.
Elgin St.
Vanier Pkwy.
St. Laurence Blvd.
Eastern Parkway
Pretoria Bridge
417
Hurdmans Bridge
Ogilvie Rd.
Queensway
Driveway
By Drive
Main St.
Riverside Dr.
Alta Vista Dr.
Belfast Rd.
Industrial Ave.
Smyth Rd.
Innes Rd.
417
CANADA
Thunder Bay
Ontario
Quebec
Quebec City
Lake Superior
Trois-Rivieres
Sudbury
Montreal
Ottawa
Kingston
Lake Huron
200 km
320 mi
Toronto
Lake Ontario
Rochester
Albany
Boston
Lake Michigan
Detroit
Lake Erie
Chicago
Toledo
U.S.A.
New York
Atlantic Ocean

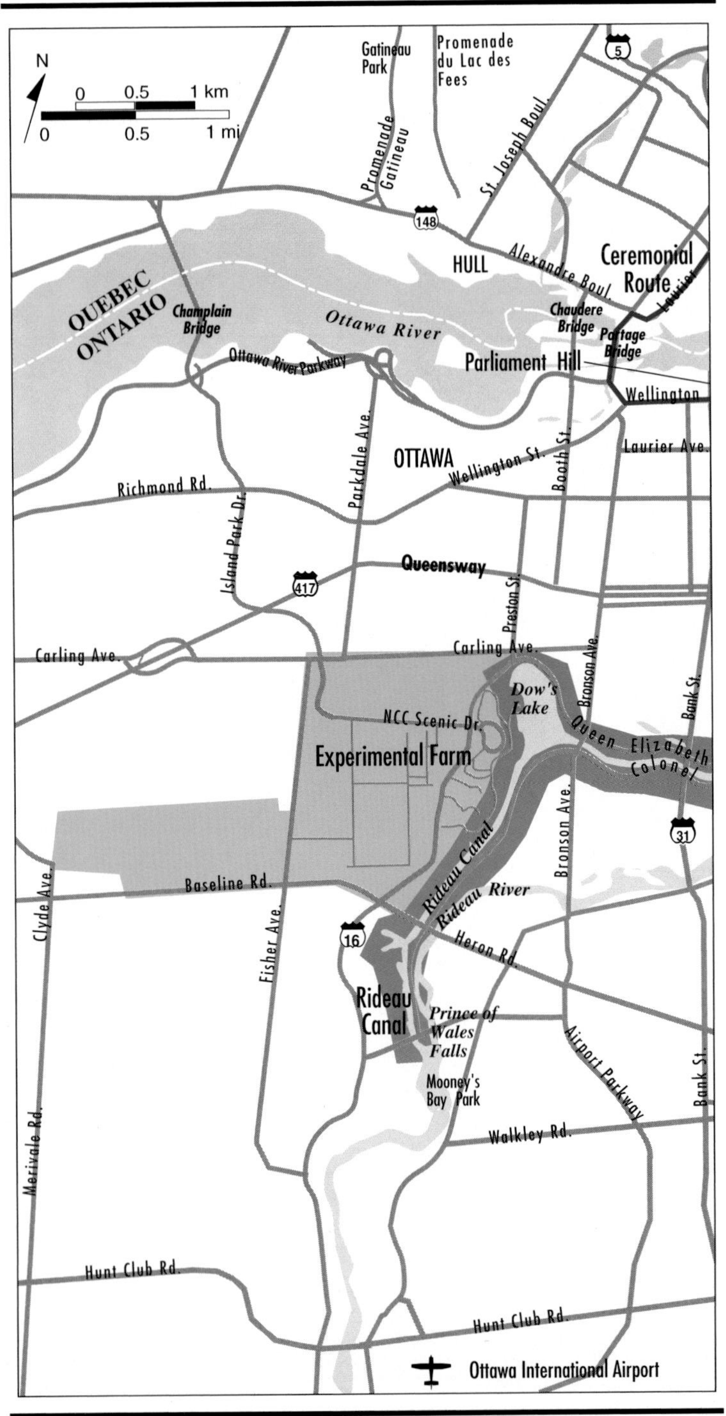
N
0 0.5 1 km
0 0.5 1 mi
Gatineau Park
Promenade du Lac des Fees
Promenade Gatineau
St. Joseph Boul.
5
148
HULL
Alexandre Boul.
Ceremonial Route
Laurier
QUEBEC
ONTARIO
Champlain Bridge
Ottawa River
Chaudere Bridge
Portage Bridge
Ottawa River Parkway
Parliament Hill
Wellington
Parkdale Ave.
Booth St.
Laurier Ave.
OTTAWA
Wellington St.
Richmond Rd.
Island Park Dr.
Queensway
417
Preston St.
Carling Ave.
Carling Ave.
Bronson Ave.
Dow's Lake
Bank St.
NCC Scenic Dr.
Queen Elizabeth
Colonel
Experimental Farm
Rideau Canal
Bronson Ave.
31
Clyde Ave.
Baseline Rd.
Rideau River
16
Fisher Ave.
Heron Rd.
Rideau Canal
Prince of Wales Falls
Airport Parkway
Mooney's Bay Park
Bank St.
Merivale Rd.
Walkley Rd.
Hunt Club Rd.
Hunt Club Rd.
Ottawa International Airport

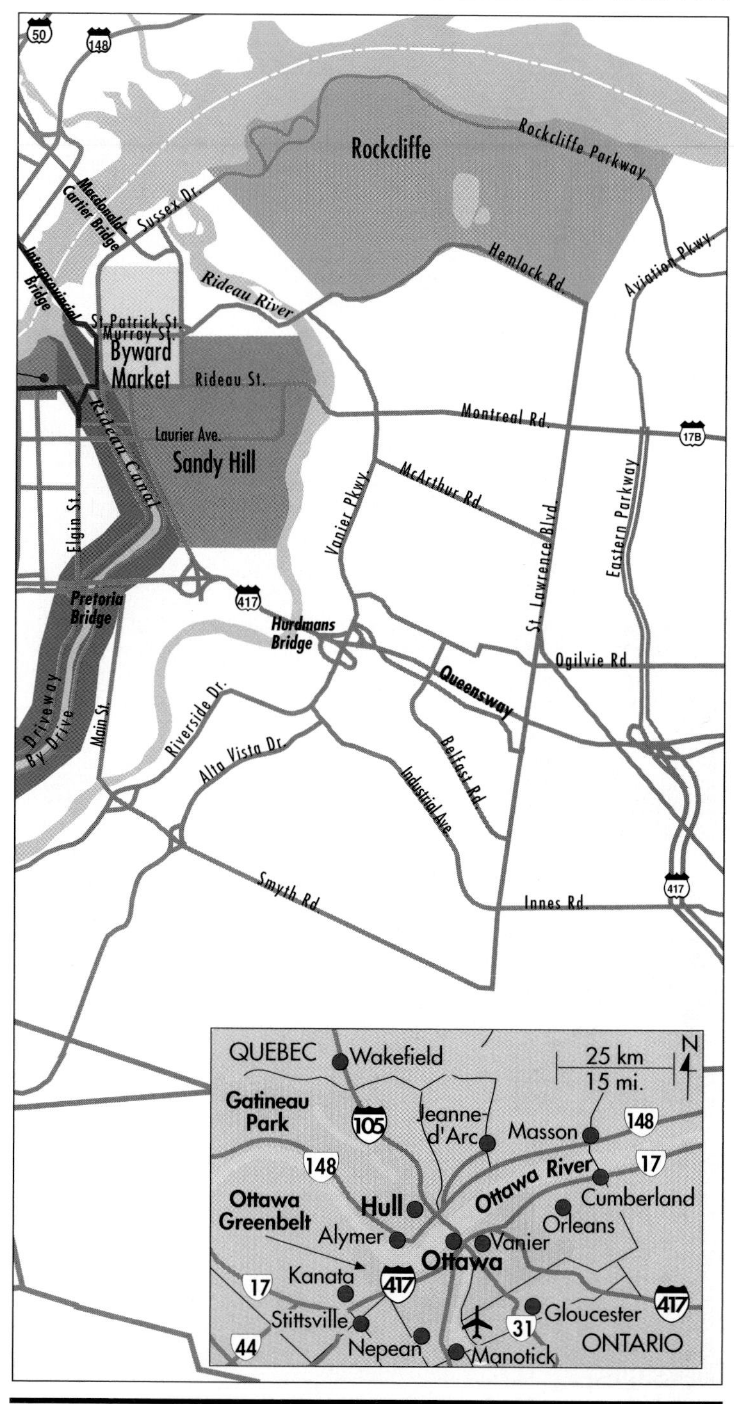
Rockcliffe
Rockcliffe Parkway
Hemlock Rd.
Aviation Pkwy.
Macdonald-Cartier Bridge
Sussex Dr.
Interprovincial Bridge
Rideau River
St. Patrick St.
Murray St.
Byward Market
Rideau St.
Montreal Rd.
Laurier Ave.
Sandy Hill
Rideau Canal
McArthur Rd.
Vanier Pkwy
St. Laurence Blvd.
Eastern Parkway
Elgin St.
Pretoria Bridge
Hurdmans Bridge
Ogilvie Rd.
Queensway
Driveway By Drive
Main St.
Riverside Dr.
Alta Vista Dr.
Belfast Rd.
Industrial Ave.
Smyth Rd.
Innes Rd.
QUEBEC
Wakefield
25 km
15 mi.
N
Gatineau Park
Jeanne-d'Arc
Masson
Ottawa River
Cumberland
Ottawa Greenbelt
Hull
Orleans
Alymer
Vanier
Ottawa
Kanata
Stittsville
Nepean
Manotick
Gloucester
ONTARIO

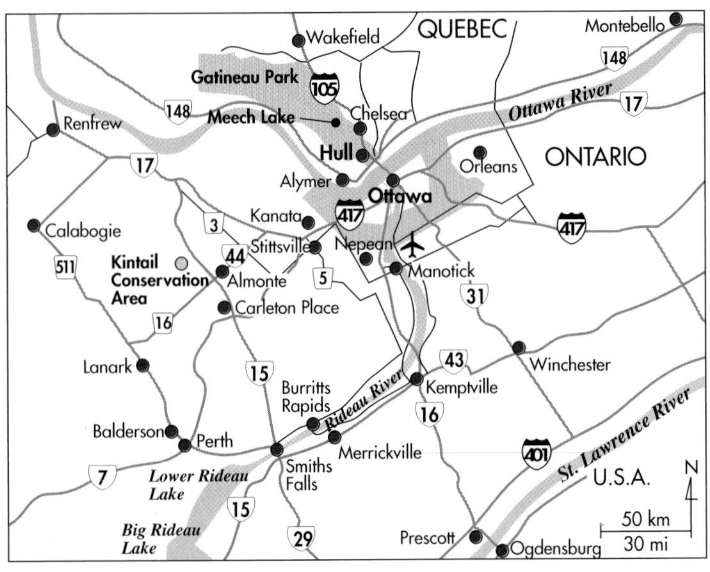

For an excursion to the beautiful Gatineau Hills and the historic villages of the area see page 146.

For a tour of Lanark County, a vibrant area, rich in history and culture see page 152.

For a relaxing drive, complete with beautiful scenery, heritage architecture and interesting shops and restaurants, see Manotick, Burritts Rapids and Merrickville at page 160.

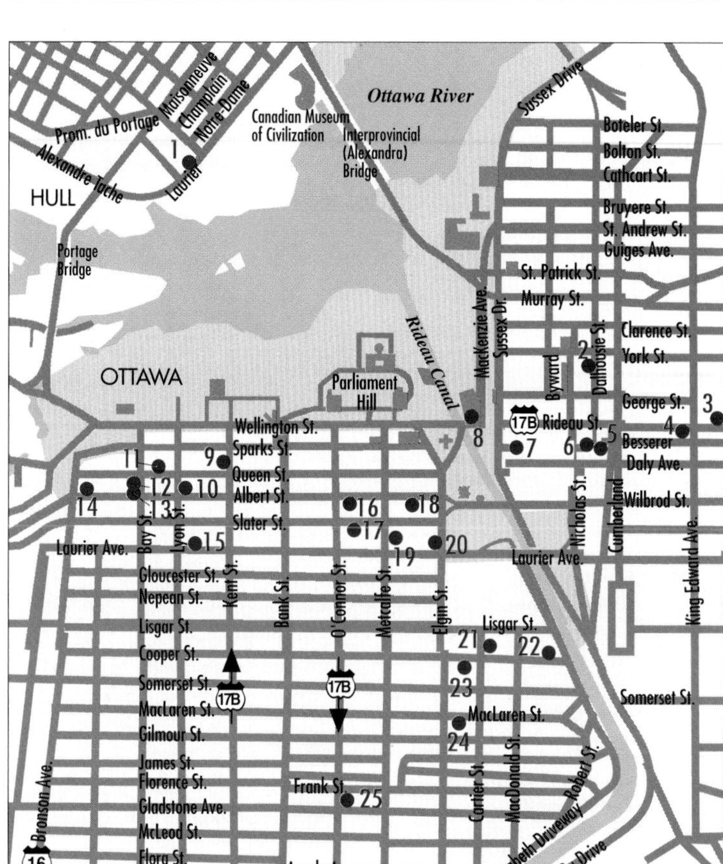


1. Clarion Hotel Centre Ville
2. Market Square Inn
3. Town House Motor Hotel
4. Quality Hotel Downtown
5. Les Suites Hotel Ottawa
6. Novotel Hotel
7. The Westin Hotel Ottawa
8. Chateau Laurier
9. Radisson Hotel Ottawa Centre
10. Citadel Ottawa Hotel and Conference Centre
11. Delta Ottawa Hotel & Suites
12. Webb's Motel
13. Albert at Bay Suite Hotel
14. Doral Inn
15. Minto Place Suite Hotel
16. Sheraton Ottawa Hotel & Towers
17. Howard Johnson Plaza Hotel
18. Capital Hill Hotel and Suites
19. Days Inn
20. Lord Elgin Hotel
21. Embassy Hotel & Suites
22. Ramada Hotel & Suites Ottawa
23. Cartier Place Hotel
24. The Business Inn
25. Best Western Victoria Park Suites
26. Super 8 Hotel Downtown Ottawa

For accommodation outside the downtown area, see Listings, pg. 176.

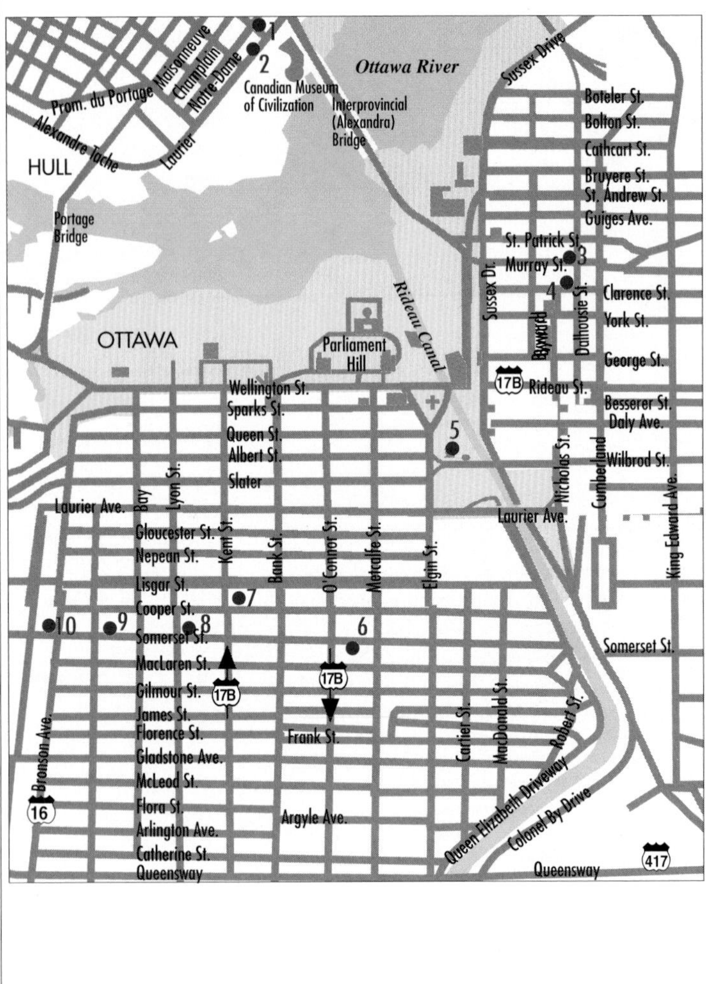


1. Le Tartuffe
2. Café Henry Burger
3. Domus
4. Clair de Lune
5. Le Cafe
6. Mamma Teresa Ristorante
7. Coriander Thai
8. Fairouz
9. Mekong Restaurant
10. Fuliwah Restaurant

**Other recommended restaurants:**

Siam Kitchen, 1050 Bank Street
Newport Restaurant, 334 Richmond Road
Geraldo's Ristorante, 200 Beechwood Avenue
Café Wisigoth, 84B Beechwood Avenue
Maple Lawn Café, 529 Richmond Road
Opus Bistro, 1331 Wellington Street
Il Vagabondo, 186 Barrette Street

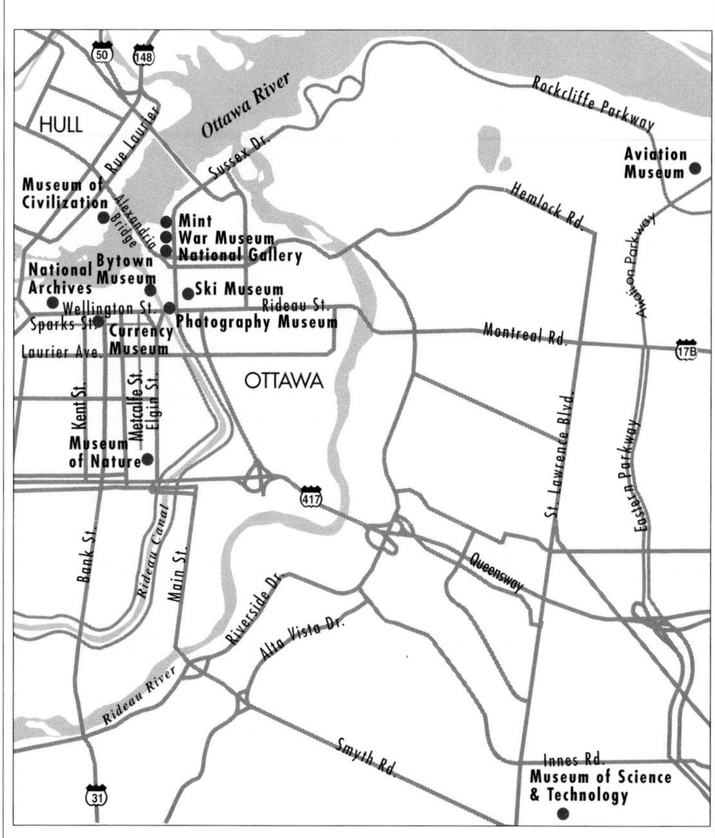


For descriptions of these galleries and museums, turn to the page numbers as listed below. For detailed information on hours of operation and phone numbers, see the Listings section, p. 184.

Bytown Museum p. 81
Canadian Museum of Civilization (CMC) p. 57
Canadian Museum of Contemporary Photography p. 81
Canadian Museum of Nature p. 65
Canadian Ski Museum p. 51
Canadian War Museum p. 82
Children's Museum (in the CMC) p. 60
Currency Museum p. 80
National Archives p. 80
National Aviation Museum p. 77
National Gallery of Canada p. 52
National Museum of Science and Technology p. 74
National Postal Museum (In the CMC) p. 60

Welcome to this guide to Ottawa, one of the top destinations for travelling Canadians as well as a growing number of international visitors!

This *Ottawa Colourguide* has been designed to enrich your visit to Canada's capital city. Ottawa is a city of layers — once a military outpost and lumber town, now a capital city, rapidly diversifying as the federal civil service shrinks in size thanks to cutbacks and decentralization. Our editors suggest you use this book to "peel back the layers" of Ottawa to experience the city with a knowledgeable Ottawa resident as your companion. The chapters in this guidebook are the work of people who know and love their city and want to share it with you.

The introductory maps offer an overview of the city, its neighbourhoods and its region. The hotels and restaurants map can help you choose the right location for your stay — and some of the best choices for a quick lunch or a fine dinner. Two chapters on the city's history tell the story of how it was that Ottawa became the country's capital and explain the significance of the canal running through its centre.

The next section of the guide presents Ottawa's best, starting with its central focus, Parliament Hill, and describing the many fine museums that together make up the feature of the city most appealing to visitors, and embracing one attraction you might not at first expect in a capital city — a farm. Our chapter on The Experimental Farm explains why it's a place not to be missed.

The Features section offers independent advice on what Ottawa offers in the way of shopping, dining out, night life and entertainment and outdoor recreation. There's a chapter on power in Ottawa, and one on Ottawa's bilingual character.

The section on Neighbourhoods and Excursions guides you through three of the city's most interesting areas, and suggests excursions you may wish to take into the surrounding region.

In the pages at the back of the guide is the listings section. Here you will find detailed information on accommodation, dining, shopping, museums, and galleries. Every significant attraction and service mentioned in the text is included in the listings, and often the listings go beyond to offer you practical information we expect you'll

find useful on the city and what it offers.

Like the other guides in our Colourguide series, this is an independent guide. Its authors and contributors have made suggestions on the sites and attractions they see as among the best in the area. No payments or contributions of any kind have been solicited or accepted by the creators or publishers of this guide.

One note of caution: While every effort was made to ensure that the guide was accurate when it went to press, things do change over time. If specific information is important to your plans (say, a particular restaurant and its hours of opening) please phone to confirm that the information in this book is still current.

If you experience something different than what you've read here — or if you find something new — please let us know. Write to the address on the copyright page (page 3).

This book has been compiled and edited by two fine and experienced editors who know and love Ottawa, Carol Martin and Kevin Burns. They recruited knowledgeable and experienced contributors and turned this book into something of a community literary project in the process. As the publishers of this book, we would like to thank Carol and David and acknowledge the work they did, and also to thank the contributors for helping us put together what we hope will be recognized as the definitive guide to Ottawa.

The photographer, editor and contributors who have created this book are:

CAROL MARTIN is an editor and publishing consultant who grew up in and around Ottawa. She was a founding partner in the independent Canadian publishing house, Peter Martin Associates. Her book for teenagers, *Martha Black: Gold Rush Pioneer*, was published in 1996.

KEVIN BURNS is an Ottawa-based writer and editor. After teaching theatre at the University of Alberta and producing radio for the CBC in Toronto, he moved to Ottawa in 1995.

DAVID BARBOUR is a freelance photographer living and teaching in Ottawa. His photographs have appeared in library exhibitions in Ottawa.

### CONTRIBUTORS

SANDRA ABMA is a freelance broadcaster known to CBC Radio listeners for her coverage of the local music scene and movie reviews.

PETER CALAMAI is a freelance journalist who has written about national politics during the terms of five federal governments.

DORY CAMERON is a freelance writer who, with her two sons, has explored the region on skis, skates, bikes and by canoe.

GORDON CULLINGHAM, former CBC producer and Publications Chairman for the Ontario Historical Society, has produced three driving tours of heritage waterways in Ontario.

LINDA DALE has been working in museum education and exhibit development for the past 15 years, primarily in topics relating to social issues and women's history

DANIEL DROLET is a bilingual francophone who has written extensively on political and language issues.

TONY GERMAN's Ottawa roots are reflected in his historical adventures for young people. He is known as a novelist, scriptwriter and popular historian.

ROSA HARRIS-ADLER is an award-winning magazine writer now completing her Master's degree in journalism at Carleton University in Ottawa.

ANDREA HOSSACK is a freelance writer and radio producer living in Ottawa while completing her Master's degree in Canadian Studies.

HOPE MACLEAN is a writer and anthropologist who has enjoyed exploring the Gatineau Hills from her home base — a summer cottage near Wakefield — for more than ten years.

PETER MARTIN returned to his roots in Sandy Hill two years ago, following a career as editor and publisher in Toronto. He is an executive member of the Ottawa-Carleton Federation of Citizens' Associations.

JULIE MASON grew up in Ottawa when Westboro was a village and the streetcars ran all the way to Britannia Park. She now lives and writes in Toronto, but enjoys frequent trips to Ottawa.

JOHN MCMANUS, an antique dealer in Merrickville, is interested in local history and architecture. He has developed and presented education programmes at Upper Canada Village.

R.A.J. PHILLIPS, a Member of the Order of Canada, in a writer and historian, former community newspaper publisher, public servant, diplomat and founding executive director of Heritage Canada.

JOE REILLY is a festival organizer and music promoter.

MARY ANN SIMPKINS is a travel writer who spent her childhood in Ottawa and now makes her home in the Glebe.

JOHN TAYLOR is Associate Professor of History at Carleton University in Ottawa. He is the author of *Ottawa: An Illustrated History* and co-editor of *Capital Cities: International Perspectives.*

JANET UREN is a freelance editor and writer who makes her home in Ottawa.

EDWINNA von BAEYER is a freelance writer and editor who is known for writing about Canadian landscape history.

RANDALL WARE is an Ottawa writer and broadcaster and Coordinator of the Canadian Literature Research Service at the National Library of Canada.

- The Publishers

# SETTING THE SCENE

# Ottawa: An Overview

Kevin Burns

Parliament Hill

Ottawa is a fascinating place of shifting power and shifting fortunes, a city of surprising transformations. Peel back the layers and you discover a lumber town, a military outpost, a place reborn upon becoming the nation's capital.

Rideau Canal

Things are not always as they seem here. The youth hostel in the heart of Lower Town was once a jail. This stern, gray edifice, once home to various felons, now provides secure lodging for travellers with limited budgets. Right next door is the Court House. No longer a venue for trial by jury, it

is now known as Arts Court — a visual and performing arts centre.

ARTS COURT

As you uncover the layers of the National Capital Region presented in this guide book, keep your map with you. To know where you are in relation to the water is important, because in Ottawa, all roads lead to water. This

is the place where the Rideau Canal — Colonel John By's engineering feat — the Ottawa River and the Rideau River meet. Divided by the canal, there was once power on one side and commerce on the other. Now the boundaries are blended in much the same way as languages and cultures are in this typically cosmopolitan Canadian city.

BUSKERS

CITY HALL

To discover Ottawa, first take a riverside walk, behind the Parliament buildings, or simply follow the canal. Then, while exploring "official Ottawa," see your reflection in the glass of the corporate towers in the

downtown core, take in the showcase homes, the manicured gardens and the embassies in Rockcliffe and Sandy Hill. Consume your way through the bustling urban

FORMER RAILWAY CENTRE, NOW A CONFERENCE CENTRE

village known as the Glebe. Take a walk through the multicultural celebration that is Somerset Heights. Enjoy the open spaces, the public parks, the gardens, the walking, hiking and biking paths. Take time to feel the excitement at Sparks Street Mall and the lively Byward Market.

I walk down by the canal and the river as often as I can, at least until the snow comes and the pathway is closed off until the spring. I find it helps me feel connected to the many layers of Ottawa. I hope it does the same for you.

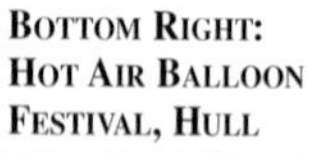

BOTTOM RIGHT: HOT AIR BALLOON FESTIVAL, HULL

# A Touch of History

Tony German

**Wright's Mill, 1823**

Hard to imagine it may be, but today's urbane, well-groomed Ottawa of stately buildings, national monuments, and civilized citizenry was once the roughest, toughest, fightingest town in all of Canada, indeed, in the whole of North America. When Lieutenant Colonel John By arrived in 1826 with a detachment of His Majesty's Sappers and Miners (engineers, in fact) and an assignment to link the Ottawa River and Lake Ontario with a canal, he found little but bush, cedar swamp, and a scattered handful of settlers. Bradish Billings had a property high on the east side of the Rideau River (near Bank Street's Billings Bridge). Abraham and Samuel Dow had farms on the west side backing into swamp, and there was a lonely inn down on the Ottawa River by the Chaudière Falls.

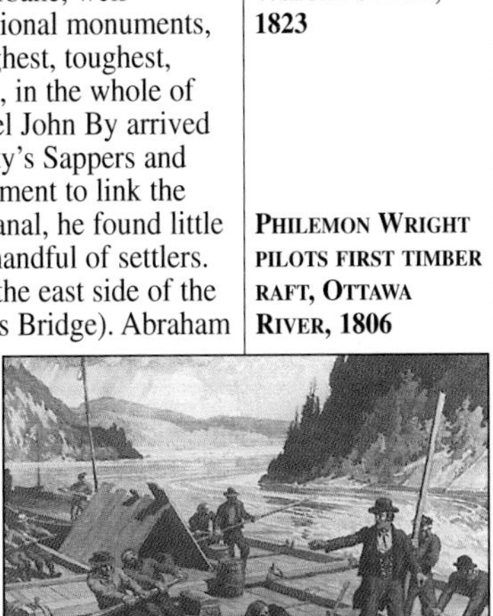

**Philemon Wright pilots first timber raft, Ottawa River, 1806**

Across the Chaudière, on the north side, was the thriving little community of Wright's Town (later called Hull). The town had been founded back in 1800 when Philemon Wright, a Yankee from Massachusetts, had arrived in the area with his family and a few settlers. There was good farmland on the northern, Lower Canada side of the river, waterpower for mills and vast stands of timber for the taking. When

**CREW OF A SQUARED PINE TIMBER RAFT, 1881**

Colonel By came on the scene, Wright's Town was well developed, and it would become a valuable source of skilled labour and supplies for his enterprise.

By 1826, Wright and other entrepreneurs were cutting giant pines by the thousands. Gangs spent the whole winter up in the lumber camps — "shanties" they were called — and, at break-up, they drove their cut down the tributary rivers to the Ottawa. Raftsmen formed the logs into gigantic rafts and floated them downriver to sell in Québec. As the century progressed, the Ottawa Valley became the world's mightiest lumber yard. Each spring, when the winter-hardened shanty boys and raftsmen came roaring out of the bush with cash in their pockets, monster thirsts, and iron fists, every river town endured a roistering, riotous, bibulous time.

### THE CANAL BUILDERS

The Rideau Canal was built in five years with a fierce winter freeze and no power machinery; it was a colossal piece of work. If you follow just that section which lies within the present city limits — from the first flight of locks, past the National Arts Centre, Lansdowne Park and lovely little Dow's Lake to Hog's Back, where the canal joins the Rideau River — you'll get some idea of the enormous amount of human muscle involved.

Most of the muscle was Irish. The Irish were the heavy labour corps of the day, and they started rolling into By's town in the spring of 1827. Mostly without families, they were a rootless, unruly lot. They overflowed their quarters along Rideau Street and, in no time, a ramshackle collection of squatters' shacks, seamy taverns and houses of dubious entertainment sprouted by the canal where the National Arts Centre stands today. This area was quickly dubbed Corkstown, although history does not record whether the name was in honour of the southern Irish seaport where many had embarked, or a tribute to the thousands of corks drawn to slake the Irish thirst. Mud-slides and cave-ins, cholera, malaria and smallpox felled many canal-builders. There was high mortality from untutored, devil-may-care use of gunpowder for blasting. And booze, the curse of the times, was certainly a factor in the demise of many more. Better than Corkstown poteen was the whisky from Squire Wright's distillery, at a shilling a gallon. A labouring Irishman earned four shillings (a dollar) a day and could afford quite enough to fuel his daily toil, and his main recreation — fighting.

Meanwhile, Colonel By laid out Upper Town, west of the canal, reserving Barrack Hill (now Parliament Hill) for the Crown. The more affluent citizens — contractors, businesspeople, artisans — took up lots in Upper Town. On the east side of the canal, across Sapper's Bridge (between the War Memorial and the Chateau Laurier in Confederation Square) was Lower Town, with some swampy and less-desirable locations. It drew working folk, mostly French and Irish Catholics. Around the Byward Market, small businesses, hotels and taverns to rival those of Corkstown sprang up, plus a corps of raffish characters, male and female, who preyed on anyone out for a night on the town. It was a roughshod, brawling little place.

**Circus, c. 1900, on Sappers' Bridge**

By opened his canal in 1832, with a triumphal passage from Kingston to Bytown in the steamboat *Pumper*. He was revered by all, including the rascals. His direction had been nothing short of brilliant. He had been a fair taskmaster and had accounted for every penny spent. Still, he was called to England to face a Parliamentary inquiry into spending more than the initial estimate — an estimate which had been made without any detailed survey. Exonerated, but smeared by the mere fact that he had been called, By received none of the honours and promotions he so richly deserved. One of the great builders of Canada — who counted his days here as the happiest in his life — Lieutenant-Colonel John By died in England after four years, miserably dejected.

### Thomas McKay

By's contractors fared far better, and a lot of them stayed in Bytown to lay a solid base in the community. Thomas McKay, a Scottish stonemason with a Midas touch, had built the first eight locks in the canal. So pleased was By with his work that he threw a banquet and ball in McKay's honour, with an ox roasted whole, and presented him with a fine silver memorial cup. McKay invested his well-earned profit in land east of the Rideau River, built an industrial enterprise at the Rideau Falls, founded the village of New Edinburgh and built his own elegant 11-room Regency villa. At Confederation, the government bought it from his heirs for the governors general to live in and called it Rideau Hall.

**Thomas McKay (1792-1855)**

### The Shiners' War

In 1833, with the canal finished and out-of-work Irish flocking in for jobs and whisky, Bytown turned into a powder keg. The French had a strong grip on lumbering and rafting jobs and a lot of them had settled in Lower Town with their families. They were the only people who were then called "Canadians." A murderous gang of Irish roughnecks who called themselves "Shiners" went after their jobs. Their leader, Peter Aylen, was a wealthy, self-made lumber baron who swaggered around at the head of his riotous mob, defying the magistrates. Beatings, arson, families driven naked into the snow, wells fouled — even people being pitched into the deadly Chaudière — these were frequent events.

A vigilante group did its best to resist. Renowned strongman and rafting foreman Joseph Montferrand finally rallied his Canadian confreres. Legend has it that, single-handed, he took on a gang of twenty Shiners on the bridge to Hull and evened the score by slinging the lot into the Chaudière. Finally, in 1837 — the year of the Upper and Lower Canada Rebellions — every honest, able-bodied man in Bytown joined the militia and the town was brought under reasonable control at last. Peter Aylen moved across to Aylmer and waxed prosperous during many years of lawful pursuits; his family name lives on today at the head of a distinguished Queen Street law firm. Many other Shiner descendants have become pillars of Ottawa society, making up in civic duty for some of their ancestors' dreadful deeds.

**Byward Market, c. 1900**

### Stony Monday

Race, religion, jobs — all were good reasons for a dust-up. Now politics became volatile as well. One Monday morning in 1849, a political group called Reformers gathered in the Byward Market to consider a "Loyal Address" for the forthcoming visit of Governor Lord Elgin. Heckling members of the Tory opposition triggered a riot, which culminated in the two sides blazing away at each other with muskets.

The Tories planned their own political gathering for the following Wednesday and took no chances. They mustered 1,700 men in Upper Town — many of them Orangemen in from the farms — with better than 1,000 muskets. Meanwhile, Reformer Ruggles Wright (son of Philemon Wright, the founder of Wright's Town and a Colonel of Militia in Hull) led 1000 armed men with three cannon across the river by boat. They mustered in the market, where they loaded their cannon with ox-chain.

Up on Barrack Hill, a quick-witted officer named Major Clements smartly dispatched 50 soldiers with two cannon to Sapper's Bridge. There, with bayonets fixed and one loaded cannon pointing up Wellington Street while the other faced down Rideau, the soldiers confronted the two advancing mobs. There were some skirmishes, and some muskets that were captured clearly came from Wright's Armoury, so Major Clements led a mounted troop towards Hull and the armoury. En route, he arrested Reformer Henry Friel, who was galloping to warn his friend Wright. Once in Hull, Clements nabbed Wright and some cronies as they were trundling out more cannon and finally restored

**Wellington Street, 1873**

order — such as it was. Lord Elgin postponed his visit for three years. Major Clements, certain saviour of countless lives, was charged in court with overstepping his authority in arresting Henry Friel. And Friel was elected Mayor of Bytown, with a street named in his honour! The whole affair went down in local memory as "Stony Monday."

### A Capital for Canada

By the 1850s, the enormous production from lumber mills at the Chaudière, and the Rideau and Ottawa River canals, made Bytown into a boom town and lumber barons into millionaires. E.B. Eddy began splitting shingles and soon made himself the world's biggest match manufacturer. J.R. Booth arrived with nine dollars in his pocket and became the biggest-producing lumber magnate in the world. Under Mayor Henry Friel, Bytown became the City of Ottawa and was incorporated on January 1, 1855.

It was during this time that the Legislative Assembly of the combined provinces of Canada East and Canada West, which had been burned out of Montreal in 1849, tired of alternating every four years between Toronto and Québec. The search was on for a permanent Canadian capital. Ottawa mayor J.B. Turgeon now tossed his city's hat in the ring. When the Legislature appealed to Queen Victoria to pick the capital, Governor General Sir Edmund Head sent her the bids from Montreal, Toronto, Kingston, Québec — and Ottawa.

With its earthy population, yowling sawmills, ankle-deep mud, rooting pigs, the stench of smoke from endless fires, and the overpowering reek of cesspools (except in blessed winter), Ottawa was an unlikely starter. Still, Head's confidential advice to the Queen was that the roaring little lumber town on the border of the two Canadas was "the least objectionable" choice, and, as "every city is jealous of every other except Ottawa," it would win "second vote of every place." Here was the classic Canadian compromise, as practiced at party leadership conventions and during affairs of state in Ottawa to this day.

Edward, Prince of Wales, laid the cornerstone of the new Parliament buildings in 1860. Then he took in the two main tourist attractions — the world-famed ride down the Chaudière timber slide and (this time incognito) the tour of the racier side of Ottawa nightlife in the Byward Market. Construction on Parliament Hill was beset by strikes and — naturally — a Royal Commission. But by 1866 the Legislature sat in the partly finished Centre Block. So

**Original Centre Block, Parliament Buildings, 1867**

much money had been spent by 1867 that there was no turning back. Ottawa became, willy-nilly, the capital of the new Dominion of Canada. In the words of historian and writer Goldwin Smith, the change from "sub-Arctic lumber village to political cockpit," had begun.

Twenty years later, Wilfrid Laurier said, "Ottawa is not a handsome city and does not appear destined to become one either." Handsome or not, by 1885 there were electric street lights, then domestic electrical service, from the first hydro station at the Chaudière. That abundant source soon powered the street cars of the Ottawa Electric Railway as Ottawa took the North American lead in public transportation. Prime Minister Laurier himself rode the streetcar daily from his home (now called Laurier House: see Sandy Hill, p. 141) to Parliament Hill.

### The Great Fire

Fires were all too frequent in the nineteenth and early twentieth centuries. In 1900, a small fire in Hull flashed out of control in a brisk breeze, gutted Hull and leaped to the enormous lumber yards across the river. Mills, lumber piles, generating stations, the whole Chaudière area, was destroyed, plus crowded working-class Lebreton Flats and a swath right out to Dow's Lake. Fifteen thousand people were left homeless. Everyone opened hearts and homes and wallets, turned to the task at hand, and rebuilt. Just two years later, in 1902, the Ottawa Valley charted record

**The Great Fire, 1900**

production: enough sawn lumber to build 175,000 modern frame houses. Ottawa's citizens might have been rough around the edges, but, from lumber baron to laundress, they knew how to get on with the job.

### Government House

At the other end of town from the Chaudière and Le Breton Flats, a succession of aristocratic British governors general and their consorts — with their coteries of dashing young officer aides-de-camp, ladies-in-waiting, secretaries and impeccably groomed administrators — turned a steadily expanding Rideau Hall into a miniature court-in-the-wilderness. There were balls and leveés, ceremonial openings of Parliament in full uniform, with ladies in jewels and feathers, "Drawing Rooms" where daughters of lumber barons and local gentry made their debut in society via a curtsey to the governor general, and the marriage stakes, where the top prize was a titled aide-de-camp. Winter was celebrated with banquets in fabulous ice palaces, skating and tobogganing parties, and skiing, introduced to Ottawa in 1887 by an English guest at Rideau Hall. Government House, as Rideau Hall was known, was the opulent hub of uppercrust society.

## INTO THE TWENTIETH CENTURY

Ottawa's real lifeblood continued to come from the forests well into this century. The springtime ritual of roistering shantymen never ceased, making this a rough town on a Saturday night. There were frequent punch-ups between French and Irish, Catholics and Orangemen, or whoever happened to be in the way. But times change. In 1906, the last great timber raft was sent down the Ottawa by J.R. Booth. Sawn lumber had begun to take over from squared timber in Booth's early days, and now pulpwood for the paper mills was in demand.

The dreadful losses and feats of extraordinary valour of the First World War brought Ottawa, and the rest of the country its first real sense of "Canadianness." The National War Memorial, conceived as the centrepiece of a masterful plan for Ottawa's development, was unveiled on the very eve of the Second World War. That war brought about the expansion of the bureaucracy, which stayed on to run big government in the new industrial age and the era of comprehensive social programs.

From wilderness to construction camp, to lumber town, to government centre, to a uniquely beautiful city, all in far less than 200 years, Ottawa has grown in harmony with its incomparable location. Colonel By's canal, which started it all, is now a winter and summer recreational gem. Government and high-tech industry have replaced the forests and rivers and mills as the city's economic base, but its people have always been its core. Recently, new waves of immigrants have added their special energies, talents and richly varied cultures to the old. And down in the Byward Market, if you decide on a night on the town, you'll still feel the beat of old Bytown's lusty heart.

**LATE NINETEENTH-CENTURY QUEEN STREET**

# OTTAWA AS CAPITAL

JOHN TAYLOR

**OTTAWA, C. 1840, PRIOR TO CONSTRUCTION OF PARLIAMENT BUILDINGS**

On the last day of 1857, Ottawa was chosen as the "seat of government" for the Province of Canada. What the Canadian parliament could not decide during the most contentious debate in Canadian history (the issue was put to a vote more than 200 times in less than a decade), a handful of the British elite did. For two more generations, Ottawa would remain a working-class town, and one of the largest woods-based operations in the world. In time, however, "Ottawa" would become less and less the name of a city, and more and more a shorthand for the exercise of power, and for the embodiment of Canadian identity (for more on Ottawa and power, see Power in the Capital, p. 114). By 1867, when the capital of the Province of Canada was converted into the capital of the Dominion, some now-familiar characters, artifacts, and attitudes were already becoming entrenched.

### INFLUENCE OF THE BRITISH EMPIRE

Until 1952 the vice-regal households were British, and, early on, they took over leadership of society. They held court in Scottish entrepreneur Thomas McKay's old mansion, which had been converted into Rideau Hall. Viscount Monck, Lord Lisgar, the Earl of Dufferin, the Marquess of Lorne, the Marquis of Lansdowne, Lord Stanley, the Earl of Aberdeen, the Earl of Minto, Earl Grey, and so on, lent tone to society, sponsored the arts and sports, and gave their names to streets, parks, pavilions, and trophies. Their political masters — Macdonald, Mackenzie, Laurier — ruled parliament and the bureaucracy from majestic buildings on Parliament Hill. Statues of these Prime Ministers and other historical figures now pepper the Hill, the first being that of Sir George-Étienne Cartier (1883-1885).

On the Hill, the Centre Block (see Parliament Hill, p. 32) was home to the Senate, the House of Commons and the elected politicians. The East and West Blocks, or "departmental" buildings, were home to the administrative branch of government: the departmental heads and the "clerks" of what was known as the "civil service." Tucked in the East Block, and now fully restored to its original glory, was the Prime Minister's office, complete with private exit, and the rooms that contained the "efficient secret" of the parliamentary system — the "Cabinet." Behind the Centre Block, overlooking the Ottawa River, is what many consider the architectural gem of Canada — the Parliamentary Library. Nearby is a reconstruction of a Victorian gazebo. These artifacts — and the activities in them — were expressions of British imperial ambitions. Indeed, the site of Parliament is the old Barrack Hill, home to the British soldiers who oversaw construction of the most expensive war measure of its day — the Rideau Canal. The canal had been built to protect the tiny colonies of Upper and Lower Canada from the Americans, the chief enemy on the horizon in the nineteenth century. (See The Rideau Canal, p. 126.)

EARLY TWENTIETH-CENTURY PAVILION, PARLIAMENT HILL

The buildings "on the Hill" were also British in their architectural expression. They were built in what was known at the time as "civil Gothic," a style believed by some to embody the genius of the British race. It was the style of the British Houses of Parliament, and is rare as a civil form. Instead, it is usually reserved for churches and educational institutions. Westminster, Ottawa and Budapest are among the few capital cities that incorporate Gothic into a national expression. For Ottawa, the Gothic style, while an expression of British loyalty, is also one that, in its rejection of the neo-classical style, shows an antipathy to things American. It is not purely British, embodying elements of the Second Empire style of nineteenth-century France, although these are best seen in the Langevin Block (1883-1889), named after Sir John A. Macdonald's Minister of Public Works, the most influential Quebecer of his day. The Langevin Block was the first federal government building off Parliament Hill and is now the real seat of power in Canada, home of the highly-secure Prime Minister's Office.

### GOVERNMENT EXPANSION

The Langevin Block was only the first building to mark the expansion of the national government, which had begun its days in Ottawa with about 300 civil servants. By the end of the nineteenth century, the government had grown to include about 1,000 permanent clerks, many of them female; by the end of the First World War it employed more than 3,000 civil servants. Several additions were made to the East and West Blocks, but it was a boom in federal buildings at the turn of the century that produced the "fab five." These castle-like buildings were designed in an "antiquarian mood" by David Ewart. They include the current War Museum, originally the home of the National Archives; the Mint; the Victoria Museum, now the Canadian Museum of Nature; and the Connaught Building. (See Canadian Museum of Nature, p.65, and More Magnificent Museums p. 79.)

PRIME MINISTER WILLIAM LYON MACKENZIE KING AT KINGSMERE

Government expansion continued until the 30s, much of it westward from Parliament Hill. New buildings included the Confederation Building, the Justice Building, and, at the end of the 1930s, the Supreme Court of Canada. The court was the first public building to be designed "out of house" — until then, all public buildings in Ottawa had been situated, designed and built by the Chief Architect's Branch of the Department of Public Works. The court is a pivotal building in other respects. Its chateau roof was favoured by Prime Minister Mackenzie King, who felt the style was an appropriate one for the capital. This accounts, in part, for the presence of that style in Ottawa's skyline. The Chateau Laurier Hotel was built during this time, along with the old Union Station, which is one of the few neo-classical buildings in the downtown core. That station was later slated to be removed but protests resulted in it being converted to its present use as a Conference Centre, and it was able to retain its place on Confederation Square.

### SHAPING A CAPITAL

In 1927, Prime Minister King put in place the Federal District Commission (FDC), to act as successor to the Ottawa Improvement Commission (OIC) of 1899. The old OIC, created under Prime Minister Laurier, had initiated the construction of many of Ottawa's parkways, but it was the FDC — with a powerful commissioner, Thomas Ahearn, and a substantial budget — that became the instrument for creating the War Memorial in Confederation Square and Confederation Park. In doing so, it effectively converted the heart of a city into the heart of a capital, by eliminating City Hall from the site along with other commercial and industrial activities. With the FDC, King had established an agency for capital planning that competed with the Department of Public Works. King's hand-picked planner for Parliament Hill in 1938, and for the entire capital region in 1950, was French architect and planner Jacques Gréber.

Gréber's 1950 plan was largely implemented by the FDC and its successor, the even more influential National Capital Commission (NCC). Both the shape and the look of the "capital" owes much to this plan, which was followed but never officially approved by the local governments. It incorporates the old imperial artifacts with massive green spaces, including most of the waterfront property in the region, the greenbelt and Gatineau Park. Gréber's plan also took into account the massive growth in the public service during the Second World War (from about 8,000 to about 45,000 employees) by expanding government offices westward from Parliament Hill and by developing satellite concentrations of government offices, including Tunney's Pasture, Confederation Heights, Carling Avenue and the National Research Council operations to the east. The National Defence Building became an outlier along the Rideau Canal.

**NATIONAL WAR MEMORIAL**

### POWER AND IDENTITY

Power relationships within the capital and among countries can be seen in buildings and planning. After the Second World War, Canada was seen as a more or less autonomous "middle power." The capital attracted dozens of embassies and ambassadorial residences, adding to the three with whom Canada had previous "external" (they weren't "foreign") relations: Britain, France and the United States. As a rule, powerful departments tend to be located close to Parliament Hill: the Prime Minister's Office, Justice, Finance and Defence. The same is also true of the powerful embassies, most notably the American, which is located across the street from Parliament Hill. This embassy will soon be moving into large new quarters a little farther away, around the corner on Sussex Drive.

Expressions of power in capitals contend with expressions of identity and participation, and, after the Second World War, these latter were given much attention. In the 1950s, the Public (now National) Archives and the National Library of Canada provided a punctuation mark at the very western end of Parliament Hill. The old Archives Building on Sussex Drive became The Canadian War Museum. Official residences were provided for the Prime Minister at 24 Sussex Drive and at Harrington Lake, also known as Lac Mousseau. Private citizens purchased Stornoway and made it into a home for the Leader of the Opposition. Local heritage was converted into national heritage with the creation of the Mile of History along Sussex Drive and the development of the Byward Market area, which linked Parliament Hill with the Prime Minister's residence and Rideau Hall. This ceremonial route included the British ambassador's residence, Earnescliffe; the former home of Sir John A. Macdonald; the French Embassy; the original National Research Council Building; and Ottawa's City Hall. By the 1960s, the External Affairs, or Pearson, Building was added to this route, and in the 1980s, so was the Japanese Embassy. (See Ceremonial Route, p. 44.)

In the 1960s, the biggest architectural expressions of identity and power were the centenary project that resulted in the construction of the National Arts Centre in Confederation Park, the successful initiative of entrepreneur Robert Campeau to break the 48-metre height barrier for commercial buildings near Parliament Hill (he got 80 metres and built the first high-rise in the downtown core), and the decision of the first Trudeau administration to bring Québec into confederation symbolically as well as in stone, concrete, brick and glass. In 1969, Trudeau and his first ministers did the latter by agreeing that the "capital" would embrace the entire "National Capital Region" on both sides of the Ottawa River. "Ottawa" would remain the "seat of government," as designated by the constitution in 1867. The Trudeau government took major steps to ensure that the capital would operate in the two official languages; it also undertook a major urban renewal operation in Hull that resulted in Place du Portage and Les Terrasses de la Chaudière, office complexes for some 25,000 public servants, as well as the Portage Bridge connection between offices on either side of the river.

### TODAY'S SHOWCASES

The final elements of what has become known as the "Parliamentary Precinct" were put in place in the 1980s and 1990s. These are the showcases of the capital: on the Ottawa side, the National Gallery of Canada, with the nearby Peacekeeping Memorial; on the Hull side, the Canadian Museum of Civilization. Our notions of the city and the capital continue to evolve. Native people have received significant recognition in both the construction and the practices of the Canadian Museum of Civilization, and, in 1996, the National Capital Commission agreed to remove the bronze native kneeling at the foot of Champlain's statue on Nepean Point. Women have yet to receive significant concrete recognition and representation in architecture and artifacts of the national capital. Meanwhile, "Confederation Boulevard," which is under construction as this is written, circles the national core. Significantly, its symbolic centre is not a building but the waters in the middle of the Ottawa River.

NATIONAL GALLERY OF CANADA

OTTAWA'S BEST

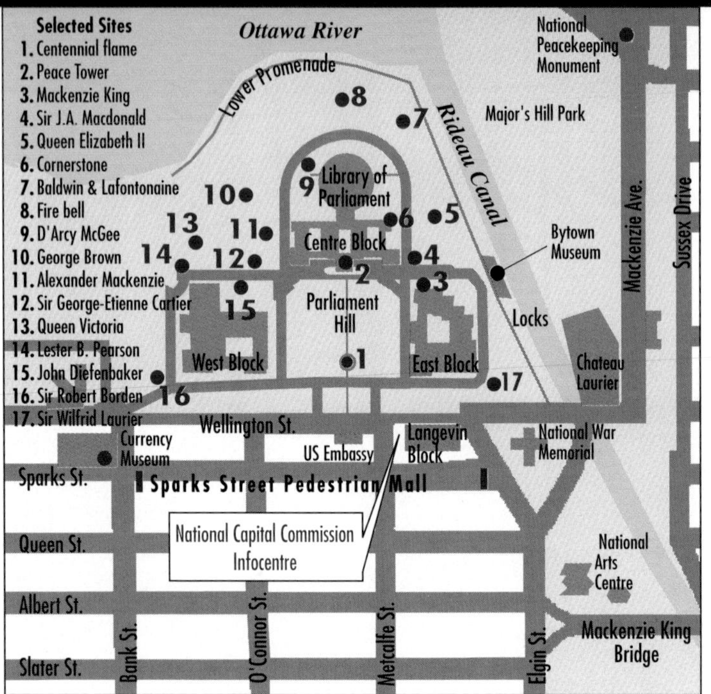


This is Parliament Hill: the heart of Canada the nation, crowded with more symbolism than its creators foresaw. It is the climactic high point of a modern city, recalling more of Canada's political past than any other place. It is a frontier in time and space on the edge of the Great Canadian Shield, reaching across most of the country into the subArctic. The Ottawa River is its boundary — a barrier or a link, as political winds dictate — between French and English cultures. Above all, Parliament Hill has embodied a country's political hopes and fears since the bold experiment of Confederation began on July 1, 1867. This is where the political future of Canada has long been written and is still being formed.

## HISTORY OF THE HILL

Before recorded history, the Hill was impenetrable bush above forbidding cliffs. Algonquin Indians passed by, camping on the flat and friendly farther shores where the Canadian Museum of Civilization now stands. This is where, in June 1613, Champlain became the first European to probe so far into the endless wilderness. His pathway along the Ottawa River provided a route for countless explorers, fur traders, and missionaries in the next two centuries. In 1800, a settlement of American immigrants founded Hull. Twenty-

PEACE TOWER AND CENTENNIAL FLAME

six years later, the future Ottawa first came alive with the sound of human voices as the building of the Rideau Canal was begun. Lord Dalhousie, Governor-in-Chief of British North America, had already acquired the future Parliament Hill, in 1823, for £750. Barrack Hill, as it was called, became the defence bastion of the northern terminus of the canal.

The settlement called Bytown quickly grew and prospered. On the southern edge of the Hill, Nicholas Sparks became the town's first private developer, shrewdly encouraging commerce and housing between Wellington Street and Laurier Avenue. In 1857, to universal astonishment, Ottawa (as Bytown was now called) was chosen as the capital of the Province of Canada. When the Dominion of Canada was created in 1867, Barrack Hill was already Parliament Hill.

## CONSTRUCTION OF THE FIRST PARLIAMENT BUILDINGS

Moving at a speed unknown to modern bureaucracy, a public competition for design of the Parliament Buildings was concluded within a year of Ottawa becoming the capital of Canada. Thomas Fuller, soon to become the foremost Gothic architect in North America, and his partner, Chilion Jones, won the competition for design of the Centre Block. Frederick Stent and Augustus Laver were to be the architects of the East and West Blocks. The Centre Block was to house Parliament and all its functions. In a monumental miscalculation, the other two buildings, which formed the sides of a large U, were thought to be large enough to accommodate Canada's entire civil service — forever. Within months of the choosing of the architects, contracts for construction were awarded for $1.095 million. The work started quickly. On September 1, 1860, the nineteen-year-old Prince of Wales (later Edward VII) laid a white marble cornerstone for the Centre Block that can still be seen at the northwest corner of the present building.

LIBRARY OF PARLIAMENT

The sounds of celebration did not last long, for haste had its price. There had been no test borings, and it was soon found that the foundations had to be far deeper than expected. No provision had been made for heating or fireproofing, and the problems of getting materials to the site had been largely overlooked. Construction was to cost three times as much as estimated. Work stopped for 18 months, while a Royal Commission studied the problem. Seventeen hundred workers were laid off, the Hill was deserted and Ottawa went into deep depression. Its suitability as capital fell into doubt. The Royal Commission's recommendations were quickly implemented, however, and work recommenced. By the autumn of 1865, 350 civil servants were moved from Québec City into their new quarters.

**Library Interior**

On June 8, 1866, Parliament assembled in its new building and almost immediately began to consider the proposals for Confederation discussed at the Charlottetown and Québec Conferences. Continuing opposition to the choice of Ottawa as capital faded as it became known that $2.6 million had already been spent on Parliament Hill. By the end of the year, the East Block was finished — four years behind schedule and with a bill that had climbed from $150,000 to $750,000 for an L-shaped structure. In 1910, a new eastern wing closed in the quadrangle.

Praise for the new structures on Parliament Hill was almost universal. "They are really magnificent," prominent Canadian politician George Brown wrote to his wife. "Fit for the British, French and Russian Empires, were they all confederated." On July 1, 1867, the decision to make Ottawa into the capital of a nation seemed glorious. At five minutes past midnight, a 101-gun salute marked the passage from province to Dominion of Canada and the Hill was lit up by bonfires and fireworks. The next morning, it was enlivened by military parades. The Governor General bestowed honours on the Fathers of Confederation. Sports and celebrations spread throughout the town until evening, when everybody poured back to Parliament Hill for more bonfires and fireworks: a tradition happily revived for Canada's Centennial and repeated each July 1.

**West Block**

### Construction and Destruction

When the Dominion became fully operational, construction was not yet finished on Parliament Hill. The Parliamentary Library, jewel of the Centre Block, was opened in 1876 with the biggest party in Ottawa's history before or since and 83,883 volumes to read. A fourth building was erected at the western end of Parliament Hill on

Peace Tower

Bank Street. In the Gothic style of the main three Blocks, but far more modest in its quiet charm, it was the first home of the Supreme Court of Canada and the National Gallery of Canada. Neither its grace nor its history could save it; in the 1950s it was demolished to provide more parking space. In the early 1960s, the West Block was brutally gutted in a major renovation. Only the exterior survives from the original structure. The interior, shorn of the first century of its history and today used for parliamentary offices, is closed to the public.

The most traumatic loss on Parliament Hill was the burning of the Centre Block on February 3, 1916. The fire was presumably caused by a lighted cigar dropped in a chesterfield by a Member of Parliament, not by German agents, as a panicky population quickly assumed. The Library of Parliament was saved by the dramatic closing of its iron doors amidst the flames of the dying building. The bell in the main tower crashed to the ground and cracked, reputedly as it tolled the eleventh stroke of midnight. It is preserved behind the Library. While Parliament met in the building that is now the Museum of Nature, plans advanced quickly for a new Centre Block to be built under the direction of gifted architect John Pearson. Fifty percent larger than the original, the new steel-framed building follows the lines of the original and is built of sandstone. Its Gothic Revival style brilliantly harmonizes with the styles of its London antecedent and the other structures on the Hill. The House of Commons was able to meet in its new quarters in 1920. The 90-metre Peace Tower, with its dramatic observation platform, its superb 53-bell carillon, and its moving Memorial Chamber honouring Canada's war dead, was finished in 1927 — just in time for Canada's Golden Jubilee.

On August 4, 1952, the Parliamentary Library was almost lost to fire once again, this time because of inadequate wiring. Flames in the roof were heroically quelled, but the damage from water poured into its interior raised serious doubts about its future. Of the 400,000 books then in the library, 150,000 were seriously damaged and 45,000 required rebinding.

Woodwork, Parliamentary Library

Every piece of ornate woodwork from the dome and walls had to be removed, numbered and sent to Montreal for restoration. After four years of intensive work, the job was done and "the most beautiful room in Canada" was dazzlingly preserved.

**TOURING THE CENTRE BLOCK**

Today, the grounds of Parliament Hill are always open. Visitors may take guided tours of the Centre Block seven days a week throughout the year, except New Year's Day, Christmas and July 1. Guided tours of the historic East Block are offered daily but only in the summer months, unless visitors request a return to an earlier regime of weekend visits during the rest of the year.

**ARCHITECTURAL DETAIL, CENTRE BLOCK**

Most tours of the Hill begin with the Centre Block. Although the original Centre Block was a magnificently imposing structure rising over a frontier town, although it held irreplaceable memories for those who toiled there, and although it embodied the history of the birth and youth of Confederated Canada, it had not been a wonderful place to work. The building that we see today is both functionally and architecturally far superior. Built with structural steel (as only the Parliamentary Library was before) and with far less wood in its interior finishing, it was designed to be less prone to fire. Its architecture is commonly accepted as the finest example of Gothic revival in North America — a reputation which sometimes leads untutored visitors from abroad to mistake it for a church, a misconception compounded by the signs along its sidewalks: "For Minister's Vehicles" (sic).

**SPEAKER'S CHAIR, HOUSE OF COMMONS**

Despite its advantages, the Centre Block has been unable to keep up with the demands of growing government. Less than half the Senators and Members of the House of Commons have offices there, and even the cabinet is spread elsewhere on the Hill, in surrounding buildings that are collectively known as "the Parliamentary precinct." Inside and out, the structure has been unequal to attacks of nature and humanity: not only has acid rain eaten away at its masonry and metal roofs but, more immediately, demands for electricity in its halls far outstrip the safe limits of supply. By the mid-1990s, massive repairs and renovations, needed for safety and planned for decades, could no longer be postponed.

It is the House of Commons that first draws in the more than half a million visitors who tour the Centre Block each year. Its rich reality far exceeds its familiar television image; it stirs the imagination of those alive to

Canadian history, who recall the moments of high drama punctuating the endless hours of routine debate. In its procedures as in its architecture, the House of Commons draws heavily from its British ancestry. Still, it has grown to be especially Canadian in its rules, its conduct, and its political character. One marked difference from its counterpart in Britain is that all 301 members have assigned seats and desks, instead of unmarked benches. Also of its own character is the Senate, its "Red Chamber" contrasting with the Commons green. The Senate cannot match the drama of the Commons, but nothing can surpass the rich ceremony that takes place in this room when the Governor General opens each new Parliament.

In concept and execution, architecture and intimate detail, no part of the Centre Block is as breathtaking as the Library of Parliament. It is a Victorian fantasy, exuberant in its colours, awe-inspiring in its proportions, yet owing much of its effect to the genius of Canadian woodcarvers who laboured over every detail of its fittings.

No other rooms in the Centre Block match the fame of the Commons, Senate and Library, but the hallways and corridors are sources of endless fascination. The name of every Parliamentarian since Confederation is inscribed in the hall near the Commons. The portraits of Prime Ministers that line the corridors are arresting, if only because of their sometimes controversial portrayals of political figures who still stir differing emotions. Attracting unanimous praise is the stone carving that ornaments every vista, inside the building and out. The carving has been painstakingly carried out by a series of Dominion Sculptors, with interruptions during the great depression and the Second World War.

**TOP: SIR JOHN A. MACDONALD'S OFFICE**
**CENTRE: CHAPEL, HOUSE OF COMMONS**

**RED CHAMBER**

CANNING HALLWAY

There are massive forms, like the imperious lion and unicorn holding shields at the front entrance; there are heraldic arms, there are gargoyles, there are floral decorations. Many faces are models, or caricatures, of well-known figures in Canadian public life. Although the exterior carving was largely completed by 1938, inside the building it took 30 years to finish even the Central Hall of Honour. The carving still continues, and perhaps it always will. Most of the interior work is done at night in order not to disturb the occupants with noise and dust. If the Centre Block were nothing else, it would still be a sculpture gallery of unending interest.

The architectural climax of the Centre Block is the Peace Tower. Unlike the previous, shorter tower, the Peace Tower of 1927 is a freestanding structure connected to the main building, unsupported by steel and rising 90 metres. Its most unusual architectural feature is the world's first two-directional elevator, which changes angle as it ascends and descends. It was added in 1981 to speed the growing crowds of visitors past the Memorial Chamber and the carillon to the observation platforms.

The Peace Tower's 60-ton carillon has 63 bells, ranging in weight from four kilograms to 11 tonnes. When the Dominion Carilloneur is at the keyboard for concerts, he plays most of the keys with a closed fist, but must use his feet to strike the larger bells. The crystal-clear tones then spread across the Hill, through the city, and into two provinces. It is a tough instrument on which to practice quietly.

PEACE TOWER

The Memorial Chamber in the Peace Tower is a richly ornamented tribute to Canada's war dead. On its walls are carved the regimental insignia of every French, British and Canadian regiment involved in the history of North America. On the Altar of Sacrifice is a Book of Remembrance, which records the names of all who died in military service in the First World War; the open page is turned daily. Those who lost their lives in later conflicts are also honoured in the Chamber.

### THE EAST BLOCK

In the context of our political past since Confederation, the East Block is by far the most interesting building in Canada. For those schooled in history, the magnificently restored rooms are enormously evocative, giving a deeper dimension to the written word. For newcomers to our story, it is a gentle lesson, well told and unforgettable. Its superb restoration makes it one of the most compelling visitor attractions in Ottawa.

Age alone lends the East Block importance. It is the only building on Parliament Hill surviving in recognizable form from before Confederation. While it has suffered many thoughtless and barbaric changes over the decades, the major restoration completed in 1982 was a model for the world. It is not a museum, but an efficient working building for modern parliamentarians. The exterior, the main entrances, and the corridors have been restored so that the visitor is transported back to early Canada. As well, four vital rooms have been painstakingly furnished in the style in which their famous early occupants knew them.

EAST BLOCK

Not only were the East Block and West Block designed to contain the whole civil service forever, but their allotments of space were sometimes carved in stone: for example, the wheat sheaves over the east entrance indicated the Department of Agriculture. The interior of each room conformed to a well-defined hierarchy for everyone from ministers to clerks. The visitor could immediately judge the influence of the occupant from the size of the room, the fireplace (from marble to cement to none), the wood carving on the doorways, the intricacies of the plaster work on the ceilings (floral pattern, plain, coloured), and the lavishness of the washbasins, provided in most rooms behind discreet green curtains. The second floor of the west and north wings were centres of political power for well over a century.

Every governor general from Viscount Monck (the first) to the Earl of Athlone (in the Second World War) had an office over the main west entrance. Until 1926, the governor general wielded London's power over the Canadian colony. One can almost sense the tension that must have existed as His Excellency delivered orders from the Colonial Office to a prime minister waiting politely with thoughts of greater autonomy. Until 1928, the governor general held his New Year's Levee in this office: the tradition of the governor being available to shake the hand of every commoner who comes to call stretches back to

RESTORED GOVERNOR GENERAL'S OFFICE

early in the French regime and continues even to this day, where it now taxes even the facilities of Rideau Hall. All the government's codes and cyphers were kept in this room until the late 1920s, and the Queen has sometimes used this room as her Parliament Hill office. It is lavish, but not large, for governors general spent most of their days in Rideau Hall. But in a nearby washroom they did have a vice-regal bathtub (not restored!).

The southwest corner office in the East Block is restored to the era of its original occupant — the first prime minister of the Dominion, Sir John A. Macdonald The British North America Act, centrepiece of Canada's written constitution, had made no provision for a prime minister. It was assumed that this would be a part-time job performed by some senior minister who already was assigned an office, so it was as Minister of Justice and Attorney General that Macdonald long occupied the southwest corner office. Though it was later used by renowned Canadians such as Lester Pearson, the office evokes Macdonald and the earliest days of the fragile Dominion, when conversations in this room determined not only the future of a transcontinental railway, but of Canada itself. Here, on May 6, 1870, Sir John suffered a severe gallstone attack; for several days he lay on the leather couch, too ill to be moved, under the care of Lady Macdonald.

Near the northern end of this west corridor is the room commonly known as the Prime Minister's Office. It was first occupied by George Étienne Cartier, Macdonald's Québec partner in forging Confederation. (Sir Alexander Mackenzie worked in the highest tower of the West Block, since known as the Mackenzie Tower.) Later, every prime minister from Sir Wilfrid Laurier to Pierre Trudeau used this office until the building was closed in 1976 for major restoration. The prime minister then moved permanently across the street to the Langevin Block. After the restored East Block was reopened by the Queen in 1982, the historic Prime Minister's Office became a museum room. Unlike Sir John A. Macdonald's office, which reflects a single famous occupant, this office was used by many leaders. It is restored to the period of 1872.

PRIVY COUNCIL CHAMBER

In the East Block is the room that most evokes our history since Confederation: the Privy Council Chamber and its adjoining anteroom. Every Cabinet of Canada met here until the late 1970s to conduct the country's business in time of triumph or disaster. Here the draft British North America Bill, which would create the

**PRIVY COUNCIL ANTE-CHAMBER**

Dominion of Canada, was studied. Here, a railway to create a country from sea to sea was repeatedly debated. The crisis of the Riel Rebellion was faced, and the peopling of the prairies was planned. In this room, conscription crises in two world wars were tensely discussed, and more Cabinet crises were weathered than histories have recorded. Indeed, until the Second World War, there was never a written record, or even an agenda, of what happened in this room: it was in fact a Privy — or private — Council. Only ministers were allowed to be present. It was Prime Minister King who finally allowed the Secretary to the Cabinet and an assistant secretary to enter, make notes and prepare minutes. Now every visitor to the East Block may enter this political shrine.

As the country and the Cabinet grew, the table was enlarged (inside the room, because it was too big to go through the door) and identical new chairs were crafted. A few pieces were brought from Québec in the 1865 move of government to Ottawa. The décor reflects the appearance of the room at the end of the nineteenth century. The ante-chamber, containing a reference library of statute books, was used partly for small meetings, but more as a smoking room when smoking was forbidden in the Council Chamber. It was the custom of addicted ministers to excuse themselves to consult on points of law, and then to slide into the haze-filled ante-chamber for a nicotine fix.

The Privy Council corridor doors of etched glass have survived from 1866, except for one that was broken long ago by a civil servant pushing a filing cabinet too enthusiastically. The new pane was so skillfully made that it is uncertain which panel was replaced; nor does history record what happened to the civil servant. In the skillful restoration completed in the early 1980s, not only were the corridors restored to recapture the early atmosphere of the building, but the stairways, some horribly vandalized by modern elevator shafts, were brought back to their early magnificence. Gone forever, however, is the antique open cage elevator near the Prime Minister's Office. During the long tenure of Prime Minister King, a lonely operator had to wait for hours each evening to convey him down one floor; for his services, he received $10 extra each month.

Apart from the four historic rooms open to the public,

Centennial Flame

the East Block continues as a working office building, mainly occupied by Senators and Members of Parliament and their staff.

**The Grounds**

A walk around the Parliamentary Grounds is a walk through history, for the main design of Parliament Hill has changed little since Confederation. A fountain was originally planned on the main walk, so early lithographers included it in their drawings of the Parliament Buildings, but it was not built. Only in preparation for the marking of the centenary of Confederation in 1967 was the more modest — and temporary — Centennial Fountain erected to enrich the celebrations. By the end of the year it had acquired a history of its own, as over 60 Heads of State had stood beside it to pay tribute to Canada. Thus it, too, became a permanent fixture.

The main grounds are the setting for many celebrations. Each summer morning at 10 o'clock, the Ceremonial Changing of the Guard takes place. The Governor General's Foot Guards and the Canadian Grenadier Guards perform this ceremony with perfect choreography for the pleasure of hundreds, and sometimes thousands, of visitors. On July 1, tens of thousands watch a showcase of performers from all parts of the country. This celebration culminates in a gigantic display of fireworks. On unscheduled occasions, large crowds gather here in political protest or to advance a cause, and are often addressed by Members of Parliament. It is very much a "people place," the heart of Canadian democracy.

Since 1885, the Hill has become home to a growing collection of statues honouring Canadian political leaders. The style of these ranges from the romantic Victorian to the majestic, to caricature. Prominent among them is the likeness of Sir Wilfrid Laurier, at the southeast corner of the Hill. Under it lie pipes of the big central heating plant servicing the Hill, the Chateau Laurier and many other buildings, making this slope Ottawa's first harbinger of spring when hundreds of crocuses mark the end of winter. Also on the Hill are a famous bronze statue of Queen Victoria

Changing of the Guard

and an equally famous likeness of Queen Elizabeth II on a favourite Canadian-born horse.

The walk by the iron fence atop the cliff edge at the back of the Centre Block offers a dramatic view across the Ottawa River, to the City of Hull and the Gatineau Hills. Just upstream are the picturesque Chaudière Falls, almost obscured by the remnants of industrial buildings erected in the middle of the nineteenth century. Immediately on the farther shore, in Québec, is architect Douglas Cardinal's bold Museum of Civilization, situated where Indian encampments and tribal battles were recorded by seventeenth century European explorers. Beside it is a limestone Digester Tower, which was once a part of the sprawling lumber mills; it recalls the nineteenth century, when Hull was a leading industrial centre.

TOP: STATUE, SIR WILFRID LAURIER
ABOVE: QUEEN ELIZABETH II, ON HORSEBACK

Finally, at the northwest corner of Parliament Hill is a delightful wooden pavilion. Originally called the Summer House, it was here that the Speaker of the House of Commons entertained amidst rich rugs, tapestries, fine food, and drink. Erected in 1877, the pavilion was thoughtlessly demolished in 1956, without any detailed records being made of the structure. In 1994 it was ingeniously reproduced by architect Julian Smith, through the generosity of the Canadian Association of Chiefs of Police and the Canadian Police Association. These organizations hold memorial services there to commemorate members who have lost their lives in the line of duty.

Today, Parliament has grown beyond the Hill itself. In far-sighted moves during the 1960s and 1970s, the federal government acquired all the private land and buildings on Wellington Street facing the Hill. Many plans have been prepared for eventual expansion, and particularly for the redirection of traffic in the Hill's vicinity. No plan has yet been implemented, however, and each step forward has been checked by budgetary realities. Though many parliamentary functions are carried on in buildings on the south side of Wellington Street, and to the west of Bank Street, Parliament Hill continues to be the special enclave that grew with Confederation. It remains firmly marked by its original fine stone and its wrought-iron fence, whose gates are never closed.

PARLIAMENT BUIDLINGS

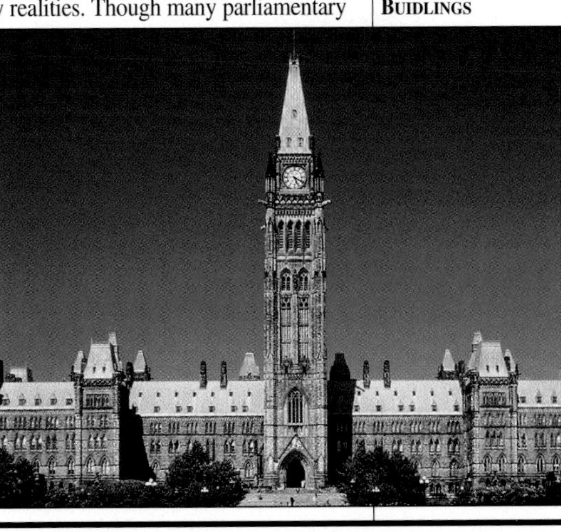

# The Ceremonial Route

Randall Ware

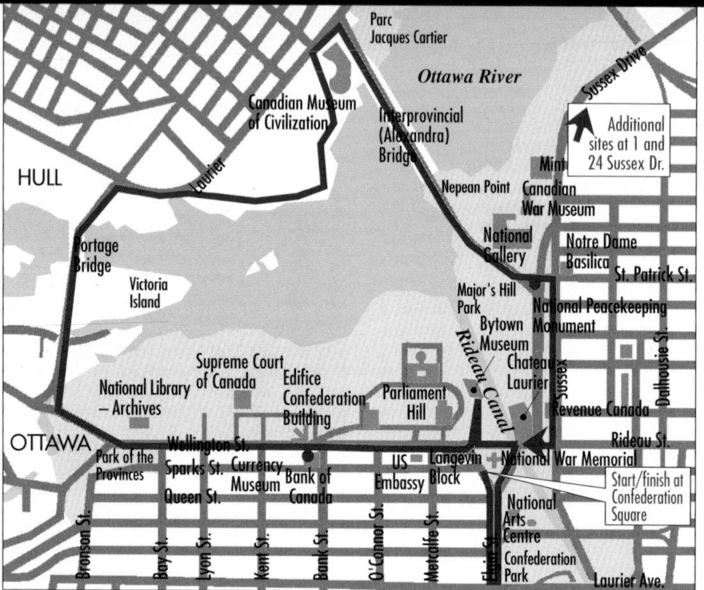


Confederation Boulevard is Ottawa's official ceremonial route, used for important occasions such as the official opening of Parliament and visits by heads of state. Along the length of the route one finds some of the capital's most distinguished landmarks as well as some of its most imposing monuments and works of art. The route takes you by many of Canada's national institutions as well as some of Ottawa's best shopping areas. The National Capital Commission divides the route by describing the side closest to the river as the Crown Side and the other side of the street which leads to commercial activity as the Town Side.

Confederation Boulevard can be walked in its entirety in a leisurely 90 minutes; do allow extra time for side trips to other points of interest that present themselves along the way. The National Capital Commission (NCC) has placed information kiosks all along the route. For the faint of foot, Capital Trolley Tours offers a two-hour tour with commentary that follows the course of the Ceremonial Route. This

is available from mid-April until mid-November.

Visitors to the capital should also be aware that an extensive renovation of Confederation Boulevard is currently underway and is expected to cause some mild disruption until the turn of the century. New sewers and roadbeds are being built and new sidewalks and lighting standards are being installed. The result will be worth the mild inconvenience. And now, let's walk!

**Confederation Boulevard**

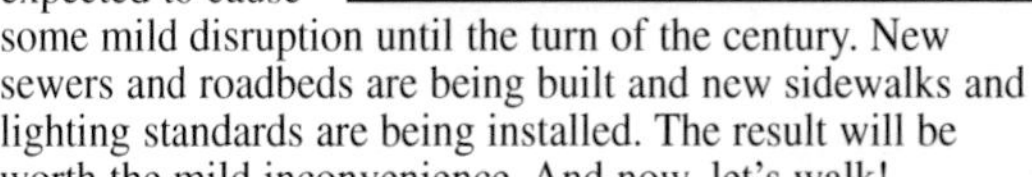

A possible starting point is the National War Memorial on Confederation Square at the corner of Wellington, Sparks and Elgin streets. Vernon March created his sculpture, the *Response*, in 1932 as a tribute to the soldiers who died in the First World War. It is the site of the annual Remembrance Day ceremonies.

Immediately south is the National Arts Centre, Ottawa's premier performing arts institution. Home of the National Arts Centre Orchestra as well as visiting French and English language theatre companies, the Centre also offers a stimulating season of dance productions and serves as the venue for the major road shows that come to town. Although forbidding looking from the outside, it does have some lovely terraces overlooking the Canal and an excellent restaurant. Immediately south is Confederation Park, site of several of the summer festivals that makes Ottawa such a popular tourist destination.

**National Arts Centre**

Back up toward Parliament Hill, alongside the Canal is the Chateau Laurier Hotel, one of Canada's great railway hotels and an architectural delight. Check out the magnificent lobby! The hotel is also home to CBC Radio,

**Confederation Park**

Museum of Contemporary Photography

whose broadcasts in English and French emanate from the seventh floor of the hotel.

Between the hotel and the Canal is the Canadian Museum of Contemporary Photography, the newest of our federal cultural institutions. This museum offers an ever changing series of exhibitions in an unusual space under the hotel and beside the locks which connect the Rideau Canal and the Ottawa River. This is one of the most beautiful vistas on this tour. It makes you understand why Colonel John By and his engineers felt it so important to create a link to the river. A short visit to the Bytown Museum, down a flight of stairs, will provide further information about the history of the area.

Confederation Building, Wellington Street

Continue westward along Wellington Street and you will see, on the north side, the East Block of the Parliament Buildings in which some of Canada's elected representatives have their offices. Cross the road and you will see the Langevin Block. This is where the current Prime Minister has his headquarters. His office overlooks Wellington Street. Stay on the south side of the street and note that the only non-federal buildings on this part of the ceremonial route are the Embassy of the United States of America and the Bank of Montreal. Money and power!

The American Embassy is scheduled to move to another less symbolic location in the next several years. Beside the Embassy, at 14 Metcalfe Street, is the National Capital Commission's tourist information centre. Stop in here and pick up maps, souvenirs or any of the excellent booklets that they have produced on subjects such as public

Off Wellington Street

BANK OF CANADA

art or guides to museums.

Although the buildings on the south side of the street are not architecturally distinguished, they do offer interesting external detail. Frescoes and figures carved into their facades demonstrate a craftsmanship seldom encountered in new buildings. If you see familiar faces on this part of the street, it is probably because the Press Building is here. Almost all of the major television networks and newspaper services have offices here. If you gaze northward across the street, you will see the Parliament Buildings with the Centennial Flame burning a short walk in from the gates. (See Parliament Hill, p. 32.)

NATIONAL LIBRARY AND NATIONAL ARCHIVES

Cross Bank Street, still on the south side, and notice a modern building which is the Bank of Canada, 234 Wellington Street. Look at it carefully and you will discover that the original building has been incorporated into the new design. In effect, the new building, two twelve-storey green glass towers, encloses the old building. Don't miss the Bank's Currency Museum, a small but stylish site that always mounts fascinating exhibitions. On the north side of the street, pass by the Edifice Confederation Building (a perfect example of how bilingualism works in the naming of public places), which houses the Department of Justice, and you will come to the Supreme Court of Canada. It is set back from the road in a kind of splendid isolation. Its severe exterior suggests probity and weightiness. Built in 1946, it has the now-green copper roof that has become the trademark style of official Ottawa. Tours of the court can be arranged.

A small but charming park separates the Court from the building that houses the National Library and the National Archives at 395 Wellington Street. Both institutions offer large and small exhibitions for the general

Museum of Civilization

public, and the Library has an active program of concerts and lectures by Canadian writers. Although the building is unattractive from without, the inside is fascinating, particularly the glass engravings by John Hutton that appear throughout the public areas. Also of note is the sculpture which sits in front of the building. *The Secret Bench of Knowledge*, by Lea Vivot, was first placed there by the artist without any official permission. It became so popular that when the artist ultimately removed it, the public demanded its return. Eventually, a donor was found and a new version of the Secret Bench now sits proudly in front of the Library. Across the road, on the south side, is the Park of the Provinces. This pleasant space is known as one of the best places to skateboard in the downtown area! It is also a popular summer lunch destination for government workers.

Pass the Library and turn onto the Portage Bridge which takes you to the other side of the river. To the right you can enjoy the magnificent vista this site offers. This

Portage Bridge

view of the Parliament Buildings is impressive for the rear-view aspect it provides of the Library of Parliament. On the walk along the bridge you will see Victoria Island and the now derelict shell of the Ottawa Carbide Company Mill, built in 1890. This island has long been the subject of a native land claim and has been occupied by a group of natives for several years. Just past the island a sign saying "Québec" indicates that you have entered another province while still on the bridge. The Ceremonial Route continues to the right at the end of the bridge. The route leads away from the lively downtown of the city of Hull, famous for its night life and its many clubs and bars. The stretch of approximately 300 metres which leads to the Canadian Museum of Civilization is, frankly, not very interesting unless you are keen to see a series of undistinguished federal, provincial and municipal government buildings. They exist, perhaps metaphorically, in separate but apparently peaceful harmony. Take the foot path at the end of the bridge and follow the river's edge to the Museum. These paths are well-used and do provide a welcome respite from the drone of traffic.

**Statue, Samuel de Champlain**

The Canadian Museum of Civilization is situated directly across the river from the Parliament Buildings by the Alexandra Bridge, also known as the Interprovincial

Bridge. Designed by Native architect Douglas Cardinal, the Museum's sinuous lines blend perfectly into the surrounding landscape. Its copper roofs reflect those of the much older buildings on the other side of the river. The inside of the Museum is equally spectacular but always in a human scale. The Museum offers exhibitions for adults and children and a regular series of cultural activities of all kinds. (See More Magnificent Museums, p. 79) There is a tourism information office located across the road from the Museum on Laurier Street.

**National Gallery of Canada**

Parc Jacques Cartier sits on the other side of the

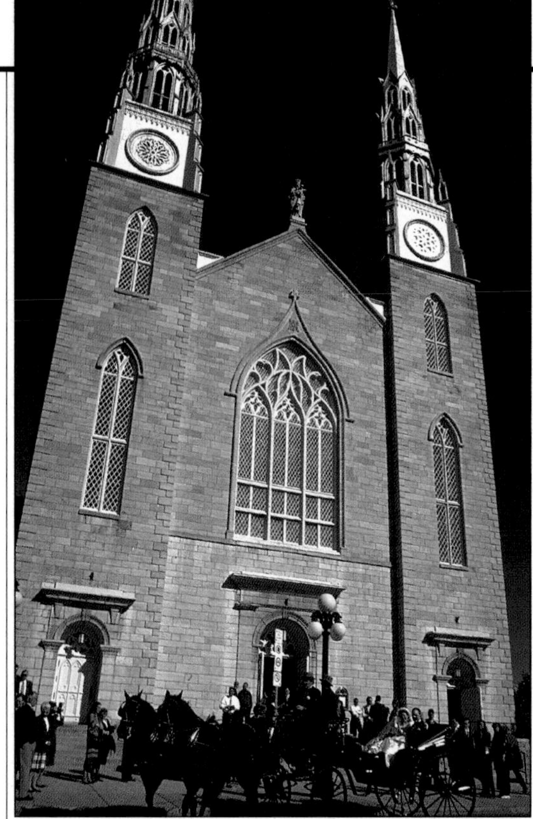

RIGHT:
NOTRE DAME BASILICA

BELOW:
PLAQUE AT RIDEAU HALL COMMEMORATES THE TWENTY-FIFTH ANNIVERSARY OF CANADIAN GOVERNORS GENERAL

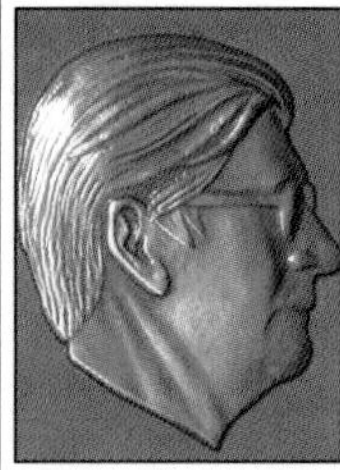

GROUNDS AT RIDEAU HALL

entrance to the bridge and is a pleasant picnic site that affords an excellent view of the river and of Ottawa on the other side. The small stone house in the park was built by Philemon Wright, Hull's founder.

The walk across the Alexandra Bridge offers exceptional views of the Rideau Falls and the course of the river. Back on the Ottawa side of the bridge, you will arrive at the conjunction of several sites of interest. Directly ahead is Major's Hill Park, where several summer festivals take place. To the left, the National Gallery of Canada, at the corner of Sussex Drive and St. Patrick Street, is a site not to be missed. But before turning into the Gallery, look up and note the statue of Samuel de Champlain and follow the short road up to Nepean Point. The sculpture of Champlain (which depicts him holding the Astrolabe upside down!) was created by

**PEACEKEEPING MONUMENT**

Hamilton MacCarthy in 1915 and pays tribute to Champlain's exploration of the Ottawa River. This magnificent site, sometimes used for summer concerts, is a photographer's dream.

The National Gallery was built in 1988 and designed by the architect Moshe Safdie. It makes extensive use of glass to allow for the maximum amount of natural light inside. The Gallery always has several different exhibitions on view and offers many musical concerts throughout the year. Directly across the street from the Gallery is Notre Dame Basilica, Ottawa's oldest surviving church. Its twin spires are downtown landmarks. Immediately beside the Gallery, at 330 Sussex Drive, is the Canadian War Museum. The Sherman Tank outside will help you to find it. Inside is a large collection of weapons, uniforms and memorabilia that details Canada's long military history. Farther along Sussex Drive, away from downtown, is the official residence of the Prime Minister at number 24. This stone mansion, built in 1868 by a wealthy mill owner, is very difficult to see from the street and is not open for tours. At One Sussex Drive is Rideau Hall, the official residence of the Governor General. The grounds are usually open for self-guided tours and scheduled tours of the residence are available during the summer months. Meanwhile, back near the Gallery, you will notice the National Peacekeeping Monument, 'The Reconciliation' at Sussex Drive and St. Patrick Street. Its imposing proportions dominate the intersection. Sussex Drive marks the perimeter of the lively market area. No national institutions here, although you can check out the Canadian Ski Museum at 457A Sussex. At the corner of Sussex Drive and Rideau Street, you will pass the Revenue Canada building, the temple of taxation. Don't look!

At the corner, to the right is Confederation Square, where the journey began 90 minutes ago. Happily, the market area is close by and coffee and other good things await.

# National Gallery of Canada

Janet Uren

*The Jack Pine*, Tom Thomson

Go to Major's Hill Park and stand in the shade of century-old trees. There, you'll find yourself at the visual epicentre of a circle of towers that defines the Ottawa skyline: the copper-green roofs of Parliament, the turrets of the Chateau Laurier, the silver-sharp spires of Notre-Dame Basilica and, most recent and most wonderful of all, the broad glass steeple of the National Gallery of Canada.

The Great Hall

The National Gallery houses the world's most important collection of Canadian art and one of Canada's finest European collections. Plan to be spellbound. In many cities, gallery-wandering is hard work. After walking through palatial rooms with one framed work succeeding another in monotonous procession, you end up with sore feet and a feeling of having done your duty to art. Not so in Ottawa. There is too much variation in the size and shape of the rooms here and in the collection itself. If you become tired, stop to refresh yourself in a tranquil corner or courtyard bathed in the sound of running water, sip coffee in the Great Hall or wander through the bookstore, piled high with bright treasures, including an array of gleaming books, prints, jewelry and creative toys for children.

A day at the National Gallery of Canada remains with you as a series of striking impressions. For that, we owe much to the architecture. Moshe Safdie of Habitat '67 fame designed the building as a kind of cathedral of light — light that is direct and stunning in the outer rooms but diffused and gentle in the galleries. Though the gallery blazes with modernity, there is a feeling of tradition about it as well.

TAIGA GARDEN

You have a choice in the huge, light-filled Great Hall — to stand fascinated at the massive windows, gazing outward into the green core of the city; or, you can turn inward, towards the galleries, in search of the *raison d'etre* for all this splendour. There are some seven sections to choose from: Canadian, European and American, Asian, Contemporary Art and Inuit Art, as well as two areas devoted to prints, drawings and photographs.

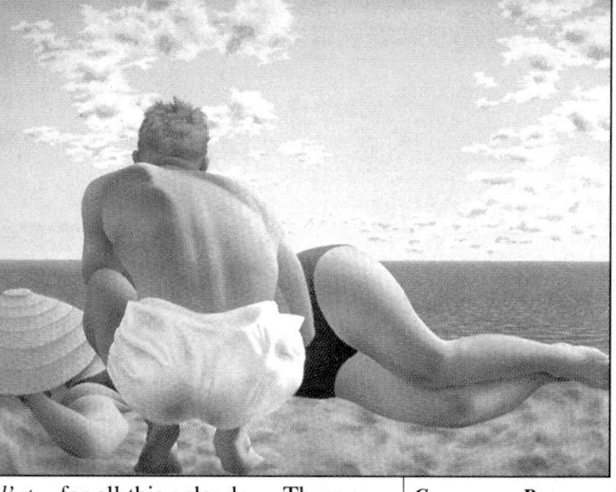

*COUPLE ON BEACH*, ALEX COLVILLE

## CANADIAN GALLERIES

The Taiga Garden is carved out of natural limestone and granite and carpeted with harsh northern species of shrub and ground cover. It is a fragment of landscape that sets the psychological stage for a visit to the rough, vivid canvases of Tom Thomson and the Group of Seven.

Most Canadians have grown up with reproductions of paintings like Tom Thomson's *The Jack Pine*, but there is no substitute for standing in front of the real thing. To see it with your own eyes rather than printed in a book is exactly the difference between sunshine and shadow. Thomson was one of a movement of extraordinary painters who captured not only the shape and colour of Canada, but also its essence, its bones. Wander further into the Canadian

*BLUNDEN HARBOUR*, EMILY CARR

*ST. MARK'S AND THE CLOCK TOWER, VENICE*, CANALETTO

galleries, and you'll find that he was not alone. Twentieth-century Canadian art, while it certainly took on a new and distinctive character with the Group of Seven, never limited itself to the styles and themes of a single school or movement. From the brooding visions of Emily Carr in the 1930s to the skewed reality of Alfred Pellan in the 1940s, from the wild colour-storms of Jean-Paul Riopelle in the 1950s to the compelling geometry of Claude Tousignant in the 1960s, the record of this century — as illustrated by the Gallery's collection — is one of inventiveness, experimentation and excitement. And that brings us to the present.

### CONTEMPORARY GALLERY

On expeditions to the National Gallery, I always look into the Contemporary Gallery. All that "contemporary" art means, really, is art that is being produced now, in our own time. When the National Gallery was formed in 1880, the collection consisted entirely of contemporary art, works that are now considered Canadian classics. The Gallery still sees the gathering of important contemporary works as central to its mission. The Contemporary Gallery — which includes works both by Canadian and international artists — houses one of the finest such collections in Canada.

*SEPTEMBER, 1975*, COLETTE WHITEN

Modern art is not easy, but neither is it boring. After watching the Gallery's provocative video — *What's This?* — I recognize that something important is happening here. It is hardly surprising to find that the vocabulary of art is sometimes strange and new. What is more important is that the artistic language of modern art echoes the novelty, chaos and erupting potentialities of our time.

An interesting aspect to contemporary art is its intense intellectualism. Today's artists are just as concerned with the message as they are preoccupied with the simplification

CONTROVERSIAL *VOICE OF FIRE*, BARNETT NEWMAN

of colour or form. And they seem capable of almost limitless whimsy. Consider a work called *September 1975* by Toronto artist Colette Whiten. Three figures — herself and two male friends — pressed their bodies, front and back, into plaster to make six negative casts. Set in double, hinged frames, the six recessed shapes stand in a circle and give the eerie illusion of having been shaped in relief to express the duality of human nature. The beautiful work conveys a powerful idea.

Perhaps the singlemost controversial work in the National Gallery's collection is *Voice of Fire*. Created by American artist Barnett Newman for the American pavilion at Expo '67, it features three vertical stripes in a pattern of blue, red and blue and cost U.S. $1.5 million in 1989. Those who dislike the painting are vocal on the subject of wasted money; however, those who like it — and there are many — see in its deceptive simplicity nothing less than the momentous objectification of thought. They say Newman was challenging the viewer to see purely and to respond intuitively without the help of external references.

And that is important, for perhaps more than anything else, today's artists are concerned to challenge. They want to force a response — even a negative one. They want to provoke discussion. They do not, on the whole, produce comfortable art, yet it is intensely thought-provoking.

**RIDEAU CHAPEL**

Be sure to visit the Rideau Chapel, a lovely, quiet place. It has an authenticity to it, with its delicate pillars and the heavenly blue-and-white fan-vaulted ceiling. For nearly a century, the chapel was part of the Convent of Our Lady of the Sacred Heart in downtown Ottawa, until the wreckers came in 1972. Thanks to the passion of the arts community in Ottawa, the decoration and furnishings of the chapel were dismantled piece by piece and stored. Years of determination and fund-raising

THE RIDEAU CHAPEL

*HOPE I*, GUSTAV KLIMT

resulted in the chapel being resurrected as part of the new gallery in 1988. The years in packing boxes have not robbed the chapel of its grace.

### EUROPEAN GALLERY

For anyone interested in the history of art, the European Gallery is filled with treasures, from Rembrandt's plump Old Testament lady — very pleased with herself — to the cold clarity of Canaletto's Venice and the magic glitter of Gustav Klimt. Chardin, Turner, Rossetti, Pissarro, Léger...the list goes on and on, reading like a catalogue of the world's great masters.

### ASIAN GALLERY

Even if time is running short, don't miss the Asian Gallery, where there is a small but fine collection of Indian sculpture. Some of these works date back to the first century A.D., making Rembrandt look like a newcomer. I am drawn to a 10th-century sandstone carving called *Ganesha Dancing*. It shows a six-armed elephant-woman dancing with plump knees bent, trunk curled gracefully and scarf floating. With braceleted ankles, a jewelled coronet on her broad elephant brow and little round belly, the frolicking Ganesha always holds me in amused delight.

### SPECIAL EXHIBITS

Every year, in addition to maintaining its permanent collection, the gallery hosts a series of special exhibits, large and small. Some of them have been real blockbusters — Edgar Degas, Emily Carr and William Morris spring to mind. For the year of Renoir, the gallery brought together some 60 of his portraits from all over the world.

That says something about the depth of activity at the National Gallery. More than a magnificent building, the National Gallery is a place where art is preserved, studied and displayed for the interest, information and delight of us all. It's a towering landmark not only on the Capital skyline, but also in the world of Canadian art.

*HEROINE FROM THE OLD TESTAMENT (ESTHER OR BATHSHEBA)*, REMBRANDT

# Canadian Museum of Civilization

Kerridwen Harvey

Canadian Museum of Civilization

Ottawans debate which is more beautiful: the stark, glass spires of the National Gallery, or the organic, curvilinear Canadian Museum of Civilization (CMC), both of which were built around the same time in the 1980s. To judge for yourself, you might choose to approach the museum by traversing the Alexandra Bridge, which leads from the gallery across the Ottawa River into Hull, and allows for a splendid view of Parliament Hill and the rugged river's edge.

The CMC was designed by architect Douglas Cardinal and the exterior of the building is arguably as impressive as many of the treasures you will find inside it. There are no straight lines in the architecture; instead, the building is composed of striking, flowing, sandy-coloured curves cut from Tyndall stone (a fossil-filled sedimentary rock). A tour of the CMC shows that the institution does not follow straight lines in its programming either; instead, it consciously blends history, culture and art, blurring the usual divisions between museums and galleries. The impressive art of Bill Reid, Alex Janvier, and other well-known Native artists is peppered throughout the Grand Hall and elsewhere in the museum; their work complements Cardinal's design. Artwork located outside the museum includes the *Kolus*

Tyndall stone (fossilized rock) forms the curves of the museum's architecture

*Sculpture*, a large, brightly painted bird by artist Simon Dick. Atop the museum, a traditional Japanese rooftop garden combines Zen design with rocks from Canada.

### Virtual Museum

The CMC was formerly known as the National Museum of Man. When it was reborn and renamed in 1989, it left its home in the Victoria Memorial Building, which now houses the Canadian Museum of Nature, and became a very different kind of museum. As befits a museum located near Ottawa, the "Silicon Valley of the North," this

Imax/Omnimax Theatre

museum is wired! CMC President Dr. George MacDonald combines the use of high technology with the desire to afford visitors an accessible, entertaining museum experience. His approach has proven popular: the museum draws over a million people a year. Even before you visit the museum, you can check out the "virtual museum" on the World Wide Web, learn what is happening at the museum, and visit "virtual exhibits" on-line. Although the closest you will get to real artifacts is images of them, the virtual museum allows visitors who can't make it to Hull to get a glimpse of what the CMC is all about. Another of the CMCs high-tech offerings is Cineplus, the world's first combined Imax/Omnimax theatre, where you can experience films in much-larger-than-life format.

### Permanent Exhibits

For all its virtual wonders, the CMC also displays many real wonders — at any one time, the exhibits display only a fraction of the museum's impressive collection of over four million artifacts. Perhaps the most impressive permanent exhibit is the Grand Hall, which was developed with

Pacific West Coast exhibit in the Grand Hall

THE GRAND HALL

the help of Native Elders and artists, and represents the culture and history of six coastal peoples. Highlights include a reconstructed archaeological dig, a Pacific West Coast long house and a Haida canoe. Totem poles, each of which tells its own story, are displayed to their best advantage in the Grand Hall's beautifully designed, river-fronting elliptical room. This room's majestic beauty makes it the site of many artistic and cultural events hosted by the museum.

Another must-see permanent installation is Canada Hall, which encompasses a walk through a millennium of Canadian history, starting in the Maritimes and travelling west. Phase I of the Hall focuses on the Atlantic provinces, Ontario and Québec from the year 1,000 and the first European contact, to 1885. Along the way, you visit a Norse landing, a Basque whaling ship, a Newfoundland fishery, a farmhouse in New France, a fur trading post and the main street of an Ontario town. Phase II will be complete in 1998, with the addition of a West Coast salmon fishing village, a logging scene, Yukon mining and more. Each installation features recreated environments, giving visitors the feeling of "being there." The CMC also produces many excellent temporary exhibits and often attracts travelling exhibits that focus on archaeology, ethnology, native art, folk art, and social history.

EXHIBITS IN CANADA HALL

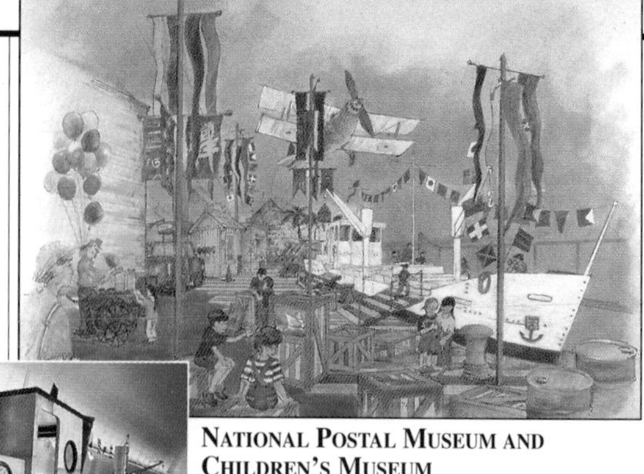

The Children's Museum

## National Postal Museum and Children's Museum

Philatelists alert! The National Postal Museum is contained within the CMC and offers regular exhibits on the history of mail in Canada and elsewhere.

The CMC doesn't forget the needs of children either. The very popular hands-on activity centre for children of all ages offers a range of family programming. This is a chance for kids to do all the things they aren't allowed to do in the museum itself: touch things, pick them up, run around and make noise. Warning, parents: this is not a place for quiet contemplation! In fact, the Children's Museum is not really a museum at all. Everything in it is a reproduction. Its purpose is to provide children with an opportunity for fun and a chance to blow off steam, which may help adult visitors enjoy the museum more thoroughly.

Stamp on Display, Canadian Postal Museum

## Ongoing Activities

There is always a lot going on at the museum, including the usual fare of guided tours, workshops, demonstrations and lectures. The CMC distinguishes itself from most other museums by employing an in-house theatre company, called "Dramamuse," which interprets exhibits with short plays, giving the visitor a glimpse of the history or lives of various peoples. Actors appear throughout the day in the various exhibit halls to deliver plays on themes as diverse as "Life in New France" and "Spirit Singers." Finally, no museum visit would be complete without a trip to the gift shop and CMC has four of them. Particularly tempting are a variety of textiles and carvings with Haida motifs — and, of course, a cyberboutique allows you to shop on-line through the Web site (you can find the site at this address on the web:http://www.cmcc.muse.digital.ca).

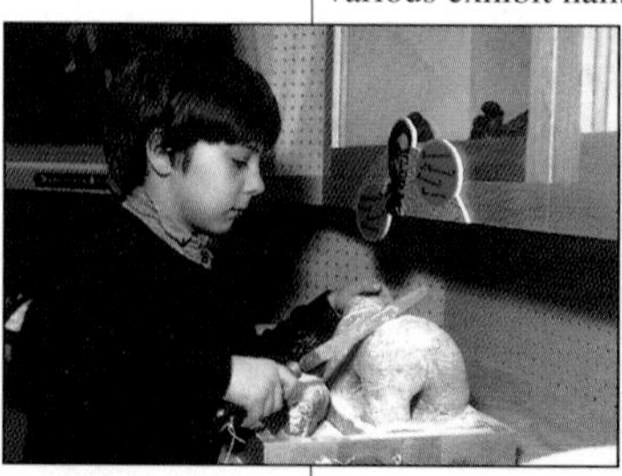

# The Byward Market

Carol Martin

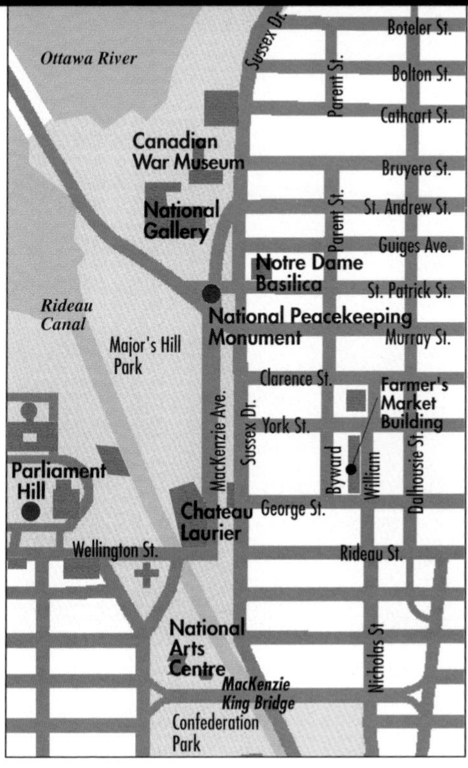


The Byward Market is situated in what is still known as Ottawa's Lower Town, but it is a focal point for the entire city, and a feast for the senses. Early in the spring, fresh maple syrup fills the stalls, soon followed by the aromatic heaps of wild garlic. All summer and fall, colourful mounds of flowers and luscious fruits and vegetables attract crowds. In the early winter there are Christmas trees and firewood. The constant bustle of activity around the market gives it a friendly air, as does the polite, "Can I help you? Vous aidez?" greeting of the stall attendants.

Chapter after chapter in this guide recommends spending time in the market. A Touch of History, (p. 19) tells of Stony Monday, when

Byward Market

Reformers and Tories faced each other over muskets and cannon here in 1849. The memory of that event still lingers, though more peacefully, in the nearby restaurant operating under the same name. Dining (p. 901), recommends eating in the market or buying fresh vegetables from its stalls. In Night Life (p. 99), music lovers are sent here for an evening's entertainment. And shopping in the market for clothes, crafts and funky gifts (see Shopping p. 84) is a quintessential Ottawa experience.

## Founding of the Market

Zak's Restaurant

The market lies in one of the oldest parts of the city. In 1826, two small villages, Upper Town and Lower Town, were laid out by Lieutenant Colonel By, one on either side of the canal. Three years later, the first market sprang up and, after a few moves, it settled permanently in its present location in Lower Town, in the shadow of Parliament Hill. It has remained a place for local growers to sell their produce ever since.

**Market Renaissance**

At some point in its life, every Canadian city has fought a battle with fire. Ottawa is no different. In fact, the present building is the fifth market building to be constructed on this site, after the previous four were destroyed by fire. The extended roof of the current building provides protection for the colourful open-air stalls that are open most of the year. And there are plans to renovate the building even further to enable the market to operate year-round. Meanwhile, the area around the market has undergone a transformation.

Until twenty-odd years ago, shopping in the farmer's market was why most people came to this part of the city. Then, in the mid-1970s, the market building was renovated, craftsmen and artisans were invited to set up shop inside, and specialty bookstores, boutiques, and fashionable cafés sprang up in the surrounding blocks. Within ten years, the Byward Market was the place to go — to eat, to shop, or just to see and be seen.

Some of the city's oldest and most interesting buildings are here. The cobblestone courtyard of the Clarendon Court on George Street, with its surrounding stone buildings, is a reminder of the days when horses and wagons, rather than cars, filled the streets and required stabling. Another building of interest is Tin House Court on Clarence Street. The elaborate tin sculpture, playfully mounted on the wall at second-floor level, was once the front of an early twentieth century tinsmith's home.

The market is an excellent place to begin a number of the tours described

in these pages. The National Gallery is a few steps to the west, and, from there, visitors can trace a route to the city's most interesting museums (see More Magnificent Museums, p. 79.) Cross Rideau Street to the south to where the Sandy Hill tour begins. If it's winter, bring your skates and enjoy the transformation of the canal into a giant outdoor skating rink. You can start out left of Confederation Square, one block further west on Rideau Street. If it's summer, examine the locks of the Rideau Canal to the north of Confederation Square, and continue along the tour route set out in The Rideau Canal by Gordon Cullingham, (p. 126.) The Ceremonial Route, (p. 44), which leads visitors on a circle tour past monuments and landmarks, starts at the square as well.

Many of the most interesting things to see and do in Ottawa begin in the Byward Market. So why not start out here with a hearty breakfast, or return for an entertaining evening — whatever your choice, you're sure to find it in the market.

# THE CANADIAN MUSEUM OF NATURE

LINDA DALE

EARTH HALL, CANADIAN MUSEUM OF NATURE

The Canadian Museum of Nature (CMN) is located in a large Victorian stone building in downtown Ottawa, just east of the intersection of Bank and McLeod streets. It was originally built as a monument to Queen Victoria in the jubilee year, 1897. As you cross the small park to the entrance, you'll pass by a full-sized Arctic elephant and a woolly mammoth. The building itself has been described as an "impressive pile of masonry." It is an unlikely setting for exhibits of bison, sharks and various creepy crawlers — but, somehow, it works. The strange grandeur of the building, with its arched windows, high ceilings, and carved wooden staircase is an attraction in itself.

ARCTIC ELEPHANT AT THE ENTRANCE TO THE CANADIAN MUSEUM OF NATURE

At the CMN, there is a lot to see and do. The museum contains seven permanent exhibit galleries: The Earth, Dinosaurs, Birds in Canada, Mammals in Canada, Rocks and Minerals, Creepy Critters, and Plant Life. The content and style of the displays vary considerably — exhibits range from displays of snakes and cockroaches to multi-media presentations on the

TYRANNOSAURUS REX SKELETON, DINOSAUR GALLERY

world's geology. Together, they offer a broad range of experiences and information about our natural world. And, perhaps because of those high ceilings, visitor fatigue is rare.

## DINOSAURS

For sheer excitement and interest, particularly for kids, it is impossible to beat the dinosaur exhibit. A skeleton of Tyrannosaurus rex presides over this hall. The CMN has wisely decided to minimize the interpretation and, instead, a number of specimens from the museum's huge collection are simply displayed. A dinosaur toe bone is available to touch. No matter how many times you see these amazing creatures, they always make a great impression.

## ROCKS AND MINERALS

The second floor contains two exhibit halls: Birds and Mammals of Canada, and Rocks and Minerals. Both these exhibits are favourites that provide a range of experiences and many beautiful things to see and learn about. As you enter the rocks and minerals exhibit, it is easy to believe that you have stepped into an art gallery by mistake. Cases feature stunning specimens from around the world. The colours, designs and shapes of these gems are dramatically lit, as if they were precious jewels.

GOLD MINE TOUR

The first gallery in this exhibit forms the introduction for a series of displays, while the back section has many interesting interactive displays. Coming from the Atlantic region, I am always impressed by the recreation of the red cliffs of the Bay of Fundy. The lighting recreates in viewers the feeling of a late afternoon sun on Kingsport Beach. Two videos provide information on the natural and geological history of the Fundy area.

A favourite display in this area is the multi-media show, "The Experimental Time Machine." It is quick, bright, and contains lots of humour. A computer talks to the commentator as it takes us back and forth in time. Lights flash on natural history display cases throughout the presentation. It is fun — and a great way to learn some geology along the way. Another visitor favourite is the gold mine tour. Adults may be wary to try it — just looking at the elevator shaft might be enough — but kids love it.

### BIRDS AND MAMMALS IN CANADA

Across the stairwell from the rocks and minerals is the Birds of Canada Hall. Dioramas of natural habitats provide the setting for displays of many different birds, from the comical puffin to the elegant sandhill crane. In the centre of the exhibit, visitors can sit and listen to bird cries. Overhead is a mirrored display of geese flying. This is a truly elegant exhibit.

CENTRE: MAMMALS IN CANADA

As you walk out of this area, you are greeted by a

TOP AND BOTTOM: BIRDS OF CANADA HALL

dramatic display of bison, the first in a series of displays on Mammals in Canada. The displays are arranged behind glass, in imitation of storefront displays. This area never fails to please children, who are fascinated by recreations of mammals such as the polar bear, shown inside his wintry setting, or the cougar resting languidly on a tree branch.

CREEPY CRAWLERS

### CREEPY CRAWLERS

On the third floor of the museum is the exhibit Creepy Crawlers, where you will see live snakes, along with displays of cockroaches, rats, eels and other small insects and animals. Acknowledging how many people react to certain insects, reptiles and mammals is part of the display technique. The entrance has a large video screen showing footage of how these creatures live.

### PLANT LIFE AND MORE

Compared to the newer halls described above, the exhibits on plant life are less exciting, but very informative. As well, the CMN recently opened an interesting exhibit on herbal remedies. In addition to the permanent halls, the museum always prepares a temporary exhibit on the ground floor. Special programs and kids' camps are offered during the summer. A gift store includes games, books and a great selection of miniature animals. Many families take advantage of the grounds around the museum for a picnic.

BOTTOM: PLANT LIFE GALLERY

# Central Experimental Farm and Agriculture Museum

Edwinna von Baeyer

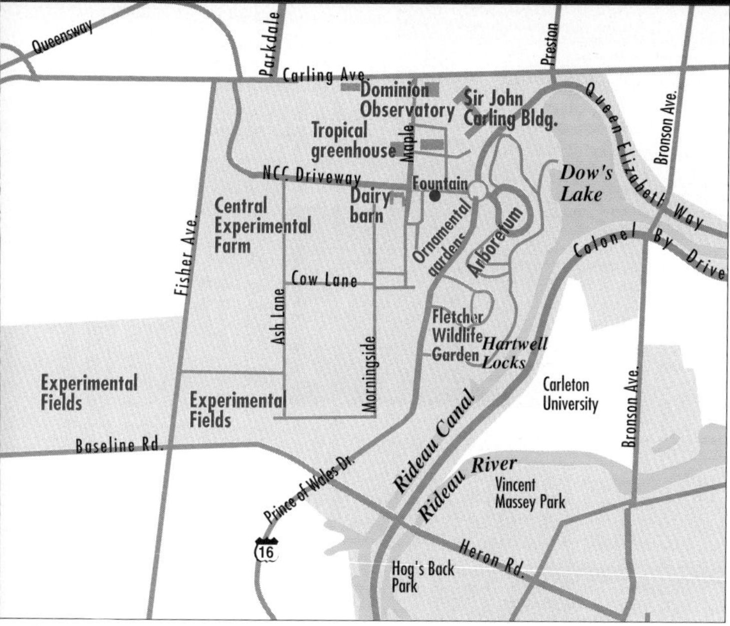

Queensway
Parkdale
Preston
Carling Ave.
Dominion Observatory
Sir John Carling Bldg.
Queen Elizabeth Way
Bronson Ave.
Tropical greenhouse
Maple
NCC Driveway
Fountain
Dow's Lake
Central Experimental Farm
Dairy barn
Ornamental gardens
Arboretum
Colonel By Drive
Fisher Ave.
Cow Lane
Ash Lane
Fletcher Wildlife Garden
Hartwell Locks
Morningside
Experimental Fields
Experimental Fields
Carleton University
Baseline Rd.
Rideau Canal
Prince of Wales Dr.
Rideau River
Vincent Massey Park
16
Heron Rd.
Hog's Back Park

With its trees, rolling lawns, flowers, barns and farm fields, the Central Experimental Farm is a rural oasis in the midst of urban hustle and bustle. Established in 1886, during Sir John A. Macdonald's second term of office, "the Farm," as it is known to locals, started out on 186 hectares of land and gradually expanded to nearly 500 hectares as the city grew around it. Its purpose was to further advances in agriculture and horticulture. Research was carried out on plant hardiness, and disease and insect resistance. In addition, innovative farm architecture was developed and technological advancements were promoted. William Saunders, a practical scientist from

Dairy Barn

London, Ontario, was the first director of the Dominion Experimental Farms system. Marquis wheat – a hybrid that helped western Canada become one of the great wheat-growing regions of the world — was developed under Saunders' direction, largely through the work of Saunders' son, Charles. For more than a century, agricultural research has been championed by the federal government through its network of agricultural research stations. The Farm is at the centre of this network. Today, you can explore the extensive grounds containing experimental fields, ornamental gardens, the Arboretum, barns and stables, office buildings, laboratories and greenhouses.

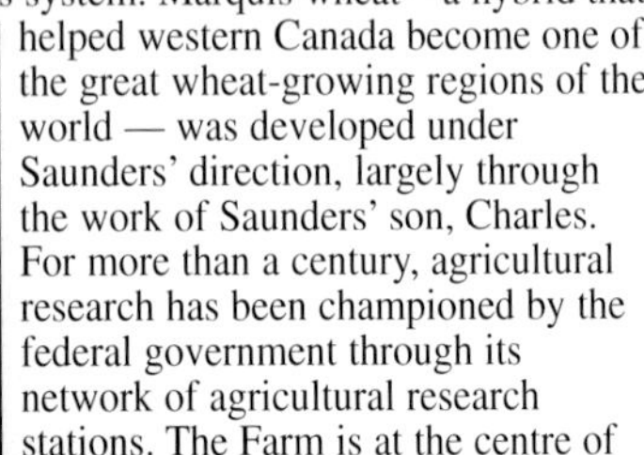

### Dairy Barn and Agricultural Museum

The Experimental Farm smell is authentic, especially when you visit the dairy barn, located to the west of the Prince of Wales Drive traffic circle on the Experimental Farm Driveway. Built in 1914, its herd of purebred dairy cows has been a favourite attraction for many years. The southeast wing, where the calves are kept, is a popular spot where you can reach into a stall and pet a calf. The barn is open from 9 am to 5 pm every day.

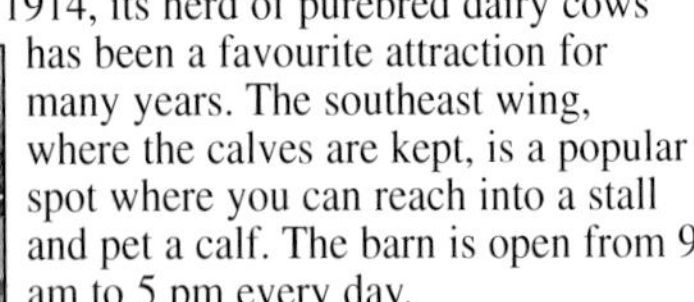

The top floor of the barn has been converted into an Agriculture Museum. Exhibits focus on farm history and advancements, such as the Amazing Potato exhibit or the display of implements past generations used to cultivate the earth. Other livestock — goats, sheep, horses, chickens – can be seen in nearby quarters. The museum complex is open from 9:30 am to 5 pm every day except Monday.

After leaving the museum, visitors

Tally Ho Wagon

can give their feet a rest and, for a small charge, climb aboard the Tally Ho wagon that boards near the front door. For over 20 years, two magnificent Clydesdales have been taking visitors for a leisurely ride around the Farm. In the summer the wagon operates from Wednesdays to Sundays; from September 1 to Thanksgiving Day weekend, it operates only on weekends. Tour times are 10 am to 12 pm, and 1:30 to 4 pm.

### Greenhouses and the Observatory

The greenhouses, which can be seen as you proceed north on Maple Drive, are on the west side of the street. Visit the Tropical Plant greenhouse and stroll around the steamy, exotic display from 9 am to 4 pm daily. Across the street is the William Saunders greenhouse, on the site of the former director's residence.

Continuing north on Maple Avenue, you will see a number of hedges. This interesting collection of shrubs, some of which were planted as early as the 1890s, are examples of properly trimmed, extremely hardy hedge material. To the east is the Sir John Carling Building, the administrative centre of the Department of Agriculture and Agri-Food, named after a minister of agriculture who served from 1885 to 1892. Further down Maple Drive, the dome of the old Dominion Observatory looms into view. The Observatory, built between 1902 and 1904, now houses geophysics instruments that measure earthquakes and tides. Its telescope was given to the Museum of Science and Technology when city lights became too bright for star gazing.

Tropical Plant Greenhouse

### ORNAMENTAL GARDENS

Horticultural research and plant breeding were major activities here as late as the 1980s. The Explorer roses that now grace our northern gardens are the Farm's latest success in producing hybrids to suit the Canadian climate. To see these roses, retrace your steps and head back to the museum/barn area. Across the driveway is the James Fletcher fountain, which commemorates the Farm's first botanist and entomologist. Turn east to enter the ornamental gardens area. Stroll around the Macoun Garden, with its flagstone-lined pond and memorial sun dial. The garden, commemorating our first Dominion Horticulturist, W.T. Macoun, is nicely framed by beds of annuals and perennials. Heading south, you will enter a floral extravaganza of massive, flower-filled test beds displaying the newest rose, shrub and flower varieties to warm the heart of any gardener. Beds of Explorer roses, a rock garden, perennial borders, and shrub collections can also be visited year round.

**MEMORIAL SUN DIAL**

Although every season has its delights in this area, spring draws out the greatest number of visitors to see the masses of blooming shrubs, bulbs and other spring flowers. Prince of Wales Drive divides the arboretum from the ornamental gardens area. On both sides is a profusion of flowering crabapple trees, many of which are hybrids developed by Isabella Preston, an internationally renowned hybridist who worked at the Farm from the 1920s to the late 1940s.

**MACOUN GARDEN PERENNIAL BORDER GARDEN**

To the west of this area are the experimental fields where the breeding of cereal grains, corn, soybeans and forage plants are conducted. Disease-resistant, high-yielding plants have been the hallmark of the Farm's agricultural breeding experiments. These fields are not open to the general public.

Experimental Fields

## Arboretum

The arboretum is a magnificent collection of trees and shrubs, established in 1887 and maintained on 35 hectares of beautiful rolling lawns bordered by Dow's Lake (seen from the northeast lookout), the Rideau Canal and, across the canal, Carleton University (seen from the southeast lookout). The well-marked paths in the arboretum lead through towering oaks, weeping willows, rolling lawns, and picturesque bridges spanning small inlets. It is open to the public.

The arboretum contains some of the oldest cultivated trees and shrubs in Canada and some of the hardiest and rarest. The Friends of the Central Experimental Farm (FCEF), a volunteer group formed to help preserve the Farm, are especially active in the arboretum area and have established a hosta garden below the two lookouts. They also run an active donor tree program, and they "map" the arboretum by labelling the many varieties of oaks, magnolias, maples and other trees. Elsewhere, they help maintain the ornamental gardens and perform a variety of other activities.

## Fletcher Wildlife Garden

Before returning to the Experimental Farm Driveway and the beginning of the tour, continue south of the arboretum for one last stop. Immediately south are the Hartwell Locks (see Rideau Canal, p.124), a historic site maintained by Parks Canada. Farther south still is the Fletcher Wildlife Garden, a 16-acre natural landscape that has been preserved and enhanced by the Ottawa Field Naturalists' Club. It demonstrates an alternative, ecologically sound gardening style that enhances wildlife habitat in urban environments. The Fletcher Wildlife Garden holds many events and offers interpretation. The garden incorporates several different habitats, including a model backyard garden, a sedge meadow, a butterfly meadow, woodlots and an amphibian pond. It is open all year round and accessible by car.

Arboretum

# The National Museum of Science and Technology & the National Museum of Aviation

Linda Dale

The Crazy Kitchen

The National Museum of Science and Technology (NMST) is located on the outskirts of Ottawa, at the St. Laurent exit off the Queensway. About ten minutes away, along the Rockcliffe Parkway, is the National Aviation Museum (NAM). An outing to these museums can easily take a day, and can include a ramble through the open spaces along the Aviation Parkway, or some small-aircraft watching at the Rockcliffe Airport. Children can also burn off energy at the NAM's playground. As well, both museums have excellent gift shops and adequate cafeterias — so plan to spend some time exploring these institutions.

## NATIONAL MUSEUM OF SCIENCE AND TECHNOLOGY

The NMST is a large museum with many interactive displays on the history of technology. It is a busy place where people learn through doing and where answers are discovered rather than taught. All this makes NMST a favourite place with children.

Permanent exhibits include: Connexions - a history of communications technologies; Love, Leisure and Laundry - a history of housework; More than a Machine - an exhibit of early automobiles; Currents of Change - marine history; Log On - an exhibit on computers; Canada in Space; Locomotive Bay - early trains; and Eureka! - an interactive exhibit. In the centre of the museum is a demonstration area where visitors participate in "hair raising experiences" and other scientific experiments. During the summer, a section of the museum parking lot is converted into a huge sandlot where children can play with simple construction machines.

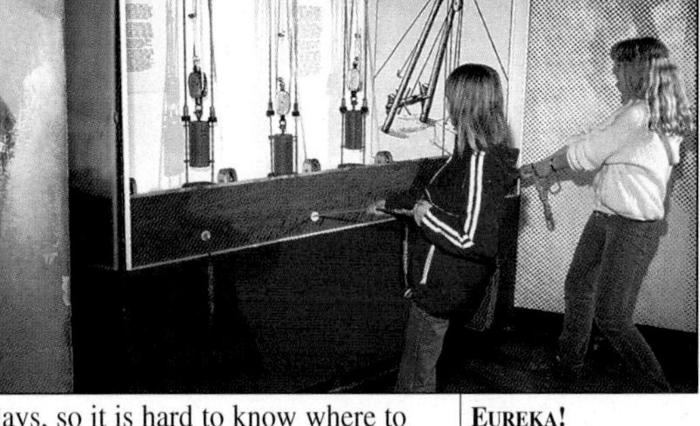

This is a museum filled with "must-see" displays, so it is hard to know where to begin. The Crazy Kitchen is the first choice of many children — walls and floors are tilted to make walking fun and, well, crazy. The Crazy Kitchen also sets the scene for Eureka!, an area where visitors can test out basic scientific principles through interactive displays.

**EUREKA! INTERACTIVE DISPLAYS**

Currents of Change offers a quieter approach to learning. Once over the excitement of the former two exhibits, many children really enjoy looking at the large boat models, including the one of the *Titanic*. There is interesting information on the features of sail, engine, and steam-powered ships. The navigators in your crew will want to use the interactive "steer the course" mechanism.

**"HOW IT WORKS" STATIONS**

Nearby is the exhibit Love, Leisure and Laundry: Why Housework Just Won't Go Away. Artifact displays, interactive displays, computer games, graphics and videos provide a history of machines developed for the home. This is an exhibit designed with the family in mind. A giant egg-beater, a talking outhouse and a child-sized-house play area are directed at younger visitors. Technical information and artifact displays of home appliances, both past and future, are aimed at adults. Videos and blow-ups of advertisements give a humorous but pointed analysis of gender roles in the home.

Connexions describes the history of communication technologies. A series of "how it works" stations demonstrate the scientific principles on which wired and wireless communication are based. The interactive displays are lots of fun: visitors can decipher messages by Morse Code, select from a variety of videos, play virtual hockey or use the walkie-talkies.

Although not physically linked to Connexions, the Log On exhibit is also about communication — in cyberspace. This is a hands-on exhibit where visitors choose among interactive games or surfing the Net. As one might expect, it is popular, though parents have been known to say, "Come on — we have a computer at home. Let's look at the displays."

Canada in Space

Just up from this area is an NMST tradition: the circular glass incubator where you can watch chicks struggle out of their eggs. Children are invited to colour or draw pictures on the tables nearby. This part of the museum provides a nice break from the more razzle-dazzle atmosphere of the rest of the building.

Before leaving the NMST, there are three more stops to make. The first is Canada in Space, an exhibit filled with interactive displays, simulations and special effects. In keeping with the topic, this area has an other-world feel, cultivated through its beautiful visuals and unusual artifacts.

Exhibits on antique cars and early trains focus on a different era in transportation history. The cars are elegant, exotic-looking creatures with rich colours, wooden dashboards and sleek lines. Visitors are invited to climb aboard one of these machines and look out at the cars, delivery wagons and buses from the early 1900s.

The Trains Exhibit

Nothing can beat the final exhibit: the trains. Both children and adults have smiles on their faces as they climb aboard the trains, look at the engine and peek in the elegant coach car. It is a great way to end a visit to this museum.

**NATIONAL AVIATION MUSEUM**

The NAM is a different kind of experience altogether. Located next to an airfield, it is dedicated to the experience of flight and the beauty of the machines that glide or race through the clouds. Unlike some aircraft museums, NAM displays real planes. It has one of the best collections in the world, particularly of pioneer and bush aircraft, and is second in reputation only to museums such as the Smithsonian in Washington.

The museum building recreates the atmosphere of an aircraft hangar, with its bright, airy feeling. Paths, or runways, lead the visitor around the aircraft on display. You don't have to know aviation history to enjoy looking at these beautiful machines. Examples include the A.E.G.G. IV, the only remaining German twin-engine bomber of the First World War; the Komet, the first rocket plane; and the Curtiss HS2L, an early bush plane. The Curtiss flying boat was found at the bottom of an Ontario lake and was rebuilt by NAM's expert technical staff.

Some of the aircraft are simply displayed while others have backdrops to provide information on the situations in which the planes were used. For those who want to know more about aviation history, the videos located throughout the hall provide background information. One of the big favourites is a video of early experiments in flying. A computer terminal provides detailed

information on the NAM's collection.

This museum also has an active programs department. The helicopter studio provides a space for children to enjoy crafts and read books on airplanes. As well, during the summer there is a day camp for kids. A virtual reality hand-glider simulator can be used for a small extra fee, and those looking for some time to rest their feet will appreciate the theatre's feature-length films. If adventure is more your style, however, try the strongly recommended bi-plane ride: for a modest fee, you can take a loop around the Rockcliffe Airport and get a sense of the experience of the aviation pioneers featured in the exhibits.

Of course, the real attraction in the museum are the old planes, such as the Lockhead Electra, similar to the plane used by Amelia Earhart on her last flight. NAM also has the only remaining bits of the famous Avro Arrow project. Many people stop to examine the Lancaster Bomber used by the Alouette Squadron during the Second World War. The Beaver No. 1 is also on display — it was the very first Beaver aircraft ever made, and was used for years in Canada's north. From its fascinating planes to its interactive programs, this museum is a treat to visit — whether you are an aviation buff or not.

# MORE MAGNIFICENT MUSEUMS

JULIE MASON

CANADIAN MUSEUM OF CONTEMPORARY PHOTOGRAPHY

From the modest to the marvellous, the quaint to the quirky, Ottawa's museums offer visitors unique opportunities for education, entertainment, quiet contemplation and noisy participation. As the nation's capital, Ottawa is home to several national museums with world-renowned collections of Canadian artifacts and art. Some of these are housed in wonderful heritage buildings that are themselves worth the visit, while others are almost hidden and hard to find. Still others, like the Canadian Museum of Civilization and the National Gallery of Canada (see Canadian Museum of Civilization, p. 57, and National Gallery, p. 52), have added dramatic new profiles to the Ottawa skyline.

With a few notable exceptions, most of the museums are clustered in the city's downtown core, within a comfortable walking distance of each other. However, don't be tempted to try to do them all in one day. While the tiny Bytown Museum or the Currency Museum are quick stops you can add to another tour, others, like the National Museum of Science and Technology, the National Aviation Museum (p. 74) and the Museum of Nature (p. 65), are more demanding and well worth their own special half-day visit. For more information on Ottawa's larger museums and National Gallery, refer to the appropriate articles in this book. In this tour, we will concentrate on smaller, but no less interesting, museums.

Aboriginal Rights Exhibit, National Library

## The National Archives and the National Library

Start your museum tour quietly, with a trip to the National Library and National Archives of Canada. These are located on the Ottawa River, just a few blocks west of the Parliament Buildings on Wellington Street. The National Archives, formed in 1872, is Canada's oldest cultural institution and home to more than 60 million documents, including maps and drawings. Every year thousands of scholars, historians, journalists, authors, even plain folks interested in their family background, visit to research part of our history.

The National Library receives at least one copy of every book, magazine and journal published in Canada, and it holds up to 3 million items, including superb collections of Canadian music, newspapers and periodicals. You can even look up your mother's Master's thesis, on microfilm, if she wrote it at a Canadian university. Like the Archives, the National Library is used primarily by scholars and researchers, but many of Canada's finest writers have read from their work through the library's public readings program.

Exhibits in the Library and Archives are usually small, temporary and often quite static, but they're treasured by book and history lovers who enjoy the opportunity to see unusual or rare volumes on specialized subjects. When leaving the Library and Archives, stroll around the back of the building to see a statue of Arthur Doughty, the first Dominion Archivist, and catch a wonderful view of the Ottawa River with the Gatineau Hills in the distance.

## Bank of Canada Currency Museum

Continuing back towards Parliament Hill, detour south to the Sparks Street pedestrian mall between Bank and Kent

Bank of Canada Currency Museum

Bank of Canada Currency Museum

Streets to find the Bank of Canada, with its twin mirrored towers designed by Arthur Erickson. Inside, the Bank of Canada Currency Museum is a numismatist's nirvana. This is the place to take your great-uncle who still keeps a shinplaster (a 25-cent Canadian banknote) in his wallet. Happily, every visitor will find plenty of interest, as the Museum has chosen to use its comprehensive collection of Canadian money to illustrate Canada's history, and the exhibits are surprisingly informative and amusing. There's also a section on world money, and some provocative exhibits that challenge ideas about the meaning and purpose of money. Collectors will want to stay all day, but this museum is probably a quick stop for most people.

### Canadian Museum of Contemporary Photography

Resume your tour at Confederation Square and look for the square archway just to the west of the Chateau Laurier Hotel to find the almost-hidden Canadian Museum of Contemporary Photography. This newest of Ottawa's museums is an offspring of the National Gallery of Canada. It is ingeniously built inside the old tunnel that used to connect the Chateau Laurier to the railway station that is now a government conference centre. In spite of the underground location, the museum has made creative use of its small space to display the work of Canadian photographers. Guided tours aren't offered every day, but it is worthwhile arranging your visit for a time when a tour is available. The museum focuses on contemporary photography, so visitors interested in photographic history in Canada should proceed to the National Gallery. If you're a would-be photographer, the bookstore is also a must.

Bytown Museum

### Bytown Museum

From the Museum of Contemporary Photography, a slight detour west on Wellington Street and down the steps at the east side of Parliament Hill will take you to one of Ottawa's oldest and smallest museums, the Bytown Museum. Its location alone — it is situated beside the Ottawa Locks where the Rideau Canal meets the Ottawa River — makes this museum worth the trip. Operated by the Historical Society of Ottawa, the museum introduces visitors to daily life during

CANADIAN WAR MUSEUM EXHIBITS

the time when the Rideau Canal was built. Housed in Ottawa's oldest stone building, which dates from 1827, the museum features the story of Lieutenant Colonel John By, who was responsible for the construction of the Rideau Canal. Children will enjoy the tiny turn-of-the-century toy store as well as the chance to watch pleasure boats move through the locks outside. The museum keeps fairly limited opening hours, so it's worth a phone call to check on times.

### CANADIAN WAR MUSEUM

To finish the tour, return to Confederation Square and go east past the Chateau Laurier to Mackenzie Street, left beside the Chateau Laurier and walk along Major's Hill Park until you catch a glimpse of the elegant glass spire of the National Gallery of Canada. Next to its elegant neighbour, the Canadian War Museum looks a little dowdy, but in spite of the limited exhibits and static displays, a visit to the museum can be a moving and memorable experience. The exhibits — which range from a real Sherman tank to a recreated First World War trench that smells of cordite — manage to celebrate the bravery and sacrifice of soldiers without glorifying war. You'll learn about Canada's participation in international conflicts from the Boer War to our more recent peacekeeping roles around the world. Sadly, government cutbacks replaced the veterans who used to serve as commissionaires with a security service, so visitors no longer enjoy hearing them tell their stories. Nonetheless, there are many tales of courage to be found in the Hall of Honour that commemorates Canadian war hereoes.

As these smaller institutions show, museums have been part of Ottawa's history for decades, and Ottawa residents are enthusiastic and knowledgeable museum-goers. They demand the best from their museums, no matter what their purpose and content. As a result, visitors to the capital have an opportunity to enjoy some of the country's finest collections displayed in fresh and innovative ways.

# Features

# SHOPPING

MARY ANN SIMPKINS

COWS SOUVENIRS

Ottawa has many interesting shopping areas where distinctive gifts and mementos can be found. Even the tourist office, Capital Infocentre, located right across from the Parliament Buildings at Metcalfe Street, is a one-stop shop. It provides not only maps and information but also a small store at the back selling a selection of sweatshirts, maple syrup candy and other souvenirs.

## SPARKS STREET MALL

Stroll one block down from the tourist centre to reach the Sparks Street Mall. Running between Elgin and Bank Streets, Canada's first pedestrian mall contains a variety of shops, including two with an excellent range of authentic native work.

In the first block, just east of the War Memorial on Elgin Street, Snow Goose displays Indian and Inuit art and crafts, such as the famous cream-and-brown Cowichan wool mitts (made by Cowichan Indians in British Columbia), wooden masks, brightly coloured jewellery inspired by the prairie landscape, horses and moose-leather statues, as well as Inuit sculpture and prints.

Canada's Four Corners, in the old stone building at the corner of Sparks and Metcalfe Streets, ranks as the city's largest supplier of top-quality Indian and Inuit work and Canadian craftwork. Leather-fringed Indian vests, moccasins, silk scarves printed

INDIAN AND INUIT ART FROM SNOW GOOSE

FOUR CORNERS

with Inuit designs, bead jewellery and pottery compete for attention with whales sculpted from wood and Inuit soapstone sculpture. On the second floor, the gallery exhibits watercolour scenes of Ottawa, Inuit prints and original art.

Even if you haven't any Irish roots, check out O'Shea's Market Ireland, on the other corner of Sparks and Metcalfe, for attractive men's and women's wool sweaters, dresses, hats, Celtic pottery pins, silver rings and twisted Irish walking sticks. Inside the old Birks Building beside Canada's Four Corners, a small gift shop, Rubynak, has humorous kitchen magnets adorned with mounties and skiing moose, and Canadian map puzzles for youngsters. Nocean, another gift shop on the mall with branches on Sussex Drive and in the Rideau Centre, carries pens, games and puzzles from Europe, as well as a few Canadian items such as toy RCMP statues.

NORMA PETERSEN WINDOW DISPLAY

For reading material about Canada or books by Canadian authors, head to Books Canada, just a little distance down the mall. Next door, Renouf specializes in publications from the federal, Ontario and Québec governments along with those published by the United Nations, the European Economic Community, and other public institutions. Easy-to-care-for clothes particularly suited for women travellers are the mainstay of Canadian designer Norma Peterson. Her small shop on the mall has an assortment of two- and three-piece outfits and dresses. The well-known English chain, Marks & Spencer, carries its own brand of men's and women's wear and various British foodstuffs — frozen steak-and-kidney pie and spotted dick pudding, for example.

The Ottawa institution of McIntosh & Watts appeals to American visitors wanting English china by Wedgwood and Royal Crown Derby. This store and its various branches also have crystal, silver and, for the collector on your list, Coalport bears and other animal miniatures. The office tower at the end of the mall, across Bank Street, is named, simply, 240 Sparks. It boasts three levels of shops, but the main drawing card is Canada's most exclusive department store, Holt Renfrew. The individual boutiques in the two-level store stock imported and Canadian designer fashions for men and women.

HOLT RENFREW DISPLAY

Heritage Buildings on Sussex Drive

## Byward Market

A more funky atmosphere permeates the Byward Market where, amidst the food stores, restaurants and pubs, there is something for every taste and pocketbook. In the heritage stone buildings along Sussex Drive, numerous boutiques feature everything from wrought-iron chandeliers to Christmas decorations.

For women's clothes, try Justine's, once a favourite destination for Margaret Trudeau, or Kaliyana for subdued hand-printed, rayon women's tops and pants by Canadian designer Yana Kalous. Local designer Richard Robinson has the Ottawa *haute couture* market cornered in his Sussex Drive salon, where you can order your own tailor-made outfit.

Art Mode Gallery

Art Mode Gallery along Sussex Drive stocks an impressive collection of predominantly Canadian art works and reproductions, many of them by artists living in the region. Pre-Columbian replicas of jewellery from Bogota's Gold Museum are the mainstay of Striking, while Julien Laframboise sells mainly his own jewellery designs at Créations Lucas. Three independent bookstores in this area cater to specialized interests: Nicholas Hoare's strength is literary books, particularly from England and cookbooks from around the world dominate at Food for Thought on Clarence. The Chapters chain has a store on the corner of Sussex Drive and Rideau Street.

Richard Robinson window display

Be sure to go down some of the side streets. On Murray Street, the all-Canadian crafts at Galerie lynda greenberg run from brightly coloured glassware to witty animal sculptures. Polanco, on Clarence Street, imports housewares and pots from Mexico, while batik clothing, jewellery and merchandise from the Far East predominate at Kulu Trading. At Lilliput you'll see a world of miniatures and dollhouses, which contrast with the tribal masks looking down at you in Giraffe African Arts. If you have trouble finding a swimsuit, venture into Puerta de Sol Sunware on

Cumberland Street, which has ready-to-wear and made-to-measure suits.

The craze for cows that swept Prince Edward Island a few years ago has landed in Ottawa: talking cow toothbrushes, along with T-shirts, socks and school bags decorated with cows riding bikes and driving cars fill the shelves at Cows Ottawa in York Street's red-brick Time Square building. In the same building, Universal Coins and Collectibles handles coins from around the world. Also along York Street, Valley Goods Company lives up to its description as an old-fashioned general store with a mix of kites, relishes, oil lamps, tea towels, and Christmas decorations. Over on William Street, Country Clover competes with two floors of throw mats, hand-made duck decoys and traditional pine furniture.

In the summer, craftspeople stake out spots on the east side of the Byward Market Building, but all year round you can find craftspeople and artists working, and selling, stained-glass lamps, women's silk tops, men's sheepskin hats and jewellery.

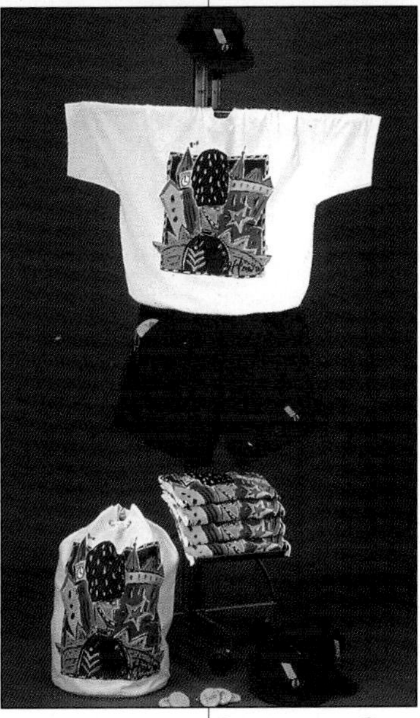

DISPLAY FROM OH YES OTTAWA

## RIDEAU CENTRE

Walk through The Bay, the large department store on George Street, cross over Rideau Street and you're in the main downtown shopping centre. The Rideau Centre houses Eaton's, another large Canadian department store. It's easy to get lost in this three-level mall filled with chain stores and a few independents. Oh Yes Ottawa and Ottawa Souvenir & Gifts sell maple syrup candy, plush toys and Ottawa t-shirts. The unique Mrs. Tiggy Winkle's appeals to children of all ages with items for the junior scientist and games that are just plain fun.

RIDEAU CENTRE

## BANK STREET AND THE GLEBE

A bigger branch of Mrs. Tiggy Winkle's is located on Bank Street in an area known as "the Glebe." Bisecting this trendy residential area, which stretches from the Queensway to Lansdowne Park, Bank Street is interspersed with new and second-hand book shops, restaurants, clothing and kitchen stores, and gift shops offering goods from around the world: Chinese figurines at East Wind, flying angels from Bali at Dilemme, gargoyles and pots for the garden at Thorne & Co., sculpted wood bowls at the all-Canadian craft shop, Snapdragon, nose rings from Thailand at True South Trading, and thick wool sweaters from Ecuador at Quichua Crafts.

THE GLEBE

Amolite Jewellery

**Antique District and Stittsville Fleamarket**

Cross the bridge beside the stadium at Lansdowne Park to enter the antique district in Ottawa South. Starting at Sunnyside Avenue, numerous small shops beckon, their windows displaying depression glass, art deco lamps, exquisite porcelain figurines and old fashioned jewellery. About 40 dealers spread out treasures that range from delicate tea cups to primitive furniture inside the basement at Ottawa Antique Market. Serious shoppers should also stop at Westboro Village along Richmond Road (between Golden and Tweedsmuir Avenues) for furnishings and ornaments, both *avant garde* and traditional, for the home.

Finally, on Sunday, spend a couple of hours roaming through Eastern Ontario's largest flea market, located in Stittsville, just west of Ottawa. The Stittsville flea market houses more than 200 vendors inside its buildings. When the weather is warm, up to 250 vendors display their wares outside and lure huge crowds with merchandise that ranges from toys to stamps to antique furniture.

# Dining

## Rosa Harris-Adler

**Rideau Bakery**

For generations, Ottawa restaurants and markets — as befits the country's capital — offered traditional Canadian fare: food in search of an identity. Meals were usually well prepared, but a little cowed, as it were. They were conventional — heavy on red meat, potatoes, and other hearty carbohydrates to help see the city's stalwart citizens through the long winters. For people with truly discerning palates, Hull, on the Québec side of the Ottawa River, was the place to go, where restaurants such as Café Henry Burger served up — and still do — first-rate elegant cuisine in the classic style. Those seemed the two options — sirloin rare or rarefied French cooking.

**Café Henry Burger, Hull**

Over the last several decades, however, Ottawa has become notably more cosmopolitan. The city is now the heart of the National Capital Region, which also encompasses Hull, Gatineau, and Aylmer; the overall population of the region is just over a million. This is a district on the move and its residents and visitors have demanded and won a more sophisticated selection of eateries and marketplaces. The change started with the influx of immigrants from every part of the globe; their impact on Ottawa dining and food shopping was immediate. Today, Ottawa establishments offer Afghani, Ethiopian, Belgian, Filipino and even

Kamal's Lebanese Cuisine, Glebe

Croatian fare. More commonplace are Lebanese, Chinese, Italian, and Thai restaurants. The following is a personal sampling. A more comprehensive list, with addresses, can be found under "Dining" in the listings in the back of the book. However, since this list is not exhaustive, the best advice is to explore, experiment and enjoy.

## Middle Eastern Food

In the first half of this century, there was a wave of immigration from Lebanon to Ottawa. As a result, the city now has a myriad of restaurants reflecting Middle Eastern cuisine. For a traditional Lebanese meal in an elegant setting, try Fairouz, at 343 Somerset Street West. The atmosphere is intimate and the menu features stuffed grape leaves, exotic soups and taboulleh ( a delectable blend of mint, garlic, tomato, parsley, onion and cracked wheat), along with taste-tempting kebabs grilled over charcoal. You'll find other Middle Eastern diners throughout the city, particularly in major hubs. Look for them in the downtown Byward Market area, in the Glebe (a tiny neighbourhood in central Ottawa) or along Somerset and Elgin Streets.

## Chinese Food

As in most other cities, restaurants with similar cuisines tend to group together. Ottawa's lively Chinatown, which runs along Somerset Street West between Bronson Avenue and Preston Street, is a case in point. If you have time to really explore the city, you'll find wonderful Chinese cooking in virtually every neighbourhood. The advantage of Chinatown is that it offers many varieties of Chinese cuisine, from Mandarin and Cantonese to the spicier Szechuan style, all within easy walking distance.

Despite the Vietnamese name, the Mekong Restaurant at 637 Somerset West serves the best Chinese food: the chef's fried eggplant is unforgettable. The decor is serviceable, the staff friendly and the prices mid-range: a dinner for two can cost under $50, without wine. There are some excellent spots for dim sum as well. A favourite is Fuliwah at 691 Somerset West, where perennials such as shu mai (pork balls), har gow (shrimp balls), sticky rice and egg tarts are done to perfection. Served hors d'oeuvres-style in groups of two or four, each dish costs between $2.25 and $3.25.

Mekong Restaurant

### ITALIAN FOOD

Located right next to Chinatown is the city's Italian neighbourhood, the heart of which is the intersection of Preston and Somerset streets. Italian cooking in Ottawa is now as diverse as the palate can handle. There are some superb restaurants that serve specialties from northern Italy and others which excel in finely prepared veal dishes.

Again, however, don't confine yourself to this part of Ottawa if you're big on Italian food. Ottawa's best-known and best-loved Italian eatery is probably Mamma Teresa's, at 300 Somerset West, where the walls are filled with photos of its famous clientele — among them Pierre Trudeau and Brian Mulroney. Prices reflect the expense accounts of its customers: expect to pay upwards of $60 for two, without wine. There are other great Italian places as far afield as Vanier, in Ottawa's east end. Geraldo's, at 200 Beechwood, is a moderately priced and pleasant place for a meal in this area.

### THAI FOOD

Recently, Thai food has gained a strong following in Ottawa, with restaurants opening up almost every day. The new Thai restaurateurs are braver about using spice than their predecessors, who were wary of shocking Canadian taste buds. Two excellent places for a meal are The Coriander Thai at 282 Kent Street, where chefs do wonders with lemon grass and peanut sauce (a dinner for two without wine is about $40), and the Siam Kitchen at 1050 Bank Street, in an area known as Old Ottawa South. The latter has reasonable luncheon specials: two can eat exceptionally well for under $20.

CHEF, DOMUS CAFÉ

### NORTH AMERICAN FOOD

Finally, for sheer fun and good basic food, try the Newport Restaurant at 334 Richmond Road. This media hangout is home to the Elvis Presley Sighting Society, a group of hacks and flacks who spread the rumour that the King is alive, well and living in Tweed, a couple of hours west of Ottawa. The offbeat ambience makes it a great place to people-watch.

### FINE DINING

Though Ottawa has not always been known for fine dining, there is now a wide range of possibilities for a visitor looking for imaginative cooking in enjoyable surroundings. Right at the centre of things, on the lower level of the National Arts Centre and with a view of the Rideau Canal, is Le Café, a pleasant and reliable spot for lunches or dinner. Chef Kurt Waldele offers a

distinctive version of Canadian cooking, featuring unusual ingredients from across the country and a wine list highlighting many of the best Canadian wines.

Nearby in the market area are several appealing spots. Clair de Lune is a well-established spot much favoured by media and political types (look for your favourite *Globe and Mail* journalist or the prime minister's alter ego, Eddie Goldenberg). They are there for the food, mainly French in inspiration and attentive to what's in season. There's a pleasant outdoor area in summer. Also in the market area is Domus, an unusual spot that grew out of a cookware store that became a café and now a restaurant. The food is very good, the atmosphere informal and very pleasant.

The chef and owner of Clair de Lune display the restaurant's fare

Mamma Teresa's, on Somerset West, is a landmark Ottawa restaurant. It offers standard Italian cuisine, moderately priced for what it is, and the spot atttracts a stream of Ottawa's movers and shakers. Slightly off the beaten track, in the west end of Richmond Road, is the Maple Lawn Café — a beautiful place recently opened in an old stone house, with an elegant garden setting in the summer. With beautifully presented and served dishes, this spot offers a surprising range of dishes. It's one of my favourites. Also in the west end is Opus Bistro, French in flavour and very bistro-like in style, with good seafood and nicely presented dishes.

Maple Lawn Café Richmond Road

Another lovely little restaurant is Il Vagabondo on Barrette Street, offering an odd combination of mostly Italian-influenced dishes by a creative chef. In Vanier,

BACKYARD CAFÉ, MAPLE LAWN CAFÉ

there's the Café Wisigoth, a lovely small French restaurant with a pleasant garden area in summer. In Hull, the Café Henry Burger, across from the Museum of Civilization, is one of the Ottawa area's best French restaurants — a long-standing favourite of many. Le Tartuffe, also in Hull on rue Notre Dame, is a small restaurant featuring fine, often unusual Alsatian influenced dishes.

### ETHNIC FOOD SHOPS

The ethnic restaurants in the region may inspire chefs to stock up on the goods necessary to duplicate some of their favourite meals at home. Ottawa has a reasonable selection of specialty shops that carry the necessary ingredients. If you are planning to cook your own truly authentic Italian meal, for example, check out Nicastro's at 1558 Merivale Road in the western suburb of Nepean. This supermarket is the best place to find such items as Italian semolina-flour pasta, prosciutto and fresh basil. For Lebanese food, the Mid-East Food Centre at 1010 Belfast Road in the city's central-east area is ideal: the smell of mint and coffee which permeates it is simultaneously exotic and welcoming. And for Chinese and Thai foods, there are well-stocked Asian groceries along the Chinatown strip, although the city's best, Hong Kong Market is farther west on the Richmond Road.

PARKDALE MARKET

### MARKETS

Ottawa has its share of supermarket superstores; the pleasant surprise is that, over the years, they have become more sensitive to the ethnic diversity of the city. The best

of these, such as the Loblaws at South Keys on Bank Street, have foods from every corner of the globe, although many have been somewhat Canadianized.

At any rate, it's far more fun to explore the city's outdoor markets and specialty grocery stores. If you're visiting sometime between May and October, head for the Byward Market in the downtown core of the city. On a fine morning, the market vibrates with hucksters and browsers and, in the summer, there's a wide variety of high-quality, fresh and imported vegetables available from the stalls. In the west end of the city, check out the Parkdale Market at Parkdale and Wellington Streets. This market is similar to the Byward, but less crowded and with a neighbourly feel. It sometimes has a more exotic selection of vegetables and is the place to go when you can't find arugula lettuce anywhere else.

**BAKERIES**

What is a meal without a good loaf of bread and a little dessert? The Rideau Bakery has two locations (384 Rideau Street and 1666 Bank Street) and the best rye in Ottawa. The Ottawa Bagelshop and Deli (1321 Wellington Street) has the best bagels, prepared Montreal-style in wood stoves. For fine French pastry, try Patisserie Francais Le St-Honore just over the river in Hull (39 Boulevard St-Joseph).

One of the best things about Ottawa is the extent to which it is truly Canadian. Many of the residents of the National Capital Region switch easily between French and English, and their palates are adaptable, too. What's more, the city has a large diplomatic community with discriminating tastes in food and Ottawa has had to grow and change to meet the challenge. Its variety and quality of dining attests to the fact that it has done so with grace, and panache.

# Night Life

Sandra Abma

**Barrymore's**

As the headquarters of Canada's national parliament, Ottawa is better known for its politicians and bureaucrats than its blues bands. One of Ottawa's best kept secrets however, is a thriving local music scene that spans all varieties of popular music, including blues, rock, jazz and folk, as well as all those musical hybrids that challenge categorization.

## Byward Market

**The Rainbow**

Amidst the crowded cafés and restaurants of the Byward Market, you'll find Ottawa's longtime home of the blues, The Rainbow Bistro. The Rainbow's dark wooded interior is reminiscent of a New Orleans honky tonk, and it is the place in Ottawa to hang around the bar and take in the latest in rollicking, party blues music. Some of the great names in blues, including

**The Rainbow**

Buddy Guy and Dr. John, have played the Rainbow's tiny stage, but the Bistro is best known for fostering a local blues scene. If you drop by on weekend afternoons you'll find resident up-and-coming and veteran blues musicians jamming and making music together.

If bands with names like Big Fish Eat Little Fish, the Voluptuous Horror of Karen Black, Chickasaw Mudpuppies, or Southern Culture on the Skids pique your interest, Zaphod Beeblebrox in the market area is your kind of place. The club features fast-rising artists in the world of alternative rock music, groups such as Jale, Chickpea and, in the earlier days of their careers, Alanis Morissette and Ashley MacIsaac. The friendly ambience of the club rises above the somewhat cheesy decor — before the Zaphod management took over, the venue was a strip club.

## Sparks Street Mall and Bank Street

The After Eight Jazz Club on the Sparks Street Mall has a dual personality. By day it's a sunny café that serves lunch to a mix of politicians, reporters and shoppers. But when the sun goes down, the restaurant takes on the more

**Alternative Rock at Zaphod's**

sophisticated atmosphere of an intimate candle-lit jazz club. The After Eight imports acts from Montreal's vibrant jazz scene. As well, a local ensemble called the Jazz Police hold forth every Monday night for a jazz jam.

At the Bank Street end of the Sparks Street Mall you'll discover a more recent addition to Ottawa's night life, the Cave. As the name suggests, this is a cavernous bar, a sort of Fernando's Hideaway, where patrons can take in a game of pool, lounge along the long cocktail bar, or cuddle and converse in comfortable nooks. Throughout the week, dj's spin a diverse range of popular, nostalgic or downright

**The After Eight Jazz Club**

weird tunes. On the weekends, cutting edge, alternative rock bands can often be found on stage.

The recently restored Barrymore's Music Theatre is located on a less-than-picturesque part of Bank Street. Like Toronto's Yonge Street, this long thoroughfare has its scuzzy areas. Still, Barrymore's is decidedly a worthwhile destination. Originally constructed in 1914 as a vaudeville theatre, the main room has all the

**Cutting Edge Rock Bands at The Cave**

theatrical hallmarks of the era: gilded chandeliers adorn the vaulted, deep red ceiling, giant ornate mirrors reflect the patrons at the tables and on the dance floor. Above the stage you'll find overhanging balconies that allow for unobstructed views of the entertainment. Over the years the theatre fell into disrepair, becoming a shabby echo of its former glory. In 1994, under new management, the theatre was refurbished and a new bar installed. The entertainment at Barrymore's is wide-ranging, everything from the classic rock and roll of Bo Diddley to the alternative rock of Britain's Radiohead, from the

reggae of Jamaica's Burning Spear to protest songs of Billy Bragg. Check the newspaper to see who is playing there.

**Irene's Pub in The Glebe**

## The Glebe

Farther south on Bank Street, in the community of the Glebe, Irene's Pub is the definition of a neighbourhood watering hole. During the week, you may find Irene pouring the beer for the locals, who will be engaged in quiet conversation along the bar, or in a friendly game of darts. A few years ago, Irene starting booking live entertainment for the weekends. This has proved so popular that recently she renovated and built a brand new, enlarged stage. Every Saturday night you'll find a wide range of acts — lots of Celtic music, country music, singer-songwriters and even raw rock and roll. In the audience there are always members of Ottawa's music community, who enjoy congregating in the casual and cozy atmosphere of Irene's.

If any one music might be said to thrive in Ottawa, it is folk, or the music of the singer-songwriter. And if any one place has supported and encouraged these original voices, it would be Rasputin's, a tiny coffee house on the edge of the Glebe. Even though it exudes the 1960s aura of granola and herbal tea, Rasputin's is not above serving you a real drink. For a long time, this was the only venue where folk singers could find a listening audience. The beleaguered singer with an acoustic guitar was more often relegated to noisy bars or behind the potted plants where they attracted as much attention and appreciation as the wallpaper. Rasputin's gave the folk singer centre stage, and along the way nurtured the careers of some of the best of Canada's acoustic musicians, such as Lynn Miles and Ian Tamblyn. The coffee-house setting of tables and mismatched chairs allows for an intimate and relaxed rapport between musician and audience.

### CONCERT VENUES

The Great Canadian Theatre Company, 910 Gladstone Street, is a popular venue for concerts in the city. It is home to the Acoustic Waves Concert Series that runs throughout the fall, winter, and spring. This is the equivalent of an indoor folk festival, featuring big name Canadian acts like Murray McLauchlan and Sylvia Tyson in an intimate setting, designed for those who want to listen. If you are looking for the big names in entertainment, the newly constructed Corel Centre, when it is not playing host to teams from the NHL, is presenting concerts from the likes of The Smashing Pumpkins, Neil Young, and the Tragically Hip.

**RASPUTIN'S**

### OUTSIDE OTTAWA

If you take the excursion to Wakefield (see Into the Gatineau Hills, p. 146) be sure to drop into the Black Sheep Inn (Le Mouton Noir), located in the picture-pretty town of Wakefield, Québec. Although somewhat off the beaten path, the Black Sheep Inn has established itself as a place to hear an eclectic and high calibre assortment of talent. Anything goes at the Black Sheep Inn, from the funky disco fever of local group the Hammerheads to acoustic concerts featuring local singer-songwriter Ian Tamblyn, or Dario Domingus, the virtuoso piper from the Andes.

For more information on entertainment and night life, consult the listings at the back of this book, and local newspapers.

# FESTIVALS

JOE REILLY

TULIP FESTIVAL

Ottawa is renowned as a city of beauty: it has fabulous architecture, historic buildings that house the treasures of Canadian culture, canals and rivers that wind through the heart of a metropolitan area dotted with parks. But the capital region is seriously underrated for its vibrant music scene and night life, for its performing arts events, and for its year-round network of exciting festivals. In fact, Ottawa has a reputation for being beautiful but boring. "It's a nice place to visit, but you wouldn't want to party there unless a political convention is in town."

WAITERS' RACE

This misconception of the capital can only be sustained by those who have never visited the region — those who haven't taken in the strains of jazz music while sprawled under an ancient maple tree in a downtown park, or joined thousands for an invigorating skate along the Rideau Canal, or danced up a storm in the shadow of the Peace Tower to the power chords of the blues. Once charmed by the festive and cultural flair of the Ottawa region, visitors tend to return again and again, often timing annual visits to coincide with their favourite festivals or special events. Indeed, one of Ottawa's best-kept secrets is the myriad of festivals that animate the capital, quite literally bringing it to life throughout the year. The challenge for the uninitiated is in deciding where to begin and what to take in.

ICE SCULPTURES, WINTERLUDE

## WINTER AND SPRING FESTIVALS

Every year, the long winter season is brightened by the appearance of one of the country's largest winter festivals. For three weekends in February, Winterlude dominates life in the capital, ushering out the mid-winter blues with all kinds of outdoor fun ranging from a giant snow park with fantastic ice slides to an international ice sculpture contest. It even includes an outdoor concert series! BRRRR! The world's longest skating rink, the eight-kilometre Rideau Canal, is the festival's focal point, playing host to community snow sculpture contests and thousands of skaters daily. Skating, skiing, all forms of winter frivolity, are part of Winterlude.

The Rideau Canal is also an important focal point for the festival Ottawans eagerly await every spring. For many, the Canadian Tulip Festival in May signals the true end of winter, ushering in the summer festival season with bright and charming tulip beds. These blossom everywhere in the capital, most notably along the Rideau Canal. The canal comes to life with a giant floating parade known as the flotilla, featuring scores of colourfully decorated boats that pay tribute to the tulips. The flowers were originally donated to the people of Ottawa in 1945 and 1946 by the people of Holland, as a sign of their gratitude for Canada's efforts in liberating Holland and for housing the Dutch Royal Family during the Second World War. Today, the celebratory sights and sounds of the Tulip Festival lure residents in droves and attract thousands of visitors to the region over the Victoria Day long weekend. Musical concerts, artisan fairs, entertainment and workshops for children are all part of the fun and merriment.

SNOW SCULPTURES, WINTERLUDE

## SUMMER FESTIVALS

Winterlude and the Canadian Tulip Festival may be the capital's best-known events, but it's really the music festivals

TULIP FESTIVAL ALONG THE RIDEAU CANAL

that animate and define Ottawa during the summer. Organized for the most part by dedicated volunteer community groups, these events promote music with zeal and passion. It is not uncommon to hear of people who take their summer vacations in order to voluntarily manage everything from ticket booths to hospitality suites to the very stages the artists perform upon. The community touch is evident in the friendly, relaxed atmosphere at the outdoor events. Even visiting artists get swept up in the informality of their surroundings, sometimes hosting workshops or simply mingling with the crowds.

The first of the major outdoor music festivals, Festival Franco-Ontarien, presents the finest in francophone culture for five days, culminating with St. Jean Baptiste Day celebrations on June 24. Artisans and theatrical comedy troupes are always part of the mix, but it's the music that is the focus, attracting huge crowds for performances by French artists from across Canada and around the world.

OTTAWA JAZZ FESTIVAL

The reunion of Québec supergroup Beau Dommage was a recent coup for the festival, and appearances by world music greats such as Manu Dibango have been highlights in the past.

One of the region's newest events, the Ottawa Citizen Bluesfest, has quickly grown into one of its most successful. This festival takes place in the first week of July and attracts tens of thousands of fans for a weekend of the blues in Major's Hill Park. Covering a wide range of musical styles from the electric blues of Chicago to the acoustic sounds of the Mississippi Delta, from Tex-Mex to gospel, Bluesfest is a non-stop outdoor party from mid-afternoon until late at night, featuring rising stars alongside the best-known names in the blues.

A cornerstone of summer in the capital, the Ottawa International Jazz Festival, takes place in the latter half of July in a ten-day marathon of great sounds. Uniquely, the Jazz Fest presents its headline attractions on an outdoor stage in Confederation Park. While many larger jazz

OTTAWA JAZZ FESTIVAL

festivals operate outdoor stages, they generally present their major attractions in clubs and prestigious theatres. Accessibility is the key for the Festival in Ottawa. Organizers pride themselves on spreading the word about jazz and gaining new fans for the music through open-air concerts and affordable passports. Series that focus on piano, vocal and *avant garde* jazz use intimate settings at the National Arts Centre and the National Gallery of Canada to ensure the right atmosphere. Of course, the clubs are hopping after hours with plenty of jazz and blues.

Surprisingly, another newcomer on the summer festival circuit is the CKCU Ottawa Folk Festival. For years Ottawa was without a folk fest despite having a strong folk music scene centered around the Ottawa Folklore Centre, Rasputin's and the Great Canadian Theatre Company's Acoustic Waves series. In 1994, the great tradition of a folk festival was resurrected by a group of dedicated folkophiles. The event has grown by leaps and bounds and is currently presented along the banks of the Ottawa River in Britannia Park. Daytime programming includes family entertainers and dozens of workshops hosted by Canadian and international folk greats, happy to guide fans through the trades of songwriting, guitar playing, step dancing or fiddle making. At night the stage is filled with music, as non-stop programming may feature up to ten acts while Mother Nature provides the perfect light show as a backdrop, complete with gorgeous sunsets and the occasional shooting star.

Another major summer music festival should not be overlooked. During the last week of July and the first week of August, various churches in downtown Ottawa play host to the Ottawa Chamber Music Festival. A smashing success since its inception in 1994, the festival has attracted sell-out audiences, season after season, with a lineup of fine local and national ensembles, as well as international stars. Chamber music fans are encouraged to be early in purchasing passports and joining the lineups for shows at this event; it keeps growing every year.

The summer is also dotted with several festivals designed to bring together and highlight the region's very active ethno-cultural groups. In early June, Italian Week takes to the streets of Ottawa's Little Italy, while in August the Caribbean community comes together to celebrate Fête Caribe with music concerts and giant parades. The Portuguese Festival is always a popular attraction and, in early July, the National Capital Dragon Boat Race Festival is a focal point for the Chinese community. In late June, the Carnival of Cultures pulls together some of these groups with many others in a giant party to celebrate the diversity of cultures in the National Capital Region.

But wait — there's more! In early June, the Canadian Museum of Nature, which houses the popular dinosaur collection, is the centre of activity for the Children's Festival de la Jeunesse. Concerts, workshops and interactive displays are presented under sprawling tents on the lawn. Inside the various theatres and halls of the museum, music concerts and magic shows, as well as theatre productions, fill the building with live entertainment. The community group that organizes the festival also presents a series of concerts at the museum throughout the year.

OTTAWA INTERNATIONAL BUSKER FESTIVAL

Other exciting events include the theatrical productions of the Manotick Fringe Festival, just outside Ottawa in the town of Manotick, during the middle of June. Look for the new Ottawa Fringe Festival later the same month. The CKCU/Sparks Street Ottawa International Busker Festival delights thousands along the pedestrian mall over the August long weekend, with hundreds of performers from across the country. Every second year the city is graced by the presence of dancers from across Canada as part of the Canada Dance Festival. This is an event of national significance, with the spotlight on the finest dance troupes in the country. Centred in the National Arts Centre, with satellite venues at places such as the National Gallery of Canada, the festival offers an excellent introduction to new troupes and choreographers challenging the very definition of modern dance.

Many groups and institutions offer an array of performing arts series in the summer months, often in outdoor settings, for free or at reasonable cost. Odyssey Theatre is Ottawa's only open-air theatre group, performing in the style of *commedia dell'arte*. For much of July and August, the group breathes life into Stratchcona Park along the Rideau River. A small visual arts gallery in Aylmer, Centre d'exposition l'imagier, produces an annual series of concerts in Parc de L'imaginaire, located near the Aylmer Marina. Presented on a quaint gazebo stage adorned by mature trees, this series features everything from children's entertainers and foot-stomping Québecois artists to entrancing world music groups.

Institutions such as the National Gallery of Canada and the Canadian Museum of Civilization have traditionally offered music performances as part of their summer programming. The National Gallery has produced a summer series known as Rascals, Roots and Rads in the outdoor amphitheatre. The free series features engaging children's entertainers (Rascals), traditional

ODYSSEY

music forms from across Canada and around the world (Roots) and challenging artists breaking new ground in jazz and alternative music (Rads). The Canadian Museum of Civilization is the centre for the Twilight Concert series of weekend performances designed to highlight Canada's cultural mosaic by presenting groups from across the nation and around the world. Whether it is country and western artists from Alberta, Acadian performers from the Maritimes, or drum and dance ensembles from Africa, it can all be found under the totems on the Museum's dynamic Grand Hall stage. During the fall and winter months, the Museum also hosts See and Hear the World, an annual showcase of performing artists from all over the globe.

The region's most dynamic stage is at Nepean Point, behind the National Gallery. The Astrolabe amphitheatre, perched atop a point overlooking the Ottawa River and Parliament Hill, is the summertime venue for concerts produced by the National Capital Commission.With the moon and the lights of the city as a backdrop, magical nights of music are generally the norm.

GOODNIGHT DESDEMONA

### FALL FESTIVALS

The summer wraps up each year in a cavalcade of colour at the Gatineau Hot Air Balloon Festival, held over the Labour Day weekend. Now recognized as one of the largest balloon events in North America, this festival has delighted large audiences for years with twice-daily launches of hundreds of balloons from around the world, and evening concerts featuring the superstars of the Québec music scene. Future plans for this growing event include the introduction of airship events.

Admittedly, things quiet down a little in the fall when the major performing arts seasons open at places such as the National Arts Centre, The Great Canadian Theatre Company and Centrepointe Theatre. In early October, every second year, the Ottawa International Animation Festival comes to movie screens throughout the capital, delighting residents and visitors alike. During November, the Lebanese community celebrates its culture during a week of festivities. And, for the film buff, the European Union Film Festival offers two weeks of films at the National Library of Canada at the end of November.

This quiet period is a necessary breathing spell for the organizers of the capital's fantastic festivals. Throughout the fall and winter months they are busily putting together lineups of entertainment to delight local residents and visitors, beginning with Winterlude in February and the Tulip Festival in May — and once again carrying through the busy, musical, magical summer of festivals in the capital.

# OUTDOOR RECREATION

DORY CAMERON

**BEAVERTAILS PASTRY DELICACIES**

There are all kinds of outdoor activities to be enjoyed in Ottawa, and most of them take visitors to interesting spots in the region, offering spectacular and unusual views of the city.

## SKATING

For outdoor skating, it doesn't get much better than the Rideau Canal, which, in the winter, becomes a wide, eight-kilometre-long, outdoor skating surface (about the size of 200 Olympic rinks). During January and February, the ice is groomed all the way from Dow's Lake to the National Arts Centre (NAC). In the morning, commuters can be seen skating to work alongside speed skaters in

**SKATING ON THE RIDEAU CANAL**

training. In the evening, the ice is lit up and it is possible to skate to the NAC (bring boots), walk a few blocks into the Byward Market for dinner, then skate back. There are warming shacks on the ice for putting on your skates in relative comfort (although they can be crowded on weekends), and there are fast food stands along the canal that serve hot chocolate and beavertails (a local delicacy that is actually a big, flat doughnut).

Ottawa also has 75 community- run outdoor rinks where visitors can join in a game of hockey or just putter around on the ice outside the hockey boards. There is also a great speed-skating oval at Brewer Park.

## Cycling

Ottawa is a perfect city for cycling: it is compact, and has pretty parks and rivers, small-town traffic, and plenty of national museums, galleries and other sites to visit. Its downtown market area has the excitement of narrow, crowded streets and outdoor cafés, while a network of 130 kilometres of recreational pathways offers quiet, car-free cycling routes all over the city. Gatineau Park, with challenging trails for mountain biking and paved roads with steep hills for touring, is just fifteen minutes by bike from downtown.

For a route that takes in the city's major attractions and avoids roads as much as possible, start at the NAC, follow the bike path around the foot of Parliament Hill past the Supreme Court and National Library buildings, cross the Portage Bridge into Hull and follow the bike path in front of the Museum of Civilization. Return by the Alexandra Bridge to Ottawa. Turn left at the National Gallery and go along Sussex, past the Mint, the City Hall, and Rideau Falls, to the Prime Minister's residence in Rockcliffe Park (see also Rockcliffe, p. 132).

For a more challenging trail ride through the forest take trails 36 and 50 in Gatineau Park.

### In-line Skating

In-line skating is very popular in Ottawa and the recreational pathways for cycling and walking provide good surfaces. The "Share the Path" map and the cycling maps supply useful information. The best time and place to in-line skate is Sunday morning on the roads closed to traffic.

### Downhill Skiing and Snowboarding

Within 15 to 30 minutes of downtown Ottawa are several small ski areas that are perfect for beginner and intermediate skiers. About an hour north of the city, Mont Ste-Marie offers longer, more challenging runs where intermediate and advanced skiers can hone their skills.

These are some favourite spots: Ski Fortune in Gatineau Park is just fifteen minutes from Ottawa and is a favourite with snowboarders. Vorlage, in the village of Wakefield about 25 minutes north of Ottawa, is a very good family ski hill. Skiing is free from 9:30 to 10 am, giving skiers a chance to try the hill. About 30 minutes from Ottawa, and a short distance past Wakefield, is Edelweiss Mont Cascade. It's a little smaller than Ski Fortune and doesn't cater to snowboarders, but it's in a very pretty part of the Gatineau hills. In the summer, Mont Cascade is a waterslide park. Finally, Mount Packenham is 45 minutes west of Ottawa in Ontario. This hill places a lot of emphasis on teaching, has a huge ski school and is a great place for beginners and kids.

### Cross-country Skiing

In a city with snow from November to March and plenty of parks, finding a good place to cross-country ski is no problem. For beginners, the Rideau and Ottawa rivers, Rockcliffe Park and the Experimental Farm are good places to start right in the city. The best place to ski near Ottawa is in Gatineau Park, which has 190 kilometres of groomed trails running over a hilly landscape of forests, meadows, lakes and river valleys.

### Birdwatching

Ottawa is a good birdwatching spot in the spring, summer, and fall.

The Britannia filtration plant is the best spot. It has a little of everything: a small lake surrounded on three sides by forest ,with the Ottawa River just to the north of it. In the fall, especially, there is a great variety of ducks and geese on the lake. To get there, take Carling west to Britannia Road. Turn right and head north to the yacht club, and then take a right at Cassels Street.

Mer Bleu, in the greenbelt, is an enormous peat bog where red-eyed vireos, yellow warblers, redstarts and white-throated sparrows can be seen most of the time. As well, the arboretum at the Experimental Farm is planted with fruit trees and shrubs with small berries that attract birds all year round. The Farm is located beside Dow's Lake, so there also are waterfowl. The Ottawa Field Naturalists Club maintains a bird status hotline (722-3050) with details of bird sightings around Ottawa.

### Canoeing, Kayaking and Windsurfing

Bound on the north by the Ottawa River and with the Rideau River and the Rideau Canal flowing through downtown, Ottawa is a wonderfully watery place for canoeing, kayaking and windsurfing enthusiasts. An exciting and different way to see the city is to rent a canoe at Dow's Lake Marina and explore up and down the canal as far as the locks at the Chateau Laurier at one end

and Carleton University at the other.

The Rideau River flows from Kingston to Ottawa. Canoes can enter the river at any of the parks along its banks, but avoid the big waterfall at Hog's Back Park and the rapids at Vincent Massey Park. The three big lakes in Gatineau Park offer long, tranquil paddles in the wilderness.

### WINDSURFING

The best windsurfing in Ottawa is at Britannia Bay on the Ottawa River, just west of downtown. It's a windy spot and there's a rigging area and a little sandy beach for windsurfers. The lakes in Gatineau Park are ideal for beginners.

### HIKING

The two best places in which to hike close to downtown Ottawa are the city's greenbelt and Gatineau Park. The greenbelt is a rural area surrounding the city's core. Mer Bleu, in the greenbelt southeast of downtown, is a huge peat bog surrounded by marshes and pine-covered sand ridges. In the area around Dolman Ridge Road there's a large network of forest trails that skirt the edge of the bog and offer hikers longer routes.

Stony Swamp, southwest of the city, encompasses a variety of habitats, from wetlands, ponds and fairly mature forests to abandoned farm land. Pinhey Forest, with its sand dunes, abandoned farm land and plantations, has some short loops of one to three kilometres, and a trail suitable for wheelchairs and strollers.

The hiking trails in Gatineau Park are longer, wilder, and more rugged than those in the greenbelt, but they're worth the extra effort.

Pink Lake is an interesting place to take kids. The boardwalk around the lake is pretty easy going. This lake is

a unique relic of the ancient sea, and signs along the boardwalk explain what makes it such a rare geological gem.

The Lusk Caves can be reached easily from the Lac Philippe campsite (trails 50 and 54). Bring a flashlight and expect to get wet feet.

### GOLFING

Within 30 minutes of Ottawa, there are more than twenty eighteen-hole golf courses and three nine-hole courses that are open to the public. They offer challenges for every golfer, from the beginner to the expert. Among them are: Eagle Creek in Dunrobin, just west of Ottawa; Mont Cascade in the Gatineau hills; Loch March in Kanata; the Dôme Golf Club in Hull, only seven minutes from downtown. There are also several driving ranges and golf schools in and around the city that will arrange lessons by appointment.

The Capital Infocentre at 90 Wellington Street, across from the Parliament buildings, has a variety of maps of the city, including speciality maps showing cycling and walking routes, parks and other interesting features. For more information about about the activities and places described in this chapter, consult the Capital Infocentre maps and the listings at the back of this book.

# Power in the Capital

Peter Calamai

Changing of the Guard

Let's call it, in deference to Star Trek, the Prime Directive of Political Power. "The paramount business of life in the capital is to get inside. Of course, there are circles within circles, and you must learn about them, later. But, for the moment, concentrate upon getting within the shining rim. Once there, you can stick, and prick, and jab, and stab to your heart's content." This is the advice given by one woman to another in *The Land of the Afternoon*, a satirical novel about power and politics in Ottawa society before, during, and after the First World War. Even seven tumultuous decades later, getting inside — getting close to power — is still what really matters here.

Commons Entrance, Centre Block

This is not true of everyone, of course. Of the more than 1,000,000 people in the National Capital Region, only a few thousand actually operate in the daily world of political power. They can mostly be found in the immediate precincts of Parliament Hill — advisers, cabinet ministers, journalists — and the nearby office towers housing senior public officials, lobbyists and consultants. For these few, the capital functions much like a village, with its own hierarchy, economy, rituals, kinship and doctrines. While the Power Village can't been seen, much less entered, by outsiders, it's as real as any culture studied by Margaret Mead or Claude Lévi-Strauss.

## PRIME MINISTERIAL STYLE

In this village, power rests with the Prime Minister (PM). Some may argue there isn't any real power anymore in the national capital, that such power is found today in the boardrooms of global corporations, at the Federal Reserve Board in Washington, or down the street from Parliament in the Supreme Court of Canada. But none of these have the absolute authority of action given the head of a parliamentary government. How the PM exercises that authority determines the behaviour of the rest of the villagers, who deal in the chief currency of power — influence. Among recent prime ministers, the village has seen quite a range of styles: Pierre Trudeau's respect for intellect rewarded the skilled debaters around the cabinet table and the policy mavens in the mandarinate, the senior ranks of the public service; Brian Mulroney's need for personal control inflated the role of process and of anyone who was a crony, while the mandarinate suffered a corresponding decline. More recently, Jean Chrétien has little time for debate about process and even less for policy arguments. His cabinet meets not to resolve policy clashes among ministries but to flag any possible political objections to decisions brokered in advance among the parties directly concerned. This prime minister cares about transactions, not philosophy, which means that the cabinet ministers with influence are those who get down to the job and get things done — whether it's privatizing the air traffic control system or taming the deficit. Those who philosophize about reforming the social safety net tend to get pushed aside.

FORMER CANADIAN PRIME MINISTER PIERRE TRUDEAU

Yet there is both a caution and a paradox at the core of this Power Village. The caution: those who proclaim their influence publicly will quickly lose any they might have had. Gone are the larger-than-life senior mandarins common in the Trudeau era and even in Mulroney's days. Nowadays, the best quality of a truly influential mandarin is invisibility, and the same goes for lobbyists. During the worst excesses of Mulroney cronyism, one consultant

DEPARTMENT OF JUSTICE BUILDING

would brag that he could get any deputy minister in town on his cell phone, and then demonstrate. Today's consultants say publicly that they simply offer advice and leave the lobbying to the clients.

The paradox: those with the most influence have the least need to actually use it. Under Jean Chrétien, the person with the most potential influence in the Power Village (other than the Prime Minister's spouse, Aline Chrétien) is John Rae, who lives not in the National Capital but in Montreal, where he is a senior executive with the aptly-named Power Corporation. Rae has been friend and adviser to Chrétien for more than 30 years and has directed all his leadership and election campaigns. He has, to borrow a phrase, the Mother of all Markers in his pocket. Yet no one can imagine John Rae actually using that marker, actually picking up the telephone and saying: "Prime Minister, you know I've never asked you for any favours before but ...." Why not? Because he doesn't have to. Simply being thought capable of exercising such influence attracts even more influence. It also attracts something just as valuable — information.

## Information and Power

Information is the commodity traded here — the gold, the frozen pork bellies, of the Power Village. That is hardly surprising; information has been essential to governance since the Sumerians first tallied stocks of grain and wine on clay tablets with the sharpened tips of river reeds. Knowing what is happening is essential in the Power Village. If a new program is being plotted in one agency, other departments need to calculate in advance whether their interests lie in support or opposition, lobbyists need to forewarn clients whose interests might be affected, ambassadors want their home governments to learn from the embassy, not from the news wires. So all day long in the Village, the players are trading information. Trading is the operative word. You can be in a temporary deficit in the information commodities market but you cannot run up a long-term debt and expect to have your phone calls returned. The players who are really skilled at this game — ministerial aides, communications consultants and journalists — are like the used-book dealers who buy up entire estates and then hive off selected lots and even individual volumes to collectors with special interests. For example, players may have no personal interest in an inside tip about some impending judgeships but suspect the same information will benefit another power player with different names on her telephone's speed-dial buttons. So a call gets made, information is traded

AMBASSADOR'S LIMO

and influence conferred or confirmed.

One drawback for visitors to Ottawa is that most of this stately gavotte of information-trading and influence-acquisition happens out of public view, or in unlikely locales. Those who arrange lunch with their MP in the Parliamentary Restaurant might be better advised to book a table at Mamma Teresa's, a downtown Italian restaurant where the density of cell phones is more impressive than the cuisine, or wander over to the Royal Ottawa Golf Club on a Sunday morning and note who regularly appears. Nor can outsiders rely on patronage appointments as a guide to membership in the inner circles. The truly influential may arrange patronage appointments for others but most intend to make real money, something no patronage appointment provides. They are loath to trade down to a sinecure with no real clout. The exceptions are the diplomatic patronage posts that provide prestige, access and a chance at lucrative corporate directorships afterwards — appointments as ambassador to Washington or Paris, or High Commissioner in London.

## SIGNS OF INFLUENCE

Historical precedent, a chauffeur-driven limo, and the corner office with the panoramic view of Parliament Hill are no longer infallible guides to membership in the inner circles. For decades, the chairman of the Canadian Radio-Television and Telecommunications Commission (CRTC) was considered a major player in the Power Village. The CRTC doles out some of the most lucrative licenses in the country and often must choose between the contending interests of other villagers (such as Power Corporation, the phone companies, and the cable-TV companies). Yet, under previous chair Keith Spicer, the CRTC's decisions were repeatedly overturned by the federal cabinet. Similarly, the seemingly unassailable influence of the Bank of Canada recently suffered a decline because of the policy obstinacy of previous governor John Crow.

THE BANK OF CANADA

If you can't trust the outward trappings, how does the Power Village know who is inside, who has reached one of the inner circles spoken of in *The Land of Afternoon*? There are ways. When a visiting head of state is feted by the Prime Minister, the truly influential can garner an invitation to dinner. Even better is being invited to 24 Sussex for a non-state dinner. The guest list for the first affair is, of course, public knowledge; attendance at the private dinner becomes equally well known, but only within the Power Village. And then there is the even more exclusive inner circle of those chosen to travel with the Prime Minister on overseas trade trips, the so-called Team Canada missions. It's not just the chance to make sales, but all those hours of unequalled access to the Prime Minister, his top advisers and the most senior mandarins.

## BEYOND THE POWER VILLAGE

Those inside the Power Village may sometimes fret over recognition of their own status or whether they have made adequate contingency for a change in the party in power, but they seldom question the rightness of this elaborate system of trading influence and information. A special provision in the budget, a federal infrastructure program, the burying of troublesome social reforms, and it all seems worthwhile. At heart, however, the Power Village is an anachronism, a holdover from the time of Sir John A. Macdonald. In this era of the "knowledge society," for example, no one with real insight into science and technology is a member of the inner circles. Institutes concerned about the medium-term have been abolished — like the Economic Council and the Science Council — or are ignored, the fate of the private think tanks.

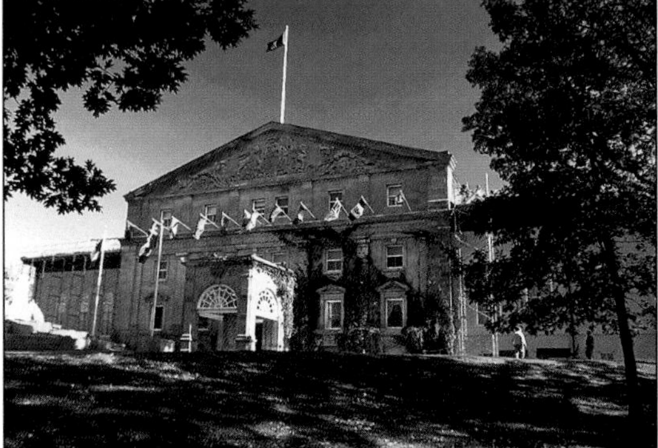

RIDEAU HALL

In the end, then, the Power Village may be as meaningless and irrelevant to today's true needs as it was to the husband and wife at the centre of *The Land of Afternoon*. Although the husband had been offered the prime ministership, the couple were so disgusted by seeing what lay on the "inside" that they moved back to Pinto Plains — a real village on the Prairies.

PRIME MINISTERIAL RETREAT AT MEECH LAKE

# OTTAWA 'EN FRANÇAIS'

DANIEL DROLET

The signs pointing to the tourist information centre at 90 Wellington Street, across from Parliament Hill, are rigorously bilingual: "Capital Infocentre de la Capitale," they trumpet. Like the signs, the services available here come in Canada's two official linguistic flavours, French and English, offering tangible evidence of a French presence in Canada's capital. Both historically and practically, the French language has been and continues to be part of Ottawa's reality — but that does not make Ottawa a fully bilingual city, not if you live here as a francophone. And the city, for the French-speaker, has several different aspects, stretching from Parliament Hill east toward Lower Town and Vanier, and farther east again to suburban Orléans.

Official Ottawa — Parliament Hill, its precincts, and the federal government buildings — is but one of those aspects, although it's the one visitors are most likely to see first. To an outsider, and particularly to non-francophones, Official Ottawa must seem rigorously bilingual. Amongst the tour guides and the official brochures and the signs on government buildings, a visitor is apt to hear and see a lot of French. It was not ever thus: only since the early 1970s, when the Official Languages Act was implemented, has the federal government made a concerted attempt to serve citizens in the language of their choice and allow francophones as well as anglophones to work in the public service in their own

ENTRANCE, CANADIAN MINT

language. The system is not perfect, and often bilingualism is expressed as, "We need to get that translated"; less often do you hear the expression, "Il faudra faire traduire ça."

## Historic French Ottawa

Look east from Parliament Hill, over the canal, beyond the Chateau Laurier and the gleaming National Gallery, and you will see the low-rise buildings of Lower Town a short walk away. The Byward Market, with its restaurants, bars and fresh produce stalls, has plenty of action — and has had it for a century and a half. This, for francophones, is historic Ottawa. It is where the community first took root. You can see it in street names such as Guigues Street and Parent Street. You can hear it in the pronunciation: Dalhousie Street is usually pronounced Dal-HOO-sie, as if it were a French word, even by anglophones.

The French-speaking community started out here in the 1830s and 1840s, when the lumber trade was Ottawa's growth industry and when lumberjacks returning from a winter in the bush camps provided a lot more local colour than most sober citizers would find acceptable today. In those days, the French and the English were often at odds with one another and legends grew up about the brawls between the two groups. The most enduring stories involve the exploits of Joseph Montferrand, a giant of a man. He came to be respected by anglophones, who changed his name to Joe Mufferaw. Folk musician Stompin' Tom Connors still sings of him today.

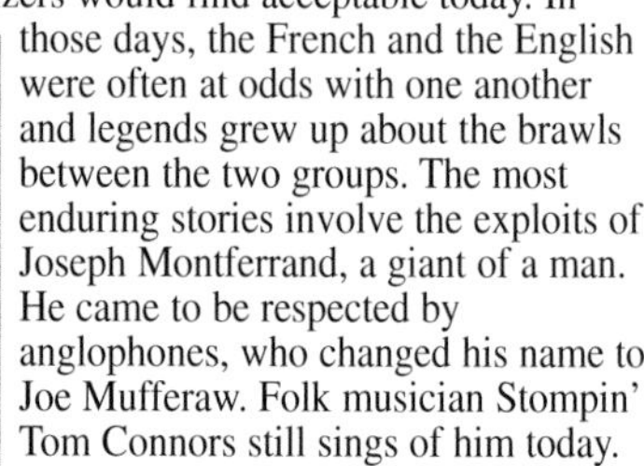

For a long time, Lower Town was the heart of French-speaking Ottawa and the site of its main institutions — the churches, hospitals and schools. It was also the site of its battles. After the brawls stopped, the fighting continued on other levels, usually over the preservation of the French language and basic rights. On Murray Street, an historic plaque outside the old Ecole Guigues relates how the school was the epicentre of a struggle against Regulation 17, which severely limited French-language instruction in Ontario in 1912. The fighters were a group of women with hat pins who kept a school inspector from closing a school that defied the law and taught in French. Thanks in part to their courage, French-language instruction became legal again in Ontario in 1927.

## French Ottawa Today

In many ways, Ottawa is a focal point for French Ontarians. The overwhelming presence of the federal government, and the bilingual Université d'Ottawa/ University of Ottawa, have made the city a place where francophones gather because there are jobs, schools, and social and cultural institutions. It is a place where French-language publishing houses have set up, where school supplies are sold for Ontario's French-language schools. But growth and suburbanization are rapidly changing Ottawa's French face. Increasingly, Lower Town, and even Vanier, the francophone bastion just east of the Rideau River, are losing their exclusively French character. For a more contemporary look at Franco-Ontarian life today, you continue the eastward journey. The destination is Orléans, a suburb just east of Ottawa's greenbelt. Most people make the 20-kilometre journey by car, via the Queensway and then Highway 17.

In 1960, Orléans was a quiet French-speaking village; today, it has mushroomed into a vast residential suburb, attracting many francophones from urban areas. In fact, Orléans is now a centre of French-language culture in the region, a venue for plays and shows, and a place where many services are offered in French. At the same time, it has attracted a large number of anglophones, and francophones are increasingly in the minority. The changing demographics mean service in French can be a hit-and-miss proposal. Francophone residents had to fight to get the accent officially put back into the community's name, and store signs often present an English-only face. Bilingualism is not a sure thing, even here: at the community's largest shopping centre, Place d'Orléans (with the accent,) you're likely to be approached in English. Yet, in the countryside just east of Orléans, the people remain largely French-speaking — for now.

### ACROSS THE RIVER

The final destination on the tour of French Ottawa is not in Ottawa at all: it's across the Ottawa River, in the cities of Hull, Gatineau, and Aylmer. The Québec shore is visible from Parliament Hill and Lower Town. From Orléans, there are glimpses of the low hills of the Laurentian Shield that rise beyond the bustling city of Gatineau. But to get to Québec from Orléans, you have to retrace your steps to Ottawa. Take the Nicholas Street exit, and follow the signs leading across the Macdonald-Cartier bridge and onto Québec's Highway 5 (the Hull Casino on Highway 5 is just a little farther along).

Over the bridge is another face of francophone Ottawa. Although there is a sizeable English- speaking community on the Québec side of the Ottawa River, it is mostly rural. Hull, Gatineau and, increasingly, Aylmer, are largely

CANADIAN MUSEUM OF CIVILIZATION, HULL

PARADE ROUTE IN HULL

French cities. Here, as in Ottawa itself, the same rigorous attention to bilingualism pervades federal enterprises such as the Museum of Civilization. The difference is in cities of the "Outaouais," the language you are most likely to hear is French.

A Franco-Ontarian is almost by definition bilingual; one would be hard-pressed to get by speaking only French. There's even an unwritten code: when two Ottawa francophones meet as strangers, in a store or at a gas station, their first contact often will be in English; it is, after all, the city's *lingua franca*. But the moment one of them detects an accent or sees a name tag, they are likely to switch to French, without missing a beat. I've lived through this ritual hundreds of times. And many other times I've tried to make the switch, only to discover that the person with whom I am dealing does not speak my language. I accept that in Ontario — as francophones we are, after all, in the minority — but I try to make sure that I do speak French with people who can speak the language.

## LIVING IN FRENCH

To live in French is to be able to attend to all the details of daily living in the language — everything from filling in your income tax return to buying a rake at the hardware store, to finding out the date of the next garbage collection. Outside Québec, this is a difficult thing to do. In Toronto, St. John's or Kelowna, few even try; the numbers just aren't there. But here, the numbers are big enough — between 18 and 20 percent of the population of the regional municipality of Ottawa-Carleton are francophones. Yet it is still difficult, particularly outside government circles. Some people just stop trying; others make a point of pushing the limits. I remember one young woman, freshly arrived from her home in the Niagara Peninsula, who marvelled at her ability to walk into any store on Rideau Street and find someone who spoke French. Still, struggling all the time to keep a language can make one weary. Sometimes, when I don't feel like making an effort to seek out a French-speaking clerk in Ottawa, I cross over the river to shop or do business. It's nice not to have to worry about language. I'm sure my anglophone friends from Québec feel the same way when they come to Ottawa. Fortunately, the "other world" is just across the river.

LE ST. HONORE BAKERY, HULL

# Tours & Excursions

# The Rideau Canal

Gordon Cullingham

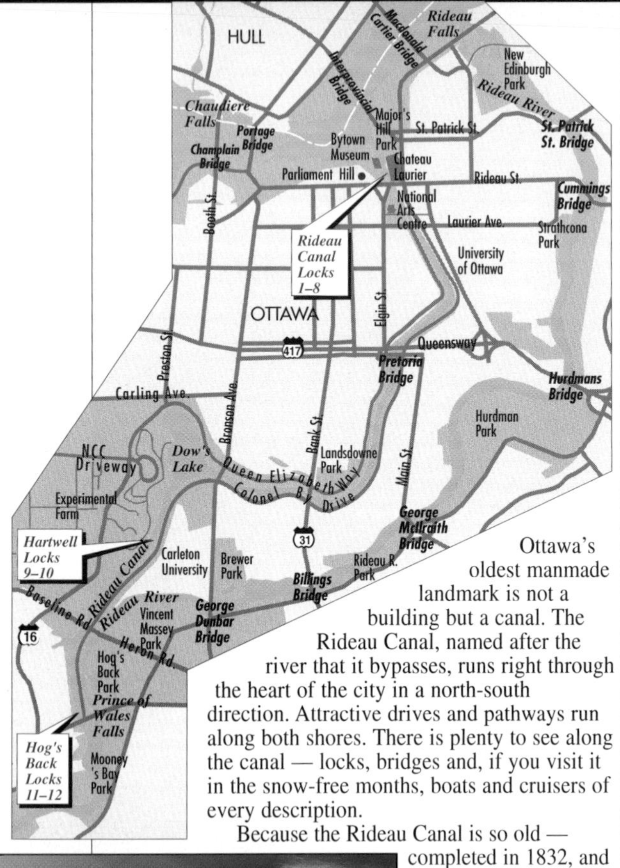


Ottawa's oldest manmade landmark is not a building but a canal. The Rideau Canal, named after the river that it bypasses, runs right through the heart of the city in a north-south direction. Attractive drives and pathways run along both shores. There is plenty to see along the canal — locks, bridges and, if you visit it in the snow-free months, boats and cruisers of every description.

Because the Rideau Canal is so old — completed in 1832, and unchanged since — it is a genuine bit of heritage inviting easy exploration. It can be approached by road or foot or bicycle at many points. The most dramatic approach is at the west end of the bridge beside the Chateau Laurier. Here lie eight locks — a giant staircase

PATHWAY ALONG THE CANAL

connecting the Ottawa River below to the plateau on what used to be a beaver meadow 24 metres above. A couple of kilometres upstream from here is a lift bridge, which rises vertically on four computer-controlled pins to allow tall cruisers to pass under. Farther along, at the Carleton University campus, are two more locks, followed by still two more at Hog's Back, although only one operates. In all, three sets of locks lie within the city limits.

EIGHT LOCKS

One of the Rideau Canal's greatest charms, and the reason for its survival, is that it has not changed since 1832, except in minor ways. Built as a single project, not several, it remains a coherent, uniform set of installations. Locks, bridges and dams have been repaired, and sometimes rebuilt, but the dimensions and operating system were retained. The mechanical handcranks (called crabs) are still operated by canal men and women, just as they always were. The exceptions are three lock stations out of the 23, where electric power was installed in a program that was soon cancelled, after the appeal of the traditional system was appreciated.

CANAL LIFT BRIDGE

## HISTORY OF THE CANAL

This intersection of the Ottawa and Rideau Rivers was a very different place when Lieutenant Colonel John By was building his canal in the 1820s and 1830s. He walked into a wilderness when he arrived in 1826, freshly commissioned by the Duke of Wellington to build a waterway from near the mouth of the Rideau River, proceeding up the river to its source, and then down the Cataraqui River to enter into Lake Ontario at Kingston. The War of 1812 was a fresh and disagreeable memory to the British government. This inland route would

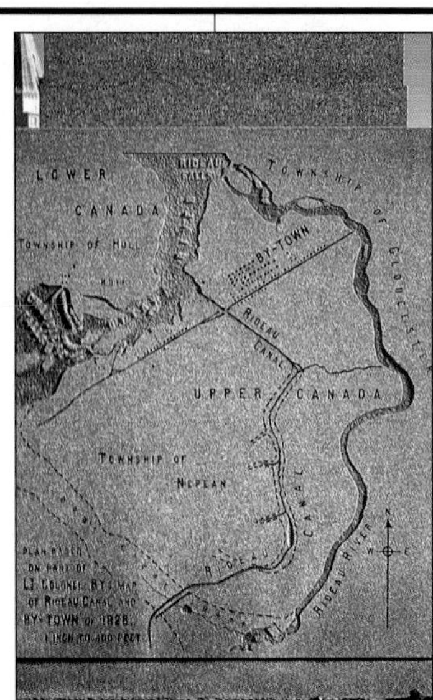


**EXHIBIT DEPICTING HISTORY OF THE CANAL**

avoid the vulnerable St. Lawrence River; it would be all-Canadian, and free of neighbouring enemies.

The waterway By produced was 200 kilometres long, raising boats on the northern section 85 metres and lowering them 50 metres on the southern. The locks themselves are all identical and unchanged. If a boat is under 30 metres long and draws less than one and two-thirds metres, it can go through them all. The dams are often picturesque, some with silvery water sliding over almost white stone forming an arch pointing upstream. The highest of the dams — at Jones Falls — rises nearly 20 metres.

In all, there are 47 locks and 23 dams (not counting the small control dams on nearby streams). The lifts of By's locks vary from less than one metre to four-and-a-half metres. The locations vary too, with the biggest one being here in Ottawa, where eight locks raise boats 24 metres. It is noteworthy that a chance visitor to this construction site in 1827 was John Franklin (not yet Sir John), the Arctic explorer who disappeared 20 years later. He accepted an invitation from Colonel By to lay the cornerstone of the third lock.

The stone for the canal had to be quarried, and the closer to the site the better. For these Ottawa locks, it came out of the bedrock around them. Quarrying was the most dangerous part of canal construction, because of the blasting that was done with antique Black Powder — gunpowder, placed in hand-drilled holes in the rock. Sometimes an inexperienced worker wasn't quick enough in beating the crude fuse to safety, with gruesome results. Hundreds of lives were lost during construction, mostly to malaria spread by the *anopheles* mosquito, others to accidents at the lock and dam sites, and especially in the quarries. Nonetheless, the calculation of water levels was mysteriously accurate, the canal's design incorporated state-of-the-art engineering, and the workers, despite their lack of training, were well-supervised. The finished product shows remarkably high standards.

Because of land disputes, Colonel By and Governor Dalhousie decided to have their new canal begin in Sleigh Bay, leading into Entrance Valley, rather than at the more obvious places both east and west along the Ottawa River. Soon, the growing encampment was disciplined by the grid pattern of streets you can still see in present-day Lower Town. These were laid out by Colonel By in the usual British, military, no-nonsense fashion. The settlement acquired the name Bytown and soon was bustling with canal workers, chiefly poor unskilled Irish immigrants along with some French Canadians who were well accustomed to surviving in these parts. Colonel By brought with him a few companies of Royal Sappers and Miners to

provide the know-how needed in the construction of dams and locks. He quartered them on what came to be known as Barrack Hill.

One of By's first challenges was to bridge the Ottawa River's awesome Chaudière Falls so that he could call on the resources of Wright's Town (now Hull) on the settled side of the river. That bridge underway, he proceeded to build a stone arch bridge over the path of his canal just at the top of the eight locks. This was the Sapper's Bridge, a stately and sturdy crossing for nearly a century. It connected Rideau Street to Sparks Street, and, when demolished to make way for the present bridge and plaza in 1912, required days of steady pounding to convince it to fall down.

**TOP: CHAUDIÈRE FALLS**

**ABOVE: BRIDGE TO HULL**

Near the location of the fourth lock, By built his "Commissariat" in 1827. The fine stone building still stands on its original site and now serves as the Bytown Museum of the Historical Society of Ottawa. Across the locks was a similar building, demolished in 1912 because of the constant vibration from the railway ledge cut above it in 1900. The year 1912 was a signal year for Ottawa, not only because of the two demolitions, but also because both the Chateau Laurier Hotel and the Union Railway Station were completed in that year. It was also the year of the sinking of the *Titanic*, which took down with it the President of the Grand Trunk Railway, who owned both buildings. As a consequence, the grand opening of the hotel was cancelled.

**BYTOWN MUSEUM**

**CHATEAU LAURIER**

On the site of the Chateau Laurier Hotel is another of Colonel By's grounds. Here he had the workshops and yards for his intensive construction project, and near the north end he built his house. The house was

COLONEL BY

destroyed by fire in the 1870s, but the National Capital Commission (NCC) has excavated the foundation and recorded its history on the site, now called Major's Hill Park. The park is at the crest of what was originally known as Colonel's Hill, but By's successor was a major, and so the hill was demoted and renamed. When the Park came along in the 1880s, it was named after the hill. It also now includes Colonel By Plaza, another of the NCCs efforts to draw attention to the history of this location. A statue of Colonel By, sculpted by Émile Brunet and first unveiled here in 1971, stands at the centre of the Plaza. It was moved and re-dedicated on August 5, 1996, the first Monday in August, a day officially declared "Colonel By Day" by the Council of the City of Ottawa.

Ottawa's hero had nothing to do with Ottawa's becoming the nation's capital. John By was long gone before that event, as was the village of Bytown. The village became a town in 1847 and was renamed the City of Ottawa in 1855. What Colonel By did was to establish this location as the head of the Rideau Canal. Even earlier, the presence of the Chaudière Falls made this the natural manufacturing site for the lumber that was ripsawn from the logs floated in grand drives down the Ottawa River.

Unlike the towering pine forests, the canal was never terribly important economically. Once built, the crews dispersed and only a fraction of the workers were employed for maintenance. But, for the period between its completion in 1832 and the opening of the first serious canals on the St. Lawrence River in 1850, the Rideau Canal had its moment of glory. This was the route to travel from Montreal to Toronto. Commercial, not military, steamers and barges would come up the Ottawa River through its canals and locks from Montreal, then pass through the Rideau waterway to Kingston. There they would off-load their cargoes to bigger ships plying the Great Lakes, reload with Canadian exports and run the

RECREATIONAL CRUISE BOAT IN CANAL

rapids down to Montreal, there to be filled up again. This was a busy triangle in those years. For several decades after 1850, the Rideau Canal survived as a local commercial waterway carrying goods to and from the interior, as well as offering fine steamers for the gentry. And, for a time, vast quantities of logs felled in the Rideau corridor were locked through just like boats. Today, these commercial uses have been replaced with thriving recreational boating, and the old canal has a new lease on life.

## WALKING THE CANAL DOWNTOWN

Because the Rideau Canal runs right through downtown Ottawa, those who stroll its banks are in the heart of the historic city. Begin by taking the staircase that descends from inside the gate near the East Block of the Parliament Buildings. Walk down past those eight locks to the Ottawa River at the bottom. At the base of the Ottawa Locks is a walking path running to the west. This traverses the whole of the Parliamentary precinct right up to the National Archives. The Library of Parliament, the Centre Block and the Supreme Court rise up above. Across the Ottawa River, the curvilinear Canadian Museum of Civilization emerges; leading towards it, the handsome Interprovincial Bridge decorates the mundane act of crossing water. In the other direction is the Bytown Museum, the oldest building in Ottawa, and, on the other side of the canal, the Chateau Laurier Hotel.

HAND-CRANKED LOCKS

Walk under the plaza-like bridge above the locks and you will come upon the National Arts Centre, with its pleasant indoor and outdoor restaurant at the side of the canal. From here you can see the old Union Railway Station, now the Government Conference Centre, infamous for its many federal-provincial conferences.

INTERPROVINCIAL/ ALEXANDRA BRIDGE

If you want to ramble farther, there is a pleasant walk of a couple of kilometres along the canal and the Driveway to the Pretoria Avenue Bridge. That's the bridge with the vertical lift — which it doesn't have to do very often, so don't wait to see it. The roadway on the other side of the canal is Colonel By Drive, a good way to leave downtown by car for the airport. Until the early 1960s, it carried train tracks. There were also once basins, or lay-bys, jutting out of both sides of the canal just above the National Arts Centre. One of them fed a system that provided washing and drinking water, sometimes flushing disease to the residents of Lower Town as it made its way to the mouth of the Rideau River.

Dow's Lake

## Dow's Lake and Beyond

This walk eventually reaches Dow's Lake, a fat bulge in the canal. The channel runs along the closest end of the lake. This wasn't always a lake, but was part of an ugly swamp, impenetrable and undrainable. By's engineers, having abandoned a fanciful idea to run the canal across an aqueduct built on the stumps of living cedar, brought in Wright's Town founder Philemon Wright to build dikes around the mess, and drain it as best he could. That diking is most evident on the left side of Colonel By Drive as you approach Carleton University.

Hartwells Locks

Beyond Dow's Lake are Hartwells Locks, and eventually Hog's Back Locks and Dam, with the scenic Vincent Massey Park on the near side of the road that passes over the swing bridge, and Mooney's Bay park and beach on the other. Hog's Back is about six kilometres from downtown Ottawa, and the canal stretches on much in the same way, but with vastly greater expanses of open water, farther up the system. It is hard to imagine what the river originally did at Hog's Back. The immense dam — barely visible now because it has been so extended — was the most troublesome to build. It collapsed three times in 1828 and 1829, almost taking Colonel By with it on the last occasion. During the spring flood, he had been standing on the

top of the arch as water carried away the unfrozen ground at the bottom. At the last moment he managed to scramble to safety. There was an investigation, and, in a response to some unsought advice from the colonial governor, By dryly observed: "I feel much obliged to your Excellency's calling my attention to the necessity of building the dams perfectly impervious to water, and I beg to state on that principle I have acted from the commencement of the work."

Ottawans are proud of their canal and its builder. Colonel By was slow in getting the recognition he deserved but, at least locally, he has now achieved the status of hero. With any luck, the Rideau Canal's owners will preserve his watery legacy. And the proud facility, built to keep out Americans, is now a heavily promoted conduit for their entry.

**HOG'S BACK**

# Rockcliffe

Andrea Hossack

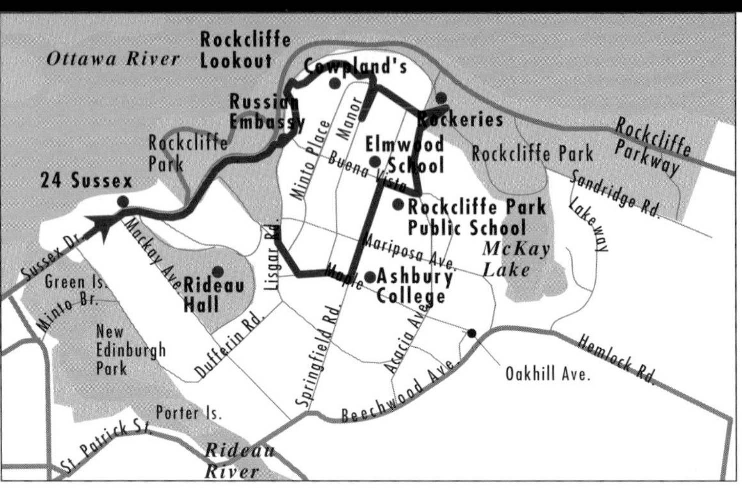


If you want to take a "Lifestyles of the Rich and Famous" tour of Ottawa, start with Rockcliffe Park. It's here in this beautiful tree-lined village that Ottawa's politicians, societal matrons and patrons, and international diplomats have held smashing dinner parties for almost a century. Rockcliffe Park is both quaint and opulent; it's a tiny-self-run village for Ottawa's elite, overlooking the Ottawa River.

Tour bus operators used to have a field day with Rockcliffe, cruising up Sussex Drive to Lisgar Road, then winding through the tiny village streets, pointing out embassy properties as they motored slowly by. The driver and guide used to head straight for the two scariest-looking official residences — the Russian residence, on Buena Vista Road, and the Iraqi residence. The Iraqi home was once recognizable for its high iron fence and the security in front of the house. Two years ago, the residents got fed up with the buses. The village's powerful little municipal council created a by-law and banned tour buses under the euphemism of "heavy vehicles." Although it was probably flattering for residents to have gawking tourists watch them go about

their showplace lives, the whole drive-by routine had overstayed its welcome.

Aside from the "star quality" of Rockcliffe Park, the village itself is a wonderful place for a walk. There is a true village atmosphere in this clean, quiet residential area. In the oldest part, the roads through the village are the same now as they were back in the early 1900s. Lawns meet the road in a natural line, without poured-concrete curbs or sidewalks. The absence of sidewalks, combined with a green canopy of towering trees, brings a feeling of simplicity and serenity to the streetscape. Walking down one of these old streets, it's easy to imagine the village back in the 1940s, when there were horses kept in stables down at the corner of Beechwood and Oakhill Avenues, and young residents would ride around the village at Christmas time, delivering gifts to friends and neighbours.

Newcomers to Rockcliffe Park buy into a community — a place where people are willing to pay a bit more for some nostalgic village life right in the middle of a big city like Ottawa. There are no churches in the village, and no commercial properties, because the people of the village don't want them there. Everyone living in Rockcliffe seems to have one car, if not five. And membership does have its privileges: Rockcliffe was protected by its own police force — a special detachment of the Ontario Provincial Police, which had a continuous contract with the tiny municipality since 1945. This arrangement only came to an end late in 1996, when Ottawa-Carleton Police Services began patrolling the village.

**PRIME MINISTER'S RESIDENCE, 24 SUSSEX DRIVE**

Pagoda-like Lookout

### Entering Rockcliffe

The approach to the village of Rockcliffe Park is spectacular. If you take winding Sussex Drive, past 24 Sussex (the residence of the Prime Minister of Canada), the Rockcliffe Parkway starts to open up, and you have an excellent view of the Ottawa River. There's a pagoda-like lookout along Sussex where you can park your car or bike and enjoy a perfect view of the sunset, or, in the early morning, a view of hot-air balloons as they're launched from across the river, in Gatineau, Québec. Though there are plenty of rocks and cliffs along this route, and even some old-growth trees clinging to those cliffs, the village wasn't named for the natural surroundings. It was named after a retired British army officer, General Rockcliffe, who lived in the village for some time. Today, the community has a population of 2,370. There are 800 homes in the village, ranging from small English-style cottages to massive mega-houses.

### Lisgar Road

Think back a couple of decades to the Cold War, and imagine what it must have been like to walk past the Soviet Ambassador's residence at Buena Vista Road and Lisgar Road. For the Russian diplomats, it was the first time they had ever lived outside a protected compound in a foreign country. Times have changed. Today, the ambassadorial family strolls through the streets of Rockcliffe Park without any high security.

U.S. Ambassador's Residence

Rockcliffe wasn't always so sedate. In the heady days of the 1960s and 1970s, when diplomat socialite Sondra Gotlieb and her husband Alan, a former Canadian Ambassador to the United States, lived there, the village was so "festive" that neighbours grumbled about the constant dinner-party noise. The Gotliebs lived on Lisgar Road, next to the Russian Ambassador.

On your way up the hill on Lisgar Road, you'll spot the sliding steel gates and rent-a-cops in front of the residence of the American Ambassador. It's now the most security-

THE STATELY HOMES OF ROCKCLIFFE

conscious residence in Rockcliffe — an ironic twist on Canada's "friendly neighbours to the south" relationship with the United States. Still, the Americans' high security is nothing compared to the kind of security that the Canadian army imposed on the village of Rockcliffe Park in 1970, during the FLQ crisis. That was the year Prime Minister Pierre Trudeau imposed martial law on the nation.

Because of the number of international diplomats in residence, Rockcliffe was kept under lock and key. Children who walked through their neighbours' properties to get to school were surprised by Canadian soldiers jumping out of the bushes, guns in hand!

TOP: COWPLAND HOUSE

ABOVE: "MEGAHOME" OF ROCKCLIFFE

### "MEGAHOMES"

Driving around Rockcliffe, you'll notice the diversity of homes — some old and some very new and opulent. There used to be a real mix of village cottages and the occasional large, historic mansion. Back in the 1960s, you could buy a modest home there for under $35,000. By the 1980s, mansion-mania had hit, and people began tearing down the cottages and replacing them with oversized dream homes. In her book *Ottawa Inside Out*, investigative journalist Stevie Cameron wrote about "ugly bunkers masquerading as homes." She discovered that "the village council have been so alarmed over these megahouses the they have recently passed bylaws restricting their size and established a high-powered 'Taste Committee' to vet designs on new developments."

With the proliferation of opulent homes, it's fun to drive around and play Queen or King for the day, deciding whether your dream home would be a stucco Tudor-style house, a crumbling old English stone "cottage," or a Hollywood fantasy like high-tech baron Michael Cowpland's gold-mirrored mansion. You can find the latter just off Minto Place, on a street called Soper Place. Built in the style of Versailles, this giant gold palace sprawls like a huge tanning salon over the lot, complete with palm trees, a pool and white Doric columns. The owner of the gold-mirrored house is one resident of Rockcliffe known for doing things in a big way: there are so many lights on the outdoor tennis courts and pool area that in summer it's constant daytime on his property. At Cowpland's last home on Buena Vista Road, the fountain was so large that when he started it up for the first time, it made a big enough noise that a neighbour thought a fire hydrant had burst and called the fire

department. If there's one mansion to see, this is by far the most extreme, but don't go on a Sunday — police have decided to barricade it on Sundays because of the hundreds of cars that have jammed into the tiny cul-de-sac, filled with curious house-gazers.

**MANOR AVENUE**

Pomp and circumstance may win the most drive-by gawkers, but the real beauty on the block belongs to the Pope. The house and grounds at 722 and 724 Manor Avenue are indicated by a sign that says "Apostolic Nunciature," or office of the papal nuncio. The house is beautifully designed — made of stone and walled-in by a stucco garden wall. As you drive down Manor Avenue and turn to the left, you can sneak a peek at the house through an arched walkway. Many Rockcliffe residents think it's the most beautiful building in the village, and should be used as the official residence of the Prime Minister, instead of 24 Sussex Drive.

MANOR HOUSE

The Pope's house was called "Manor House" when it was built by the Keefer family. The Keefers were friends of Thomas McKay — the stonemason who built Rideau Hall on Sussex Drive, now the home of Canada's Governor General. Around 1930, the Manor House was sold to Senator Cairine Wilson. She and her husband lived there for 30 years and raised their family. After the Senator's death in 1962, her family sold the Manor House to the Pope. His representatives have made some changes: a separate residence was added for the nuns who live there now, and the playroom for the Senator's children has been

transformed into a small chapel. The timeless beauty of this graceful construction overlooking the Ottawa River remains intact, and the style of the house and its surrounding landscaping evoke the image of an English country estate.

Rockcliffe School

### The Rockeries and the Schools

Despite the mega-house trend, which involved some tearing down of trees, Rockcliffe Park has managed to maintain its green, mature-tree ambiance. Visitors who seek out greenery can take a scenic walk through the Rockeries, a formal garden open to the public and maintained by the National Capital Commission. The residential streets are kept up to standards set by the local environment committee — just one of the yuppie committees for the health and well-being of the village.

Every village has its school. Never a place to skimp on resources, Rockcliffe Park has three: Ashbury College, which is a private junior and senior school, Elmwood, an all-girls school, and Rockcliffe Park Public School, where the annual Rockcliffe Book Fair takes place. The villagers of Rockcliffe Park are very proud of their fairs, which include the fall Book Fair, an antique fair and an art fair. As a tourist, you certainly won't find souvenir stands, or even a general store. Too tacky, too pedestrian. Remember: this is not a real village, it's a kingdom of the elite — a setting for Canada's version of "Lifestyles of the Rich and Diplomatic." But if you like to soak up a bit of history and practice a bit of voyeurism, you'll be welcome to stroll through the parks and walk down the streets — as long as you haven't arrived in a tour bus.

# Sandy Hill

Peter Martin

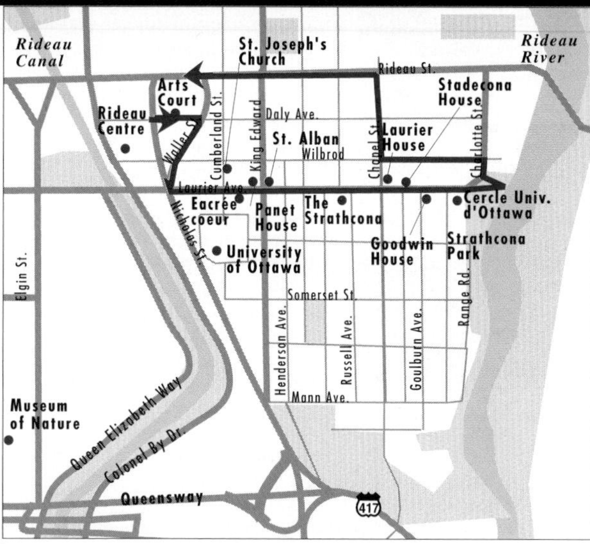


Sandy Hill, where the sudden prosperity of post-Confederation Ottawa is lovingly preserved in stone and brick, is almost an island. It's bound on the west by the Rideau Canal and on the east by the Rideau River. From north to south, Sandy Hill is the area between Rideau Street and the traffic cacophony of the Queensway (Highway 417). For many of its residents, Sandy Hill is also a state of mind. Hill dwellers are ferocious protectors of heritage architecture. They fight for and, to a degree, obtain quiet streets with overarching canopies of trees. They treasure their parks and green spaces. And they have very strong community loyalties; both their local newspaper and their community association have decades of uninterrupted existence — rare longevity for wholly volunteer institutions.

The Sandy Hill community is also, perhaps, a model for the nation in its ability to bridge the "two solitudes." First languages in this community are very roughly 60 percent English, 30 percent French, and 10 percent "other." It is very difficult to be a successful politician in Sandy Hill if French is not your first language, and almost impossible if you are not comfortably bilingual, but issues that divide the community are never along language or ethnic lines.

**Royal Oak Restaurant**

University of Ottawa

## History of Sandy Hill

From its beginning in 1828, when Louis-Theodore Besserer was granted a large tract of empty land south of Rideau Street, Sandy Hill has been primarily residential. Streets were laid out in the 1840s and people began to settle there, including Besserer himself, whose splendid 1844 house still stands at the brow of the hill at Daly and King Edward avenues. Development was slow until Confederation brought new money flooding into Ottawa to pile atop the riches accumulated by the lumber and railway barons of those low-tax days. A walking tour of Sandy Hill will call your attention to some of the very large and expensive houses erected in those salad days. I will not elaborate on a puzzling aspect of many of these dwellings: officialdom — encompassing politicians, judges, senior civil servants — was very poorly paid in Victorian times, and I have always wondered how so many of them could build so splendidly in Sandy Hill. Whatever hints of corruption echo down through the decades, the fine buildings remain to please residents and visitors alike.

The other, quite separate, engine of development for Sandy Hill was its university. Université d'Ottawa / University of Ottawa was founded by the Oblates as Bytown College in the 1840s. In 1866, the bilingual college obtained university status. Today, Ottawa U fills much of the western side of Sandy Hill between King Edward Avenue and the canal (actually, it's separated from the canal by Colonel By Drive and the Transitway), from Stewart Street to the Queensway. Though there have been the inevitable town-gown conflicts, the university's presence enriches Sandy Hill, with students adding a somewhat raucous note to local life and staff and faculty providing an intellectual and cultural element to the community.

Despite the grand old buildings, Sandy Hill is not rich as Rockcliffe is rich. Incomes are, in fact, below the Ottawa-Carleton average (the level is brought down by the large student population), but an air of comfortable prosperity does characterize the community. The prosperity is not equally shared. Some of Sandy Hill's fine old buildings are now rooming houses, others are given over to "special needs" housing, and vast wealth is hard to find. The later-built, non-Besserer part of the community south of Laurier Avenue is very middle class. Still, the man you see buying a bag of milk in one of Sandy Hill's many corner stores may be a Member

Commercial Strip, Sandy Hill

of Parliament, the woman dropping her dry cleaning off in the little commercial strip on Laurier Avenue may be head of her department at Ottawa U, and the jogger in Strathcona Park could very well be an Assistant Deputy Minister, or even a diplomat. There are about 30 embassies, chanceries and official residences in Sandy Hill (some of which you will see on your tour).

### Starting the Tour

Sandy Hill is best savoured on foot or by bicycle. You'll miss a lot of surprising (and sometimes amusing) detail if you drive. And be warned: on-street parking in Sandy Hill is generally limited to one hour; best leave your car behind, or park in one of the lots on Rideau Street at the northern edge of the community.

Bike Path, Rideau River

The tour starts at the corner of Nicholas and Daly, just southeast of the Rideau Centre. Here, at 2 Daly Avenue, is Arts Court, a fine stone building dating from 1870. It was the Carleton County courthouse until 1988 when it reopened as Ottawa's municipal arts centre. Inside are music and dance studios and art galleries. You can get program information at the reception desk in case you want to drop back later. Take a look at the stone building just behind Arts Court. Now Ottawa's youth hostel, this used to be the municipal jail (tours are available and you may well be told ghost stories). Canada's last public hanging was held in the jail's enclosed yard, behind the high stone wall just south of the main building. Also here in 1869 James Patrick Whelan was swung, before a large appreciative crowd, for the cold-blooded assassination of Thomas d'Arcy McGee.

### Laurier and King Edward Avenues

Back now to Daly, walk east, cross Waller (careful, heavy traffic: it's the main truck route through Ottawa), then walk

Arts Court

south to one of the formal entrances to the University of Ottawa. This was the western end of Wilbrod Street, but it has been closed to traffic and embellished with "heritage" street lights by the university. Turn right and walk south to Laurier Avenue. As you go, a wide lawn fringed with mature evergreens is on your left, the majesty of Taboret Hall on your right. A stylized rendering of the columns of Taboret form the University's logo.

At Laurier Avenue, the university's new "Grande Allée" leading into the heart of the campus is ahead of you. But save the campus for another time. Now, head east along Laurier. A block away at Cumberland Street, there's a church to the north and a church to the south. Both are Roman Catholic. Both have burned down twice and both have been rebuilt. The present St. Joseph's, with an English congregation, dates from 1932 and is stone-built in traditional style. Sacrée Coeur, which had Sir Wilfrid and Lady Laurier in its congregation, last burned in 1978; its present incarnation is very different from the usual gothic or romanesque churches in old neighbourhoods.

You are still on Laurier Avenue's north sidewalk. Take a moment to look ahead of you. You will see a few remnants of canopy trees that once graced the avenue; restoration of the canopy is part of the official plan for the rebuilding of Laurier Avenue and restoring the thoroughfare to some of its earlier glory. Walk on to King Edward Avenue. This very busy street was scheduled to become an expressway back in the 1970s, but local residents fought the planners to a standstill and managed, among other achievements, to save Panet House. This is a fine stone building on the northeast corner. After demolition was averted, it was restored by Sandy Smallwood, the aptly-named heritage developer who has worked extensively in Sandy Hill, and was acquired by the Chalmers Foundation as home for the Canadian Conference of the Arts.

Cross King Edward Avenue and look northwest down the hill. You can see, at the northwest corner of King Edward and Daly Avenue, the Anglican church of St. Alban the Martyr. Dating from 1867, it counted Sir John A. Macdonald among its congregants. The church was planned with a tall steeple, but excavation revealed

**Elegant Row Houses**

(surprise!) sand below the topsoil and the steeple was cancelled. Steepleless, the church is now much as it was in the years after Confederation; recent restoration work has brought out its English village-gothic charm.

Walk now a few feet north on King Edward Avenue and take a look at the lovingly maintained rowhouses of Martin Terrace and Linden Terrace. Built around the turn of the century, mostly for well-to-do civil servants, these dwellings are a feast for the eye, with fascinating architectural detail and, in season, splendid flower gardens behind their iron fences. Back now to Laurier Avenue and continue to stroll eastward.

### LAURIER HOUSE AND SURROUNDING AREA

Three blocks past King Edward you'll be at the north end of Sweetland Avenue. The whole first block of Sweetland, south from Laurier, has been given a "heritage" designation; every building on the block, representing a very wide range of design and style, is officially protected, even the somewhat dilapidated, flat-roofed boxy residence at the corner of Sweetland and Osgoode Street.

Another time, walk down Sweetland and explore the southern half of Sandy Hill (community centre, parks, tennis courts, playing fields and arenas, corner stores and restaurants). Now, though, you're still walking east on Laurier Avenue. On the southeast corner, Laurier and Russell Avenue, railway contractor George Goodwin's 1900 blond brick mansion has 33 rooms. In the Second World War, it was used by the Women's Army Corps and had six jail cells in the basement. This impressive mansion is now lovingly maintained as national headquarters for St. John Ambulance.

LAURIER HOUSE

A block further east, at Chapel Street, you come to the essential Sandy Hill building — Laurier House, Sir Wilfrid's Ottawa home. When Lady Laurier died, Mackenzie King moved in. Most accounts say Lady Laurier willed the property to King, but this is not quite accurate. She gave the house to the Liberal Party as a residence for the party leader, but King, in his wily, acquisitive way, took it as his own. In the long run, no harm was done, as King in turn gave the house to the nation. It is now managed by the Department of Canadian Heritage and is open to the public (entry used to be free, but a small admission charge was imposed in 1996). Visitors can view well-maintained period furniture and decor and inspect the study King created for himself on the third floor. It was here that our prime minister consulted

Strathcona Fountain

the spirits of his mother and other departed souls. Laurier House also features a recreation of Lester B. Pearson's study, though Pearson never lived here.

Long before Laurier and King lived in Sandy Hill, Sir John A. Macdonald enjoyed the sprawling stone splendour of Stadacona Hall, behind the iron fence a little farther along Laurier Avenue. How could a lawyer from Kingston afford a place like this? Never mind, he could and he did. And there were peacocks on the lawn in his day. Later the building became the Belgian Embassy, and in 1996 it became the chancery of the High Commission of Brunei. The Sultan of Brunei is the world's richest individual and the sultanate is his personal fief. Sandy Hillers expect Sir John's house will be well maintained.

So, too, will the massive early twentieth-century apartment building on the south side of Laurier Avenue, the Strathcona. Prime Minister John Diefenbaker lived here for a while, as did Tommy Douglas, Leader of the New Democratic Party. Subsequently the building was somewhat neglected, but it has found new life in the hands of Sandy Smallwood, the heritage developer mentioned earlier for his restoration of Panet House.

## Strathcona Park and Beyond

A little farther on is Range Road, in sight of Strathcona Park, Sandy Hill's magnificent green space on the Rideau. Across Laurier Avenue to the south side is Le Cercle Universitaire d'Ottawa, a luxurious private club. The building was once the mirror-twin of Laurier House but renovations over the years have made the two mansions look as different as can be.

Strathcona Park

Now cross. You are at the Strathcona Fountain. Imported from England in 1909, the fountain had long been inoperative and dilapidated when it was restored in 1995. In season, you are soothed by the splash of falling water as you gaze out over the green expanse of Strathcona Park. If you have time, go down the wide steps into the park. In the north corner, almost beneath the Russian Embassy looming above, is the stage where Odyssey Theatre performs plays in the mask style of *commedia dell'arte*. At the water's edge, a paved path takes you south along the Rideau River bank as far as the Queensway and Hurdman Bridge. You are sure to see ducks. If you're lucky you will see the royal swans, or perhaps a muskrat or a great blue heron. Red-winged blackbirds and aggressive gulls will trill and screech.

There are a few spots along this river bank where the city disappears and you are alone with primordial nature.

If you don't have time to stroll down into the park, take a look at the massive building around the curve on Charlotte Street. It was here that the Cold War began on the night Igor Gouzenko defected with spy documents from the Soviet Embassy. The building you see is not the one of Gouzenko's day. That one, a mansion built for the son of lumber baron J.R. Booth before it became the embassy, burned to the ground in 1956. The Soviets rebuilt in a kind of bunker style and the Russians have subsequently humanized it a bit by adding new vertical windows to the front.

One of the witnesses of the embassy fire on New Year's Day in 1956 was Senator Norman Paterson, who lived around the corner at 500 Wilbrod Street. Sadly, the Paterson House, one of the most imposing mansions in Sandy Hill, was virtually abandoned, and, by 1990, was falling into ruin. Then Sandy Smallwood (remember him?) and partners acquired the property. They restored it to its turn-of-the-century opulence and sold it to the Natural Law Party. It is now their national headquarters and they will welcome you if you want to tour the building.

**RUSSIAN EMBASSY**

Walking tours are tiring, and now might be the time to take a bus back to the Rideau Centre. You can wait at the nearest stop or you can walk north on Charlotte to Rideau Street for more frequent service. However, if you're still going strong, head back west on any of the four streets between Laurier Avenue and Rideau Street. Each of them offers delights for the senses — great trees, splendid gardens, fine buildings. And, as you walk along, be sure to look up. More often than not, the builders of Sandy Hill's heritage homes lavished as much attention to detail at the roof-line as at ground level. There is still much to see – so come again to Sandy Hill, a community where people have a proud sense of place.

# Into the Gatineau Hills

Hope MacLean

To really appreciate the beauty of the Gatineau Hills and the historic sites in the villages of the area, allow yourself at least half a day. This trip starts in busy downtown Ottawa and takes you to the contrasting rural idyll that lies across the river. The drive from Ottawa to the village of Wakefield is just 25 minutes by highway, but allow several hours to explore the side roads and walk through the villages.

Autumn in the Gatineau Hills

## History of the Gatineau Hills

A trip to the Gatineau Hills is a trip through history. Geologists say that these hills, with their unusual high, rounded shapes, are the remnants of one of the oldest mountain ranges in the world, ground down by thousands of years of ice, wind and water. The first inhabitants were the Algonquin Indians, who today have a large reserve in Maniwaki, an hour north of Ottawa. Traditionally, this was their hunting grounds. From the seventeenth to the nineteenth centuries, the Ottawa River was a highway for the fur trade, and the Indians brought their furs down the

Ottawa River

Gatineau River to trade.

The first industrial development was logging. In 1800, lumber baron Philemon Wright founded Wright's Town and developed his lumber interests. Loggers moved up the river systems in search of stands of virgin red and white pine. In winter, they left their families, and moved to shanty camps in the bush; in spring, the logs floated down the Gatineau River to Ottawa. By the 1830s, Irish settlers were moving up the river, clearing the land to raise horses and fodder for the lumber camps. Shortly after, French settlers and trappers established their own nearby towns, such as Ste-Cecile-de-Masham. Today, towns such as Chelsea and Wakefield are mainly English-speaking, and visitors can be assured of service in both French and English. Both these villages are centres for artists and craftspeople inspired by the beauty of the Gatineau Hills.

## From Ottawa to Hull

The tour begins on Albert Street in the centre of Ottawa. Follow it down to Booth Street (named after a nineteenth-century lumber baron) and turn right. On either side are the large open fields of Le Breton Flats. At one time this was a thriving community of small wooden houses built for workers in the Bytown lumber mills. In the 1960s, in a fit of civic pride, Ottawa expropriated whole communities, bulldozed homes, and has never been able to decide what to do with the land since.

The Merchants of Wakefield

Continue on Booth Street to the Chaudière Bridge, taking note of the buildings of the E.B. Eddy Company, one of the last lumber companies in Ottawa. They still make fine paper here. From the metal, arched bridge, the curving stone shelfs of the Chaudière Falls can be seen. At one time, voyageurs portaged around this boiling cauldron of water; now the falls have been harnessed to provide hydro-electric power. On the right, there is a good view of the Parliament Buildings.

Across the bridge, on the left, are the cut-stone buildings of the Eddy Plant, which dates from 1892. On the northwest corner are the tall red-brick and glass towers of Terrasses de la Chaudière. These buildings were erected during the Trudeau era to house federal government departments and declare a federal presence in Hull. Turn left at the lights onto Alexandre Tache Boulevard, then go one block and turn right onto Montcalm Street. Note the picturesque little Théâtre de l'Isle, set on an island in the middle of Brewery Creek which runs through Hull. A few blocks beyond is a renovated 94-year-old stone

Hull Waterfront

pumphouse that houses the Ecomuseum of Hull. This museum focuses on the geology and wildlife of the local area. Across the bridge, turn right onto the ramp for Highway A50 and observe the Hull Casino, with its dramatic location on a triangular point that juts out into a lake made in a former rock quarry. From the highway, admire the magnificent fountain gushing high into the air.

Bridge Entering Hull

## Chelsea

Exit just past the casino onto Highway A5 going north to Maniwaki. The escarpment of the Gatineau Hills rises sharply, about 300 metres above the valley. Exit at Chelsea and turn left to Old Chelsea, a small community that once was a way station for lumberers and farmers travelling up the valley. Now it is a chic bedroom community for those who savour country life, within fifteen-minutes' drive of Parliament Hill. There are fine restaurants, an art gallery and craft shops. At the corner of Chelsea Road and Scott Road is the former Dunn's Hotel, a green-and-white, two-storey building with a large verandah, dating from the late 1800s. Behind it is the old pioneer cemetery maintained by the Historical Society of the Gatineau, where early settlers, such as Asa Meech, are buried.

Chelsea is also a jumping-off point for winter skiing, and summer swimming and hiking in the Gatineau Park. The National Capital Commission maintains a visitors' centre at the edge of the village. Stop to pick up guide books and maps for the trails and visit the small museum for an overall view of the park and its ecology (see Outdoor Recreation, p. 110.) If you arrive after October 15, be sure to ask at the visitors' centre which roads and sites are open.

Hull Casino

## Gatineau Park and the Mackenzie King Estate

If you have time, plan an expedition into the park. The biways in Gatineau Park are open to vehicles from spring through fall. In winter, they are open to skiers only. Worth a visit is Pink Lake. Despite its name, it is really milky-green and its unique ecosystem is a remnant of an ancient glacial lake. Nearby parkways lead to the Champlain, Huron and Brulé lookouts, which offer magnificent views across the Ottawa Valley.

The not-to-be-missed highlight of the park is the Mackenzie King Estate, where the former Prime Minister rested from the stresses of running the country by walking his dog Pat on the 230-hectare grounds. King actually had several residences on the estate, which he used at different times. Kingswood is a small cottage by the lake, which he enlarged over the years. Stroll down to the boathouse to admire the formal steps leading to the lake, and imagine visitors stepping daintily into canoes to paddle the quiet waters of Kingsmere Lake.

Moorside is a much grander house, with formal gardens and a sweeping entrance; it was used for entertaining when King was Prime Minister. The lawns are dotted with magnificent pine and spruce trees, and trails lead off to the artificial ruins of "King's follies." In Moorside itself, there is a museum upstairs and a tearoom downstairs. The tearoom is open all year and offers sandwiches, cakes and old English scones that visitors can enjoy in dark wood-panelled elegance, warmed by a tall stone fireplace. The third building on King's estate is the Farm, his winter residence. This building is not open to the public, as it is now the official residence of the Speaker of the House of Commons.

**Mackenzie King's Follies**

## Meech Lake

Follow the road past the visitors' centre, as it winds past ski hills and comes out on the exquisite Meech Lake, one of a chain of three long lakes that form the heart of the Gatineau Park. The others are Harrington Lake (Lac Mousseau), official summer home of the current prime minister, and Lac Philippe, which is entered through the north end of the park.

Drive up the south side and admire the Meech Lake Conference Centre high on a cliff overlooking the south end of the lake. Here, in 1987, Prime Minister Brian Mulroney isolated the provincial premiers until they hammered out the constitutional deal known as the Meech Lake Accord. Continue past cottages and beaches until you reach

**Kingswood**

the guarded barricade that controls the entrance to the prime minister's estate.

### WAKEFIELD

After exploring Gatineau Park, return to Chelsea, turn left at Scott Road, and take Highway A5 north to Wakefield. As you come down the hill, admire the jewel-like setting of this charming village, tucked in amongst the high hills beside the Gatineau River. Founded in the 1830s, Wakefield has many historic buildings still in use today, despite a fire which destroyed part of the town in 1904. Nearby, archaeologists have discovered an Indian burial ground. Until the early 1990s, the bay in front of Wakefield was filled with logs, which were floated down the river to Ottawa. This reminder of the lumbering tradition ended when a new factory in Maniwaki was built to chip logs, intended for pulp and paper, so they could be shipped by truck instead. There are still many who regret the passing of the tranquil sight of logs floating gently down the river.

MEECH LAKE CONFERENCE CENTRE

At the intersection of Valley Drive and River Road is one of the oldest buildings in Wakefield. Upstairs, in Place 1870, is the original town meeting hall, which later became a theatre, complete with miniature wooden stage and tiny dressing rooms to one side. Later a projectionist's booth was built at the back, and the theatre became a cinema. Now it is an antique shop (open on weekends only), which perfectly preserves the theatre's historic character.

An antique steam train arrives in Wakefield most summer afternoons. The train runs between Hull and Wakefield, and winds along the Gatineau River; its route is at its most beautiful in late September and October, when the scarlet and gold of the sugar maples blanket the hills. The rail line to Wakefield was built in 1891 when travel by horse and wagon was difficult among the steep hills. It was continued on to Maniwaki by 1903, and, for many years, carried goods and commuters, as well as cottagers in summer and skiers in winter. As road travel improved, rail travel declined, and finally the Canadian Pacific Railroad ceased service in 1986. Wakefield is now the end of the line, and the working diesel train has been replaced by a tourist steam train. The 1907 engine, which was still in use to haul freight, was purchased in Sweden and shipped to Canada.

WAKEFIELD MILLS

The train turns around at the north end of town on a hand-powered turntable. The mechanism is so delicately balanced that just four people can move the engine. Immediately south of the turntable is the old railway station, now a restaurant. Its platform is a terrace, with a magnificent view of the bay, and the kitchen is in the former ticket-master's office.

Continue north to Gendron Road and turn right to see the covered foot-bridge. When the 70-year-old bridge was burned by an arsonist in 1984, the village began to raise funds to replace its beloved bridge. Finally, in 1996, two new trusses were floated by barge across the bay and lifted onto the old piers. The giant beams were sawn from old booms that once encircled logs floating down the river.

Return south through the village to visit interesting shops and galleries, and don't miss the chance to visit the grave of Prime Minister Lester B. Pearson, winner of the Nobel Peace Prize. In keeping with Pearson's modest and self-effacing style, he is buried in a simple country cemetery. Turn up Mill Road and proceed along the rapids of the LaPeche River. Cross the small bridge over the dam and continue up the hill on a winding gravel road. The tiny cemetery perched on top of the hill is marked by a Canadian flag. Pearson's grave is under a large black stone on the northeast side of the cemetery, close to the forest. A few stones over lies Eric Morse, the well-known writer on northern canoe routes.

On the way back down, stop at the historic Wakefield Mill, which was formerly a museum, but is now closed. It started out as a grist mill in 1838, and was then purchased by the MacLaren family, who added a saw mill, a woollen mill and a general store. Facing it across the river is a large red-brick Victorian house, once the MacLaren home. Beside the mill rushes the waterfall which powered the mill. These buildings are owned by the National Capital Commission, and you can stroll around the grounds.

To return to Ottawa, follow highways 105 and A5 which cross the mountain, revealing a final magnificent view of the Gatineau Hills and the city of Ottawa.

WAKEFIELD-HULL-CHELSEA STEAM LOCOMOTIVE

CLOCK TOWER AT THE ALMONTE POST OFFICE

This Lanark County tour takes visitors to a vibrant area full of historic sites, pioneer cemeteries, conservation areas, towns, museums, festivals and studio tours. The county is rich in history and culture, and well worth more than one short visit. Tourists are catered to in Eastern Ontario, and visitors will readily find guides to car, bus and walking tours as they travel the region.

In the nineteenth century, Lanark County was a successful and prosperous region. It had been first settled by United Empire Loyalists at the end of the eighteenth century, and then, early in the 1800s, by demobbed British soldiers, and Irish and Scottish settlers. The region benefitted from the manufacturing boom of the day, which was fuelled by its forests, dairy products and woollen goods. The beautiful stone houses built by Scottish stonemasons for successful businessmen still dot the countryside and add to the charm of the small towns. Many of them now house museums, restaurants and shops, since tourism, arts and crafts have, for the most part, replaced industry in the region's economy. Lanark County is also proud to be know as the Maple Syrup Capital of Ontario.

## ALMONTE

The first leg of the tour takes you from Ottawa to the charming town of Almonte. Leave Ottawa by way of the Queensway (Highway 417) travelling west and follow it to the end, passing a big Ikea on the left, then the Bayshore Shopping Centre on the right and finally Ottawa's new sports arena, the Corel Centre, on the left. (If it is a Saturday, you might first plan to take in the gigantic flea market at Stittsville. In that case, turn onto Highway 5 just before the Queensway ends.)

To reach Almonte, continue along Highway 17 to Highway 44 and turn left towards the town. Rolling countryside, boggy wetlands and attractive stands of evergreens provide the scenery along the way. As you pass, note Peter Robinson Road, which commemorates the man who supervised the settlement of Irish immigrants in this part of the country in 1823. At Almonte, follow Highway 44 all the way into town, watching for Mary Street on the right just before going over the second bridge. Turn here and follow it for two blocks to the end at Rosamond Street.

LEFT: MISSISSIPPI VALLEY TEXTILE MUSEUM

ALMONTE ROSAMOND WOOLLEN COMPANY

Our first stop, the Mississippi Valley Textile Museum, is right in front of you, housed in what used to be the Rosamond Textile Mill. Almonte's great potential in the early nineteenth century lay in the cheap power that could be produced from the Mississippi River falls, which dropped about 20 metres at this spot. In 1851, James Rosamond, an Irish immigrant, arrived at the village of Waterford, as it was then called. He had already established a woollen mill at nearby Carleton Place and went on to build two more here. The town was renamed Almonte after the Mexican general Juan Almonte, whose championing of Mexican independence against American aggression appealed to the town's inhabitants. During the following decades, Almonte became the hub of Canada's woollen industry, and for a time its name was synonymous with fine woollen goods throughout the world. By 1890, more than 500 people were employed in the Rosamond factories.

Here are the original offices of the period, with their old wooden floors and pressed tin ceilings. The history of the

THE FOUNDING OF ALMONTE

The sawmill and grist-mill completed here on the Mississippi River in 1823 by Daniel Shipman provided the nucleus around which a community known as Shipman's Mills had developed by 1824. About 1850 two town plots were laid out here - "Victoria" by Edward Mitcheson and "Ramsayville" by Daniel Shipman. They were combined in 1853 as "Waterford", which in 1855 was renamed "Almonte", probably after Juan N. Almonte, a famous Mexican general and diplomat. The opening of several woollen mills and the completion of a railway to Brockville fostered the growth of Almonte, which by 1870 was one of Ontario's leading woollen cloth manufacturing centres. Incorporated as a village in 1871, with a population of about 2000, Almonte was proclaimed a town in 1880.

manufacture of woolen goods can be traced through the machinery on display — carding machines, bobbin winders, looms and knitting machines. There is also a display of early home sewing machines. Special exhibitions of quilts, felt hangings and other related crafts are on view during the year. Books and pamphlets on nearby historic sites are available in the gift shop. The museum is open from mid-May to mid-October, Tuesday to Friday, from 8:30 am to 4:30 pm, and on request at other times.

After leaving the museum, follow Mary Street back to Highway 44 and turn right over the bridge. Take the next left onto Mill Street and park again. Mill Street is a short, congested street, full of historic buildings, including the Victoria Woollen Mill,which now houses a café and gallery, gift and antique stores and Ottawa Valley Books, another good place for additional information on the surrounding area. At the top of the street sits the imposing heritage building that was once the post office, designed in 1889 by Thomas Fuller, architect of the original Centre Block on Parliament Hill (see Parliament Hill, p. 32). Walk behind the building along Little Bridge Street, under the train bridge and past the Visitor Information Centre. Turn left at Bridge Street and pass the municipal offices to a tiny park on the edge of the Mississippi River where you can rest on the millstone bench and read the verse that begins "Stranger sit and rest and dream." On the way back, cross Little Bridge Street to see *The Volunteer*, Almonte's war memorial sculpted by Robert Tait McKenzie.

**The Millstone Bench in Almonte**

**Kintail**

## Mill of Kintail

When it's time to leave, go back to Highway 44, turn left and continue the equivalent of a block to the Metcalfe Conservation Area. Here the Mississippi River broadens into a peaceful bay, while a little farther out its energetic rapids continue to roll and tumble — a good place to pause, enjoy the view, and eat a picnic lunch.

After leaving the Conservation Area, continue along Highway 44 to Highway 15. Turn right and take it north for a visit to the museum at the

Naismith Family Home

Mill of Kintail. Follow the clearly marked route to the mill, but, before turning left at the Clayton Road, continue a few metres farther along to read the plaque dedicated to Dr. James Naismith, the inventor of basketball and a favourite son of the region. Beyond it is a beautiful stone house, his boyhood home.

Less than a kilometre along the Clayton Road, don't miss the curious, weathered, hand-carved sign on the left. It commemorates the day in 1860 when the Prince of Wales, later King Edward VII, paused to drink from the spring among the cedars. He was in Canada to lay the cornerstone for the Parliament Buildings in Ottawa.

The Mill of Kintail is a beautifully located Conservation Area, with a field of apple trees, picnic tables and a children's playground. There are about three kilometres of trails — pleasant for walking during most of the year and for skiing during the winter months.

Baird's Mill

Baird's Mill, as it was originally known, was a stone grist mill operating with water power from the Indian River, a tributary of the Mississippi River. It was part of the land on which Dr. Robert Tait McKenzie played as a boy, sometimes with James Naismith — the two were boyhood friends. Tait McKenzie, born in 1867, the year of Confederation, was the son of Scottish pioneers. He went on to become a champion athlete, a noted surgeon and a gifted sculptor — a renaissance man of his day. His expertise in anatomy is evident in many of his sculptures — heroic representations of athletic figures. After the First World War, McKenzie created a number of famous memorials and commemorative medals for Scotland, the United States and Canada,

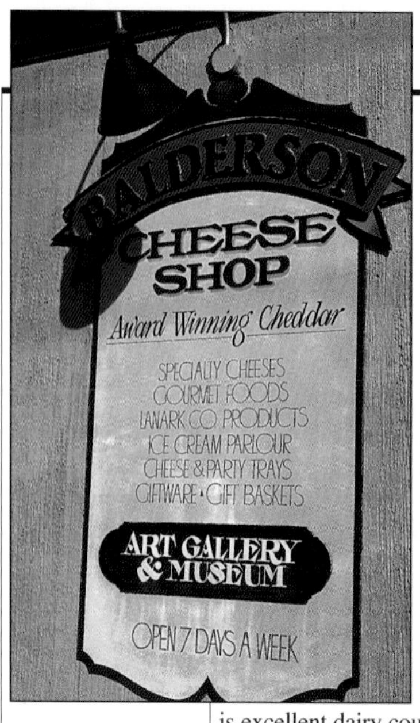


including the one mentioned above in Almonte. At the mill, visitors can see examples of his work in the museum operated by the Mississippi Valley Conservation Area.

### Lanark and Balderson

After leaving the mill, turn right when you return to the Clayton Road and follow it to the end. Then turn left onto County Road 9 and then right on County Road 16 and, finally, left at Highway 511, heading south to Perth. The route takes you through the village of Lanark, home of the famous Glenayr "Kitten" sweater factory. A little farther on, at the village of Balderson, stop at the Balderson Cheese Shop for one of its famous ice cream cones and to see an amazing array of kitchenware and gifts — and, of course, to buy some of the local cheese. Lanark is excellent dairy country and at one time small cheese factories could be found every few miles. Now only the Balderson Cheese Factory, founded in 1881, remains.

### Perth

After turning left at Highway 7 in Perth, continue to the next stop light and turn right on Wilson Street West. Follow Wilson into the centre of Perth, pass Foster Street, and turn into the municipal parking lot on the left. There is plenty to see and do within easy walking distance.

Perth was founded in 1816 by the British Army. The Rideau Canal was still in the planning stage and this strategic spot was seen as a good place to station troops in the event of attack by the Americans. It is situated on the

Tay River and its central core lies on an island between the Tay and the Little Tay Rivers.

The earliest settlement in the Perth region was on land awarded to United Empire Loyalists in the late 1780s. Although they and the Scots, who arrived as a result of immigration programs, were the earliest settlers here, they were soon outnumbered by the Irish. The village lacked the water power so important to the early success of Almonte, but benefitted first from a connection to the Rideau Canal via the Tay Canal, and later from the Canadian Pacific Railway in the 1880s.

The town's slow growth (its motto is "Make Haste Slowly") in the twentieth century was a blessing in disguise. The beautiful stone buildings, which might otherwise have been sacrificed to progress, remained standing. They were renewed in the 1980s as part of a Heritage Canada pilot project, one which commits it to preserving the historic, architectural characteristics of the city without turning it into a living museum. The result is the architectural jewel that is Perth today.

Walk back to Wilson Street and turn left. At the end of the block is an imposing stone factory, Code's Felt Mill. Part of the building dates from 1842, and felt is still manufactured on the premises. Around the corner is Code's own beautiful house at 50 Herriott Street. Across the street from the mill is Code Park, originally a drying field for felt from the factory, separated from Stewart Park by the Little Tay River, but joined by a small foot bridge. Below the bridge the stream rushes by and, to the right, a row of charming stone condominiums can be seen in what was originally a small factory.

**CODE'S MILL, PERTH**

**HERRIOTT STREET, PERTH**

Walk back up Wilson to Foster Street, turn right and one block over right again onto Gore Street East. The next two blocks are an architectural delight. Just a few steps from the corner at 11 Gore Street East is the Perth Museum, formerly the home of one of the town's most illustrious citizens, Roderick Matheson, and considered to be one of the finest houses in Perth. The museum is furnished in the style of the period with a pioneer kitchen and second-floor drawing room. On the third floor is an eclectic collection typical of small-town museums, with items ranging from a case of Anasazi native pottery

**CONDOMINIUMS, PERTH**

from the southwestern United States to the dueling pistols used in the last fatal duel fought in Canada. This duel took place in Perth. One curious item is a fragment of the famous Mammoth Cheese produced in Perth in 1892. The cheese was about two metres high, nine metres around and weighed almost 10,000 kilograms! After being exhibited at the World's Fair in Chicago, it was displayed throughout Great Britain and finally carved up and sold. This crumbling bit is all that remains.

Turn left after leaving the museum and enjoy the well-maintained heritage architecture in every direction. For

PERTH MARKET

information on a more detailed tour of the town's famous buildings, drop into the Valley Bookshop in the next block. Then you might want to stop at Stony's restaurant and, in fine weather, enjoy a cool drink on the outside balcony that hangs over the Little Tay.

Continue for another block, passing a sign marking the entrance to the Rideau Trail, a 300-kilometre hiking trail that runs between Kingston and Ottawa. Turn left on Basin Street for a view of the attractive new market building sitting on the edge of the Tay River Basin. Then walk past it to Drummond Street East and turn right over the bridge where the Little Tay joins the Tay itself. On the left hand side of the street are the Summit, the town's first brick house and, in the next block, Perth's first Anglican church, followed by the Palladian-styled District Court House and Registry Office, both built in 1872.

Backtrack a block and turn left onto Harvey Street, walking one short block back to Gore, passing the

McMARTIN HOUSE, PERTH

ostentatious, cupola-topped McMartin house on the left, now owned by the Ontario Heritage Foundation and used as a centre for Perth's senior citizens. Take a moment to pause at the corner and smile at the Butcher's Edge with its famous sculpted cow gazing out the window.

One block farther along Gore Street is the dignified Town Hall. Just past it, Market Street leads back to Stewart Park. From here you can cross the foot bridge and walk back up Wilson Street to the car park.

To return to Ottawa, retrace your way back to Highway 7 and follow it east or, for a longer trip, continue on to Merrickville and pick up the Rideau tour there (see Manotick, Burritts Rapids & Merrickville, p. 160.)

PERTH FOOTBRIDGE

# Manotick, Burritts Rapids & Merrickville

John McManus

Manotick Murals

A drive along the Rideau River, through the villages of Manotick, Burritts Rapids and Merrickville, is a pleasant change of pace for visitors to Ottawa. Heritage architecture, rural beauty and interesting shops and restaurants are found along the way.

## Manotick

Begin by following the Rideau Canal along either Prince of Wales Drive or the Driveway to Highway 16 South. From here, it is fifteen minutes to the turnoff for Manotick, down County Road 13. A series of murals on the side of a building welcomes you to the village. Park the car and enjoy the village on foot. A two-block stroll down Mill Street, on the left, takes the visitor past shops and businesses on a landscaped street to Dickinson Square. Here Watson's Mill, Dickinson House and an adjoining drive shed have been preserved as the headquarters of the Rideau Valley Conservation Authority.

Watson's Mill

Manotick was just a tiny settlement

Lindsay & McCaffrey

on the canal until Moss Kent Dickinson, the King of the Rideau, moved here from Bytown. In 1859 he and Joseph Currier, his partner in the timber trade, built the mill on Long Island. Manotick was not lucky for Currier. After his wedding, he was showing his wife Ann Crosby around the new mill, when her skirts became entangled in the turning machinery and she was killed. After the tragedy, Currier left Manotick for New Edinburgh where he built 24 Sussex Drive, now the residence of the Prime Minister. Dickinson, however, prospered in Manotick. During his career as a forwarder, he commissioned 16 steamers and 84 barges and tugs. He also built a sawmill, a planing mill and a woollen mill on Long Island, projects that assured the growth and prosperity of the village. A plaque, interpretive signs and a cairn at the mill tell his story.

Back on the main street, the visitor finds a collection of pubs, tearooms, gift shops and galleries. Under the intriguing sign "Lindsay and McCaffrey, General Merchants," a contemporary clothing store operates from the virtually unchanged nineteenth-century premises of a general store.

The Miller's Oven

**Burritts Rapids**

After returning to the car, continue through Manotick on County Road 13, following the river. Turn right onto Roger Stevens Drive (County Road 6), left at Highway 16, then right on Dilworth Road (County Road 13) at the sign for Merrickville. After less than a kilometre, turn left onto the Fourth Line Road (County Road 5). Continue past the Rideau River Provincial Park and take County Road 2 to Burritts Rapids and Merrickville.

Burritts Rapids is one of the industrial hamlets that developed around sites with water power during the last century. It is now a quiet residential village. This land along the Rideau River was part of the Crawford Purchase, a parcel bought from the Mississauga Indians in the early 1780s for United

**Bridge at Burritts Rapids**

Empire Loyalists. It was not surveyed until 1791, and two years later, Steven Burritt, a Vermont Loyalist, was granted the land on which the village now stands. By 1796, other Loyalists were settling on lots south of the Rideau River. Construction of the Rideau Canal was influencing growth in the 1820s when Henry Burritt subdivided a river lot and began selling village properties to new arrivals.

The first of a series of permanent bridges was built in 1824, the locks for the Rideau Canal just a few years later, and the first grist mill in Burritts Rapids was erected in 1831 by Terrance Smith, whose son later founded Smiths Falls. John Strachan French, the son of an important Loyalist settler on the St. Lawrence, bought the mill in 1840 and soon he had a store, a saw mill and a shingle mill. Ten years later, a woollen mill, which continued to operate until fire destroyed it in 1950, was built by Alexander Kerr. Inns, stores, and trade shops also flourished, but the economic changes that occurred when the village was bypassed by the railway sent most of the businesses into a decline in the late nineteenth century. Today, only a few of these commercial buildings survive.

**Christ Church, Burritts Rapids**

**Burritts Rapids General Store**

A number of attractive buildings do still remain in Burritts Rapids. Christ Church, completed in 1832, has been in continuous use ever since. The Methodist Church (built in 1851) is now a private residence. A store built by J.S. French in 1841 now serves as the Community Hall. Nineteenth-century houses of stone, brick and clapboard still grace the village. Examples of the smaller workingmen's houses from the nineteenth century are increasingly rare today, but in Burritts Rapids six or seven remain and are still in use as family homes. Historic plaques at Christ Church and the Community Hall tell of the building of the Church and about the founding of Burritts Rapids. As well, there are interpretive signs for the walking trails that are maintained along the Rideau Canal banks, which

Farmhouse near Merrickville

run east to the locks and west to the end of the island. In the village, the General Store offers a variety of goods, of which ice cream cones are a specialty.

## Merrickville

Back in the car, cross the Rideau Canal at Burritts Rapids, turn right and follow County Road 23 to Merrickville. This tree-lined route winds past fine examples of period architecture in log, stone and brick. It continues through Andrewsville, once a thriving community with busy mills and now a ghost town, and past two early graveyards. This is a favourite route for cyclists, who comment on the courtesy shown by motorists sharing the road.

Block House, Merrickville

At Highway 43, turn right to Merrickville. Known as the best preserved nineteenth-century village in Canada, Merrickville has more than 100 historic and heritage properties. So many of these buildings have been designated as significant, that Merrickville has the highest ratio of such properties in Ontario. A number of them are featured in *Merrickville, Jewel of the Rideau,* a book by historian Larry Turner.

Merrickville's first inhabitant, Roger Stevens, a Vermont Loyalist, settled at the Great Falls on the Rideau in 1790 and built a sawmill. He sold it to William Merrick who, by 1803, had also built a grist mill. He was followed in business by his sons, who added a woollen mill, a shingle mill, another grist mill, an inn and a store. Soon others were attracted to the area and, by mid-century, tanneries, foundries, more stores, professional offices and trades shops were serving

United Church

a population of 1,000. As the need for water power declined, industry waned in Merrickville. During the past three decades, however, many of the houses and buildings have been rehabilitated and a new life has begun for the village. Before beginning to explore, you may want to pick up the map of the village available from any of the local stores.

At the main intersection of the village, you are surrounded by restored stone buildings. The Merrickville Blockhouse, built for the defence of the Rideau Canal route by Colonel By's engineers, houses the Blockhouse Museum. Parks Canada grounds stretch east along the three locks and the swing bridge, and west to the Depot, an early warehouse that is now home to the Friends of the Rideau. Kitty-corner to the Blockhouse is the Merrickville United Church, a twentieth-century stone structure. Just east, the Sam Jakes Inn provides accommodation and meals in a house built in 1861. Back at the corner, the Arron Merrick Building has been restored as a shopping gallery and commercial space. Opposite is the massive Jakes Block, with a restaurant, a pub, an antique and art gallery, apartments and shops.

Photographs and feature articles on the walls of Harry McLean's Pub tell the story of Merrickville's most colourful resident. When H.F. McLean moved to Merrickville in 1920, he had a reputation for completing construction projects in difficult terrain and had been instrumental in providing rail service for troops in the First World War. McLean built rail lines through Northern Ontario from his base in Merrickville for the next two decades and bought both the Arron Merrick house and the Jakes Block. However, he is remembered chiefly for his eccentricities. He kept a private zoo, held children's parties, donated generously to local projects, ran a team of huskies, partied long and hard, and during bouts of roistering sometimes caused riots by throwing money out of hotel room windows to appreciative crowds on the street below.

Public Library

St. Lawrence Street, leading south from the canal, features historic buildings, stores, restaurants, boutiques and a shopping arcade. A restaurant with a Dickens theme occupies an early stone building that housed the

Mechanics Institute, the 1850s forerunner of today's public library. Next door, the Charles Holden Store (built around 1850) still operates as a general store. Two blocks down the street, the City Hotel, built in 1856, houses an English-style pub and, opposite it, a stone house has been converted to a gift shop and residence. Many other buildings of architectural note line St. Lawrence Street as far as the southern boundary of the village.

**ST. LAWRENCE ST.**

Don't fail to visit Merrickville's side streets. Tearooms, art galleries, antique stores, gift shops, artists studios and artisan workshops dot the area on either side of St.

GLASS BLOWER, MERRICKVILLE

Lawrence Street and can be easily located using the village map. Many houses of historic and aesthetic interest, restored and rehabilitated over the past few years, are also located on the map.

### NORTH MERRICKVILLE AND SMITHS FALLS

North Merrickville, on the other side of the river, is also worth visiting. A nineteenth-century foundry, in continuous operation for more than a century, and a working boatyard occupy industrial buildings that once housed water-powered machinery. Parks Canada has stabilized the ruins

MERRICKVILLE BOAT YARD

of the Watchorn Woollen Mill that burned in 1954, after 106 years of operation, and has landscaped part of the island as a memorial to Merrickville's industrial past.

Highway 43 west from Merrickville leads to Smiths Falls, 20 kilometres away. Travellers might be interested in visiting the Heritage House Museum, the Railway Museum that celebrates Smiths Falls' history as a railroad centre, the new Rideau Canal Museum and the Hershey chocolate factory.

## RETURN TO OTTAWA

To return to Ottawa, take County Road 2 (Donnely Drive) back to Burritts Rapids from North Merrickville along the north shore of the Rideau Canal. Art galleries, riding stables, bed and breakfasts, and artisan shops can be seen along the way, as can some of the most impressive architecture in the area, including three two-storey, late Georgian stone houses. Two barns copied from model barns built by the Ottawa Experimental Farm at the turn of the century, as well as a good example of an early Ontario cottage, add interest to the drive. Once back at Burritts Rapids, head east to Highway 16 and back to Ottawa.

Other great colourguides include:

$19.95

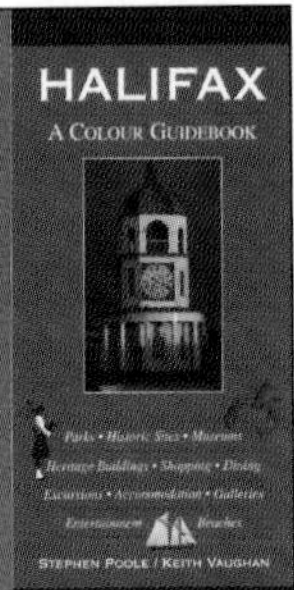


$12.95

The Living History series — books on leading heritage reconstructions and actual towns in a full-colour, larger-size format:

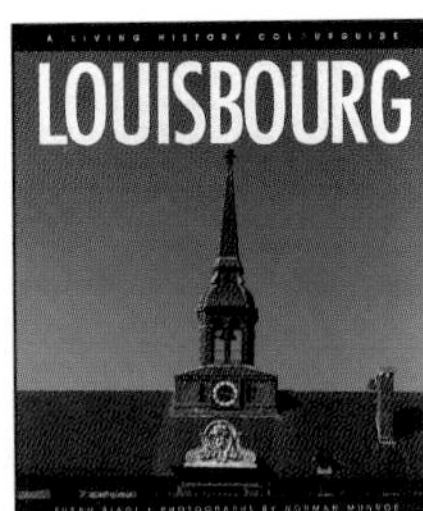


$16.95

# Contents

# GETTING THERE

## BY AIR

The Macdonald-Cartier International Airport serves the Ottawa area from outside Canada and other Canadian areas. For information call (613) 998-1427. It is located in the south end of the National Capital Region. The Airport Parkway will take you to downtown Ottawa in about 20 minutes. The airport is served by the Ottawa Transit System (bus route 96) and by a shuttle service to downtown hotels. For information about the shuttle service call (613) 736-6689.

Some of the airlines providing service to the Ottawa area are: Air Canada (including Air Alliance, Air Ontario, Air Nova and Rapidair) (613) 247-5000; American Airlines, 1-800-433-7300; Bearskin Airlines, 1-800-465-5039; Business Express (Delta Airlines Connector), 1-800-363-2857; Canadian Airlines International (including Inter-Canadian, Canadian Partner and Canadian Regional), (613) 237-1380; First Air, (613) 738-0200; Greyhound Air, 1-800-661-8747; KLM, (613) 567-4747; Northwest Airlines, 1-800-225-2525; Pem-Air, 1-800-267-3131; USAir, 1-800-428-4322.

The Ottawa region is also served by the Gatineau-Ottawa Executive Airport, 1700 Arthur Fecteau, Hull (819) 663-0737, and West Carleton Airport (613) 839-5276.

## BY ROAD

Whether approaching by car or bus, you get to Canada's National Capital Region by one of a number of routes. The main routes are Highways 417 (from the west), 17/417 (from the east) and 16 (from the south) in Ontario, and 148 in Quebec.

If you are travelling by bus, you will arrive via the same routes. Out-of-town buses arrive in Ottawa at the Voyageur Colonial Bus Terminal, 265 Catherine St., Ottawa, (613) 238-5900 or (613) 238-6668. In Hull, out-of-town buses arrive at the Voyageur Colonial Bus Station, 238 St-Joseph Boulevard, Hull, (819) 771-2442.

## BY RAIL

Ottawa is served by the VIA Rail Canada System rail network that provides service across Canada (with connections to the Amtrak system through Niagara Falls, New York). Passengers will arrive at the Ottawa Station, located at 200 Tremblay Road, Ottawa; (613) 244-8289.

# TRAVEL ESSENTIALS

## MONEY

Currency can be exchanged at any Ottawa bank at the prevailing rate. If you use a small local branch, it is probably wise to call ahead to confirm its capacity to exchange any currency other than American funds. There are currency exchange booths at the airport, and at many of Ontario's Travel Information Centres near the U.S./Canada border. Canadian Travel Information Centres can exchange Canadian dollars for most major international currencies, and vice versa. If you wish to exchange a large amount, or to exchange a less common currency, telephone ahead to ensure the Centre can serve you. Canadian currency consists of bills with denominations of $5, $10, $20, $50, $100 and up. Unlike the United States, Canada has coins for the lower denominations: the one-dollar (loonie) and two-dollar (twoonie) coins.

Most major North American credit cards and travellers' cheques are welcome in Ottawa, including American Express, Carte Blanche, Diner's Club, EnRoute, MasterCard, and Visa. Many stores and services will accept U.S. currency, but the rates they offer will vary. It is probably wise to shop around for the best rate, exchange your money, and then make your purchases. Many merchants participate in a "Fair Exchange Program," which ensures a favourable rate on the U.S. dollar. If you want to find out the "Fair Exchange" rate of the day, you can call the Royal Bank of Canada at 1-800-769-2511.

American visitors may also use bank or credit cards to make cash withdrawals from automatic teller machines that are tied into international networks such as Cirrus and Plus. This may also apply to some European visitors. Before you leave home, check with your bank to find out what services your bank card provides you.

## PASSPORTS

American visitors may be asked to verify their citizenship with a document such as a passport, or a birth or baptismal certificate. Naturalized U.S. citizens should carry a naturalization certificate. Permanent U.S. residents who are not citizens are advised to carry their Alien Registration Receipt Card. Citizens of all other countries, except Greenland and residents of St. Pierre et Miquelon, must have a valid passport. Some may be required to obtain a visitor's visa. For details, please consult the Canadian embassy or consulate serving your home country.

## CUSTOMS

**Arriving**
You may bring in any reasonable amount of personal effects and food, and a full tank of gas. Special restrictions or quotas apply to certain specialty goods, and especially to plant-, agricultural- and animal-related products. All items must be declared to Customs upon arrival. Items may include up to 200 cigarettes, 50 cigars, 400 grams of manufactured tobacco and 400 tobacco sticks. Visitors are also permitted 1.1 litres (40 oz.) of liquor or wine, or 8.2 litres (24 x 12 oz. cans or bottles) of beer.

You may bring in gifts for Canadian residents duty-free, up to a value of $60.00 (Canadian) each, provided the gifts do not consist of alcohol, tobacco, or advertising material. For more detailed information, please see the federal Customs (Revenue Canada) website at http://www.rc.gc.ca, the Customs information booklet "I Declare", or write to Revenue Canada, Customs Excise and Taxation, Travellers' Directorate, Tariff Policy Section, 191 Laurier Ave. West, Ottawa, Ontario, Canada K1A 0L5.

**Departing**
What you can take with you will be affected by the customs regulations of the country of your destination. For detailed customs rules for entering or re-entering the United States, contact a U.S. Customs office. Copies of the U.S. customs information brochure "Know Before You Go" are available from U.S. custom offices or by mail. You can also call the U.S. Embassy (U.S. Citizen Services) in Ottawa at 1-800-529-4410, or U.S. Custom Information in Ogdenburg, New York at (315) 393-1390.

Travellers from other countries should check on customs regulations pertaining to their own country before leaving home.

## TAXES

**Goods and Services Tax (GST)**
The federal Goods and Services Tax (GST) is 7%. This is a value-added consumption tax that applies to most goods, food/beverages and services, including accommodations. Visitors to Canada qualify for the GST Visitors' Rebate Program. This allows you to be reimbursed for the GST you have paid in Canada. You must keep your receipts. To get information or to receive Visitor Rebate Forms call Revenue Canada at 1-800-668-4748.

**Provincial Sales Tax (PST)**
The Ontario Provincial Sales Tax (PST) is 8%. It is added to any goods you buy, but not on services or accommodation. In most cases, the GST and PST are not included in the listed prices for goods and services. The taxes will be added on at the cash register as you pay.

**Room Tax**
A 5% provincial tax (in place of the PST) is added to most tourist accommodation charges, as well as the 7% GST.

**Food Service**
In restaurants, 7% GST and 8% PST will be added to the food portion of your final bill. In addition, a 10%

provincial tax on alcoholic beverages will be added to the 7% GST on your final bill.

### GUIDE AND INFORMATION SERVICES

- Access Ontario (Provincial Government Information), Rideau Centre. Hours: open 9 am to 5 pm, Monday to Saturday (closed 1 pm to 2 pm on Saturday). Information: (613) 238-3630 or 1-800-268-8758.
- Capital Infocentre, 90 Wellington St., Ottawa (across from Parliament Hill). Hours: open daily, 9 am to 5 pm from September through May; Open daily 8:30 am to 9 pm May through September. Information: (613) 239-5000 or 1-800-465-1867; info@ncc-ccn.ca.
- La maison du tourisme, 103 Laurier St. (Corner of Laurier and St. Laurent), Hull. Hours: open weekdays, 8:30 am to 5 pm; weekends, 9 am to 4 pm. Information: (819) 778-2222.
- Ottawa Tourism and Convention Authority (OTCA), 130 Albert St., Suite 1800, Ottawa, Ontario K1P 5G4. (613) 237-5150, web site: www.tourottawa.org or www.ottawa.touch.com.

## GETTING ACQUAINTED

### TIME ZONE

Ottawa falls within the Eastern Standard Time Zone.

### CLIMATE

The following are the average high and low temperatures in Ottawa in Celcius and Fahrenheit.

Celcius High/Low
Fahrenheit High/Low
January: -6°C to -16°C/21°F to 3°F
February: -6°C to -16°C/22°F to 3°F
March: 1°C to -9°C/33°F to 16°F
Aprill: 1°C to -1°C/51°F to 31°F
May: 19°C to 7°C/66°F to 44°F
June: 24°C to 12°C/76°F to 54° F
July: 27°C to 14°C/81°F to 58°F
August: 25°C to 13°C/77°F to 55°F
September: 20°C to 9°C/68°F to 48°F
October: 12°C to 3°C/54°F to 37°F
November: 4°C to -3°C/39°F to 26°F
December: -4°C to -13·C/24°F to 9°F

Average annual precipitation: 85.6 cm./34.3"

## TOURS

**Bicycle**
- National Capital Cycling Tours, 75 Nicholas St., Ottawa K1N 7B9; (613) 235-2595.
- Rent-a-Bike (Chateau Laurier), 1 Rideau St., Ottawa K1S 8N7; (613) 241-4140; email: cv842@freenet3.carleton.ca

**Boats**
- The Ottawa Riverboat Co. Ltd., #100 - 30 Murray St., Ottawa K1N 5M4; (613) 562-4888; fax (613) 562-7364.
- Paul's Boat Lines Limited, 219 Colonnade Rd., Nepean K2E 7K3; (613) 225-6781; fax (613) 228-8310.

**Bus**
- Capital Trolley Tours, Box 1162, Station B, Ottawa K1P 5R2; (613) 729-6888, 1-800-823-6147 (Canada only); fax (613) 729-7444.
- Gray Line Ottawa, #101 - 1335 Carling Ave., Ottawa K1Z 8N8; (613) 725-1441, 1-800-440-9317.
- Piccadilly Bus Tours, 39 Beaumaris Dr., Nepean K2H 7K5; (613) 820-6745; fax (613) 232-2821.

**Day Trips**
- Oakroads, 241 Tudor Place, Ottawa K1L 7Y1; (613) 748-0144; fax (613) 748-3782.
- Voyageur Colonial Ltd., 265 Catherine St., Ottawa K1R 7S5; (613) 238-5900, 1-800-668-4438 (Canada only); fax (613) 238-6964; info@voyageur.com

**Nature/Adventure Tours**
- Canadian Voyageur Adventures, 40 Cymbeline Dr., Nepean K2H 7Y1; (613) 820-5488, 1-800-833-5055.

- Meta Adventures Inc., 381 Apple Tree Lane, Ottawa K1K 2R3; (613) 744-7464, 1-800-844-0075 (Canada only); fax (613) 744-6971.
- Ride the Rideau Adventure Tours, Box 456, Manotick K4M 1A5; (613) 797-7656.
- Wild Places Nature Excursions, CP 221, RPO Perkins, Val-des-Monts, PQ J8N 7X1; (819) 671-2209.

**Seaplane**
- Air Outaouais, 192 Beaulac, Aylmer, PQ J9H 5G8; (819) 568-2359; fax (819) 243-7934.

**Train**
- H.C.W. Steam Train, 165 rue Deveault, Hull PQ J8Z 1S7; (819) 778-7246, 1-800-871-7246; fax (819) 778-5007.

**Walking Tours**
- Ottawa Walks, 1536A Beaverpond, Gloucester, ON K1B 3R5; (613) 692-3571; fax (613) 692-0831.
- Ottawa's Haunted Walks, 99 Seneca St., Ottawa ON K1S 4X8; (613) 730-0575.

# GETTING AROUND

## TRAVELLING IN OTTAWA

**Public Transportation**
There are two city bus systems in the National Capital Region — OC Transpo (Ottawa-Carleton) and Société de transport de l'Outaouais (STO). You can transfer between them along Rideau and Wellington Streets in Ottawa, and around the Portage Bridge area and at Place d'Accueil on Maisonneuve Boulevard in Hull.

Ottawa-Carleton on the Ontario side of the Ottawa River is served by buses operated by OC Transpo; (613) 741-4390. STO operates buses in the Outaouais region on the Québec side of the Ottawa River; (819) 770-3242.

**By Car**
A valid driver's license from any country is good in Ontario for three months. You should carry evidence of your car's registration (a car rental agreement will suffice). If you are driving into Ontario or importing a vehicle, bring with you its registration documents, and either a Canadian Non-Resident Motor Vehicle Liability Insurance Card (obtained from your insurance agent), or the insurance policy itself. If you are driving a rented car, keep a copy of the rental contract with you.

Speed limits are measured in kilometres per hour and vary depending on the type of road, with 400-level controlled-access highways having the highest limit. Speed limits on most highways are 80 to 90 kph, and 100 kph on freeways. On city streets the normal speed is 50 kph unless otherwise posted. Seat belt use by passengers and drivers is mandatory in Ontario. In Canada there are strict laws prohibiting driving while under the influence of alcohol.

One kilometre equals about 5/8 of a mile. To convert from kilometres to miles, multiply the kilometres by 0.6; to convert from miles to kilometres, multiply the miles by 1.6. In Canada metric measurements are used for motor fuel. Prices are per litre. One litre equals about one-quarter of an American gallon, or about one-fifth of an Imperial gallon.

**Car Rentals**
There are a number of car/truck rental agencies operating in the Ottawa region. They offer different rates and services. It is probably wise to call several of the agencies to get information on their current rates before booking. Here is a list of some of the agencies: Alamo, 1-800-327-9633; Avis, (613) 238-3421; Budget, (613) 729-6666; Discount (613) 234-0809; Dollar (613) 235-9333; Enterprise (613) 566-3277; Hertz (613) 241-7681; National Tilden (613) 232-3536; Myers (613) 225-1260; and Thrifty (613) 238-8000.

# ACCOMMODATION

What follows is a good cross-section of the accommodation options available in Ottawa. The emphasis is on accommodation in the downtown area, but we have provided some selections from other areas of the city and a few regional alternatives. The Hotel Map shows you the location of the hotels in the downtown area.

Ontario Tourism provides information on attractions throughout Ontario. They will also arrange reservations for accommodation. You can contact the Ontario Travel Information Centre at 1-800-ONTARIO (1-800-668-2746) (for information in French the number is 1-800-268-3736) or www.travelinx.com. You may also contact the Capital Infocentre , 90 Wellington St., Ottawa; (613) 239-5000 or 1-800-465-1867. In addition to making accommodation reservations, these offices will provide tourist information and maps.

Approximate prices are indicated, based on the average cost at time of publishing, for two persons staying in a double room (excluding taxes): $ = $50-$90; $$ = $91-$180; $$$ = above $180.

If you are not able to plan your accommodations in advance, or you are looking for hotel savings during the off-season, try using the services of the Diners' Club Hotel Savings Hotline at 1-800-567-8850. You do not have to be a Diners' Club member to use this service. It offers a range of hotel options at good rates, but only for reservations for same-day accommodation. During busy periods, you cannot rely on this service to have any inventory of rooms. The Ottawa Tourism and Convention Authority's Visitor Information Centre will also provide assistance in arranging accommodations. The Centre is located in the National Arts Centre at 65 Elgin Street. For a small fee, the Visitor Centre has a last-minute booking service designed to help find a room in one of the participating hotels, motels, inns or bed and breakfasts which have vacancies.

## HOTELS: DOWNTOWN

- Albert at Bay Suite Hotel, 435 Albert St., Ottawa ON K1R 7X4; (613) 238-8858, 1-800-267-6644; fax (613) 238-1433; web site: http:// www.absuites.com. Suites with kitchens available. Business services available. Fitness centre, sauna, whirlpool. $$
- Best Western Victoria Park Suites, 377 O'Connor St., Ottawa ON K2P 2M2; (613) 567-7275, 1-800-528-1234; fax (613) 567-1161; web site: http://www.vpsuites.com. Complimentary continental breakfast. Fitness centre, sauna. $$
- Capital Hill Hotel and Suites, 88 Albert St., Ottawa ON K1P 5E9; (613) 235-1413, 1-800-463-7705; fax (613) 235-6047. $
- The Business Inn, 180 MacLaren St., Ottawa ON K2P 0L3; (613) 232-1121, 1-800-363-1177; fax (613) 232-8143. Fitness centre, whirlpool. $-$$
- Cartier Place Hotel, 180 Cooper St., Ottawa ON K2P 2L5; (613) 236-5000, 1-800-236-8399; fax (613) 238-3842; www.suitedreams @cartierhotels.com. Close to shopping and major tourist attractions. Fitness centre, indoor pool, sauna, whirlpool. $$
- Chateau Laurier Hotel, 1 Rideau St., Ottawa ON K1N 8S7; (613) 241-1414, 1-800-441-1414; fax (613) 562-7031. Next to Parliament Buildings. This is the classic Ottawa hotel; stay here if you can afford it and you're looking for a downtown location. Rooms on the west side overlook Parliament Hill and the Peace Tower. Some rooms are smaller than you might expect, so don't hesitate to ask for something larger if you find yourself in something too small. Fitness centre, indoor pool, sauna. $$-$$$
- Citadel Ottawa Hotel and Conference Centre, 101 Lyon St., Ottawa ON K1R 5T9; (613) 237-3600, 1-800-567-3600; fax (613) 237-2351. Close to Parliament Hill and major attractions. A good value location. Fitness centre, indoor pool. $-$$
- Days Inn Ottawa City Centre, 123 Metcalfe St., Ottawa, ON K1P 5L9; (613) 237-9300, 1-800-329-7466; fax (613) 237-2163. Indoor pool, coffee shop. Family/weekend rates available. $$
- Delta Ottawa Hotel & Suites, 361 Queen St., Ottawa ON K1R 7S9;

(613) 238-6000, 1-800-268-1133; fax (613) 238-2290. Fitness centre, indoor pool, two-storey waterslide , children's creative centre, sauna, whirlpool. A pleasant up-scale location, a little to the west of things. $$

- Doral Inn, 486 Albert St., Ottawa ON K1R 5B5; (613) 230-8055, 1-800-26-DORAL; fax (613) 237-9660; http://www.comnet.ca/~doralinn. Walking distance to Parliament Hill and attractions. Kitchenettes available. $$
- Econo Lodge (Parkway), 475 Rideau St., Ottawa ON K1N 5Z3; (613) 789-3781, 1-800-263-0649. $
- Embassy Hotel & Suites, 25 Cartier St., Ottawa ON K2P 1J2; (613) 237-2111, 1-800-661-5495; fax (613) 563-1353. Free in-room movies. Fitness centre, sauna. $-$$
- Howard Johnson Plaza Hotel, 140 Slater St., Ottawa ON K1P 5H6; (613) 238-2888, 1-800-446-4656; fax (613) 235-8421. Downtown Ottawa within walking distance of major shopping centres and museums. $$
- Lord Elgin Hotel, 100 Elgin St., Ottawa ON K1P 5K8; (613) 235-3333, 1-800-267-4298; fax (613) 235-3223. Overlooking National Arts Centre and Ottawa Congress Centre. Though the building dates from several decades ago and the rooms are small, they've been well renovated. Room rates are reasonable and the location is great for access to Parliament Hill, the downtown area and the market. Fitness centre. $$
- Market Square Inn, 350 Dalhousie St., Ottawa ON K1N 7E9; (613) 241-1000, 1-800-341-2210; fax (613) 241-4804. Located in Byward Market. Walking distance to Parliament Hill, National Gallery and museums. Formerly a Holiday Inn, located on the east edge of the market. Outdoor pool. $-$$
- Minto Place Suite Hotel, 433 Laurier Ave. W., Ottawa ON K1R 7Y1; (613) 232-2200, 1-800-267-3377; fax (613) 232-6962. CAA/AAA Four Diamond Award all-suite hotel. Fitness centre, indoor pool, sauna, whirlpool. $$-$$$
- Novotel Hotel - Ottawa, 33 Nicholas St., Ottawa ON K1N 9M7; (613) 230-3033, 1-800-NOVOTEL; fax (613) 230-7865. Fitness centre, indoor pool, sauna, whirlpool. Medium size rooms in a recently built hotel; fairly well located for downtown Ottawa. $$
- Quality Hotel Downtown, 290 Rideau St., Ottawa ON K1N 5Y3; (613) 789-7511, 1-800-228-5151; fax (613) 789-2434. $$
- Radisson Hotel Ottawa Centre, 100 Kent St., Ottawa ON K1P 5R7; (613) 238-1122, 1-800-333-3333; fax (613) 783- 4229. Located two blocks from Parliament Buildings and close to museums and shopping. Fitness centre, indoor pool, sauna, whirlpool. Good location, large and well-appointed rooms. $$
- Ramada Hotel & Suites Ottawa, 111 Cooper St., Ottawa ON K2P 2E3; (613) 238-1331, 1-800-267-8378; fax (613) 230-2179. Suites available with kitchen and dining room. Fitness centre. $$
- Sheraton Ottawa Hotel & Towers, 150 Albert St., Ottawa ON K1P 5G2; (613) 238-1500, 1-800-489-8333; fax (613) 238-8497; web site: http://www.sheraton.com/665. Some kitchenettes available. Fitness centre, pool. $$
- Les Suites Hotel Ottawa, 130 Besserer St., Ottawa ON K1N 9M9; (613) 232-2000, 1-800-267-1989; fax (613) 232-1242. Located adjacent to Rideau Centre Mall and close to Byward Market. Fitness centre, indoor pool, sauna, whirlpool. $$-$$$
- Super 8 Hotel Downtown Ottawa, 480 Metcalfe St., Ottawa ON K1S 3N6; (613) 237-5500, 1-800-800-8000; fax (613) 237-6705. Minutes to Parliament Hill. Morning newspaper. Indoor pool. $$
- Town House Motor Hotel, 319 Rideau St., Ottawa ON K1N 5Y4; (613) 789-5555, 1-888-789-4949; fax (613) 789-6196. $
- Travelodge Hotel, 402 Queen St., Ottawa ON K1R 5A7; (613) 236-1113, 1-800-578-7878; fax (613) 236-2317. Located near Parliament Hill. $
- Webb's Motel, 1705 Carling Ave., Ottawa ON K2A 1C8; (613) 728-

1881, 1-800-263-4264; fax (613) 728-4516. Family owned and operated. Close to downtown. $
- The Westin Hotel Ottawa, 11 Colonel By Dr., Ottawa ON K1N 9H4; (613) 560-7000, 1-800-228-3000; fax (613) 234-5396; web site: http://www/westin.com. Walking distance to Parliament Hill. Attached to Ottawa Congress Centre and Rideau Shopping Centre. Includes continental breakfast. Fitness centre, indoor pool, sauna, whirlpool. This is the contemporary version of the Chateau Laurier, the fanciest of Ottawa's new hotels. $$-$$$

## HOTELS: OTTAWA EAST

- Butler Motor Hotel, 112 Montreal Rd., Ottawa ON K1L 6E6; (613) 746-4641, 1-800-267-1595. Continental Breakfast. Pool. $
- Chimo Hotel, 1199 Joseph Cyr St., Ottawa ON K1J 7T4; (613) 744-1060, 1-800-387-9779; fax (613) 744-7845. Fitness centre, indoor pool, sauna, whirlpool. $-$$
- Comfort Inn, 1252 Michael St., Ottawa ON K1J 7T1; (613) 744-2900, 1-800-221-2222; fax (613) 746-0836. Continental breakfast provided. $
- Mirada Inn, 545 Montreal Rd., Ottawa ON K1K 0V1; (613) 741-1102, 1-800-267-1666; fax (613) 741-1102. Outdoor pool. $
- Travelodge Gloucester/Ottawa East, 1486 Innes Rd., Gloucester ON K1B 3V5; (613) 745-1133, 1-800-578-7878; fax (613) 745-7380. Pool. $
- WelcomINNS, 1220 Michael St., Ottawa ON K1J 7T1; (613) 748-7800, 1-800-387-4381; fax (613) 748-0499. Continental breakfast included in price. Fitness centre, sauna, whirlpool. $

## HOTELS: OTTAWA SOUTH

- Adam's Airport Inn, 2721 Bank St., South, Ottawa ON K1T 1M8; (613) 738-3838, 1-800-261-5835. $-$$
- The Southway Inn, 2431 Bank St., Ottawa ON K1V 8R9; (613) 737-0811, 1-800 267-9704; fax (613) 737-3207; http://www. southway.com. Near airport. Fitness centre, indoor pool, sauna, whirlpool. $$

## HOTELS: OTTAWA WEST

- Best Western Barons Hotel, 3700 Richmond Rd., Nepean ON K2H 5B8; (613) 828-2741, 1-800-528-1234; fax (613) 596-4742; web site: www.bestwestern.com/ thisco/bw/66050/66050_b.html. Business services. Fitness centre, outdoor pool. $$
- Best Western Macies Hotel, 1274 Carling Ave., Ottawa ON K1Z 7K8; (613) 728-1951, 1-800-528-1234; fax (613) 728-1955; web site: www.bestwestern.com /thisco/bw/66023/66023_b.html. Fitness centre, outdoor pool, sauna, whirlpool. $$
- Embassy West Hotel, 1400 Carling Ave., Ottawa ON K1Z 7L8; (613) 729-4331, 1-800-267-8696; fax (613) 729-1600. Outdoor pool. $
- McKellar Park Apartment/Hotel, 1983 Carling Ave., Ottawa ON K2A 1E9; (613) 722-4273; fax (613) 725-1336; web site: http://www.magi.com/~stride. Kitchens available. $
- Richmond Plaza Motel, 238 Richmond Rd., Ottawa ON K1Z 6W6; (613) 722-6591; fax (613) 728-1402. $

## HOTELS: REGIONAL

- Clarion Hotel Centre Ville, 35 Laurier St., Hull PQ J8X 4E9; (819) 778-6111, 1-800-567-9607; fax (819) 778-8548. Fitness centre, pool. $-$$
- Holiday Inn Plaza La Chaudière, 2 rue Montcalm, Hull PQ J8X 4B4; (819) 778-3880, 1-800-567-1962; fax (819) 778-3309; crowneplaza@igs.net. Some kitchenettes available. Fitness centre, pool. $$
- Monterey Inn, 2259 Hwy 16, Nepean ON K2E 6Z8; (613) 226-5813, 1-800-565-1311; fax (613) 226-5900. Waterfront property on Rideau River. Fitness centre, outdoor pool, sauna, whirlpool. $-$$
- Motel Adam, 100 Greber, Gatineau PQ J8T 3P8; (819) 561-3600, 1-800-757-2326; fax (819) 561-2008.

Pool. Some kitchenettes available. $

- Renfrew Inn, 760 Gibbons St., Renfrew ON K7V 4A2; (613) 432-8109, 1-800-668-0466. Fitness centre, pool. $
- Rideau Heights Motor Inn, 72 Rideau Heights Dr., Nepean ON K2E 7A6; (613) 226-4152, 1-800-256-0825; fax (613) 226-8655. Complimentary coffee, danish and morning paper. $
- Sam Jakes Inn, 118 Main St. E., Merrickville, ON K0G 1N0; (613) 269-3711. Victorian building (1860) and decor. Non-smoking. Price includes continental breakfast. $$

## INNS/GUESTHOUSES: CENTRAL OTTAWA

- Albert House Inn, 478 Albert St., Ottawa ON K1R 5B5; (613) 236-4479, 1-800-267-1982; fax (613) 237-9079; 73354.3271@compuserve.com. Downtown heritage inn. Breakfasts included. Complimentary refreshments day and evening. Some in-room jacuzzis. $-$$
- Auberge McGee's Inn, 185 Daly Ave., Ottawa ON K1N 6E8; (613) 237-6089, 1-800-2MC-GEES; fax (613) 237-6201. Breakfast provided. Victorian ambiance. $$-$$$
- Auberge Wildflowers Bed & Breakfast, 376 Wilbrod St., Ottawa ON K1N 6M8; (613) 565-1887, 1-800-278-4966; fax (613) 565-7751; http://www.terraport.net/pnp/wf.htm. Full breakfast. $
- The Carmichael Inn & Spa, 46 Cartier St., Ottawa ON K2P 1J3; (613) 236-4667; fax (613) 563-7529. Non-smoking only. Breakfast included in rate. $$
- Cartier House Inn, 46 Cartier St., Ottawa ON K2P 1J3; (613) 236-4667; fax (613) 563-7529. Non-smoking. Continental breakfast provided. $$
- Gasthaus Switzerland Inn, 89 Daly Ave., Ottawa ON K1N 6E6; (613) 237-0335, 1-800-267-8788; fax (613) 594-3327; switzinn@magi.com. Centrally located in a restored (1872) building. No smoking. Rates include breakfast. $-$$
- Paterson House, 500 Wilbrod St., Ottawa ON K1N 6N2; (613) 565-8996; fax (613) 565-6546. Elegant accommodations. Continental breakfast included. $$
- Rideau View Inn, 177 Frank St., Ottawa ON K2P 0X4; (613) 236-9309, 1-800-658-3564; fax (613) 237-6842. Full breakfast included. $

## BED AND BREAKFAST FACILITIES: CENTRAL OTTAWA

- Ambiance Bed & Breakfast, 330 Nepean St., Ottawa ON K1R 5G6; (613) 563-0421. $
- Auberges des Arts, 104 Guigues Ave., Ottawa ON K1N 5H7; (613) 562-0909; frameus@magi.com. Near museums and Byward Market. $
- L Auberge du Marché, 87 Guigues Ave., Ottawa ON K1N 5H8; (613) 241-6610, 1-800-465-0079. Near Byward Market, and one block from the National Gallery. $
- Auberge The King Edward B&B, 525 King Edward Ave., Ottawa ON K1N 7N3; (613) 565-6700. Designated heritage home. Victorian atmosphere. $
- Australis Guest House, 35 Marlborough Ave., Ottawa ON K1N 8E6; (613) 235-8461; fax (613) 594-3327. Bus/train pickup. $
- Beatrice Lyon Guest House, 479 Slater St., Ottawa ON K1R 5C2; (613) 236-3904. Owner occupied. Families welcome. $
- Blue Spruces, 187 Glebe Ave., Ottawa ON K1S 2C6; (613) 236-8521; fax (613) 231-3730; 71242.1561@compuserve.com. An elegant, luxurious home. $
- Brighton House Bed & Breakfast, 308 First Ave., Ottawa ON K1S 2G8; (613) 233-7777. Early Canadian pine. $-$$
- Brown's Bed & Breakfast, 539 Besserer St., Ottawa ON K1N 6C6; (613) 789-8320; fax (613) 789-8320. Non-smoking. Close to all attractions. $
- Bye-The-Way Bed & Breakfast, 310 First Ave., Ottawa ON K1S 2G8; (613) 232-6840; fax (613)

232-6840. Air/train pickup. $

- Canal View Bed & Breakfast, 54 Queen Elizabeth Dr., Ottawa ON K2P 1E3; (613) 234-7569; fax (613) 234-7569; http://www.achilles.net/~bb/499.html. Excellent view. $
- Echo Bank Bed & Breakfast, 400 Echo Dr., Ottawa ON K1S 1P3; (613) 730-0254. Heritage house. Near canal. Swimming pool. Open 1 May - 29 August. $
- Haydon House, 18 The Driveway, Ottawa, ON K2P 1C6; (613) 230-2697. Walking distance to Parliament Hill. $
- Helen House, 168 Stewart St., Ottawa ON K1N 6J9; (613) 789-8263. $
- Henrietta Walker's Bed & Breakfast, 203 York St., Ottawa ON K1N 5T7; (613) 789-3286; fax (613) 789-3286. Excellent location. Good breakfast. $
- Laurier Guest House, 329 Laurier Ave. E., Ottawa ON K1N 6P8; (613) 238-5525; fax (613) 739-4444. Next to Laurier House. $
- Maison McFarlane House, 201 Daly Ave,. Ottawa ON K1N 6G1; (613) 241-0095; fax (613) 241-4559; mcfarlan@hookup.net. Heritage house (1868). $-$$
- Mayfields Bed & Breakfast, 167 James St., Ottawa ON K1R 5M4; (613) 233-4902. Good hospitality. $
- The Olde Bytowne Bed & Breakfast, 459 Laurier Ave. E., Ottawa ON K1N 6R4; (613) 565-7939; fax (613) 565-7981. Heritage Victorian home. $
- Robert's Bed & Breakfast, 488 Cooper St., Ottawa ON K1R 5H9; (613) 563-0161, 1-800-461-7889. Century-old home. Woodwork and stained glass. $
- Voyageurs Guest House B&B, 95 Arlington Ave., Ottawa ON K1R 5S4; (613) 238-6445; fax (613) 236-5551. Homey and friendly. $
- Waverley House, 166 Waverley St., Ottawa ON K2P 0V6; (613) 233-0427. Close to museums, canal. $

### HOSTELS/UNIVERSITY RESIDENCES: OTTAWA

- Carleton University Tour/Conference Centre, 1125 Colonel By Dr., Ottawa ON K1S 5B6; (613) 788-5611; fax (613) 788-3952. $
- Ottawa International Hostel, 75 Nicholas St., Ottawa ON K1N 7B9; (613) 235-2595, 1-800-461-8585; fax (613) 569-2131. Downtown. Formerly the Carleton County Jail (1862-1972). $
- University of Ottawa. 100 University, Ottawa, ON K1N 6N5. Near intersection of Laurier Avenue East and King Edward. (613) 564-3463 or (613) 564-5400; fax (613) 564-9534. $
- YMCA-YWCA of Ottawa, 180 Argyle St., Ottawa K2P 1B7; (613) 237-1320; fax (613) 233-3096. $

## DINING

Historically, Ottawa was not known for its restaurants, but this has changed over the past two decades. Now Ottawa not only boasts the national capital, but also some very good dining establishments. The following is a select list of the restaurants mentioned in the chapter on Dining. The restaurants are listed by category (eg. Asian) and sub-category (eg., Chinese). The map on page 10 shows the restaurants listed in this section.

Approximate prices are indicated, based on the average cost, at time of publication, of dinner for two including wine (where available), taxes and gratuity: $ = under $45; $$ = $45-$80; $$$ = $80-$120; $$$$ = $120-$180. L = lunch service. Credit cards accepted are also indicated: AX = American Express; MC = MasterCard; V = Visa.

### ASIAN

**Chinese**

- Fuliwah Restaurant, 691 Somerset St. W.; (613) 233-2552. Authentic Cantonese and Szechuan dishes. Dim Sum served daily. L/D/T-O, $$, AX/MC/V.
- Mekong Restaurant, 637 Somerset St. W.; (613) 237-7717. The chef's fried eggplant is unforgettable. L/D, $$, AX/MC/V.

**Thai**

- Coriander Thai, 282 Kent Street;

(613) 233-2828. Good. Nice in summer.
L/D, $$, A/MC/V.

- Siam Kitchen, 1050 Bank Street; (613) 730-3954. Reasonable luncheon specials.
L (except Sunday)/D, $ AX/MC/V.

## EUROPEAN

**Italian**

- Geraldo's Ristorante, 200 Beechwood Avenue, Vanier; (613) 747-0272. Moderately priced. Closed on Sunday.
L/D, $$$, AX/MC/V.

## MIDDLE EAST

**Lebanese**

- Fairouz, 343 Somerset Street West; (613) 233-1536. Kebabs are house specialty. Intimate Lebanese restaurant in heritage home. Reservations recommended. Closed Sundays. L(except Saturday)/D,$$,AX/MC/V.

## NORTH AMERICAN

- Newport Restaurant, 334 Richmond Road; (613) 722-9070. Good basic food. Home of the Elvis Presley Sighting Society. Offbeat ambience.
L/D, $, AX/MC/V.

## FINE DINING

- Le Café, Lower level of the National Arts Centre (corner of Elgin and Wellington Streets, 1 Confederation Square); (613) 594-5127. Canadian ingredients and wines. Pleasant spot, especially in summer or during the winter skating season. Closed on Sundays. No smoking. Reservations suggested, particularly at lunchtime.
L/D. $$$, AX/MC/V.
- Café Henry Burger, 69 Laurier Street, Hull; (819) 777-5646. Across from the Museum of Civilization in Hull. Located in a home once inhabited by Henry Burger. Elegant French cuisine in the classic style. Outdoor terrace.
L/D, $$$, AX/MC/V.
- Café Wisigoth, 84B Beechwood Avenue, Vanier; (613) 748-1286. Lovely French restaurant. Garden area in summer. Closed Sunday. L (except Saturday, Sunday)/D, $$$, AX/MC/V.
- Clair de Lune, 81B Clarence Street; (613) 241-2200. Roof-garden and outdoor terrace in summer. Live jazz on Saturdays. Imaginative menu that changes with the season.
L/D, $$-$$$, AX/MC/V.
- Domus, 87 Murray Street; (613) 241-6007. Interesting little place. Grew out of a cookware store. Very good food. Market setting. No smoking.
L/D, $$$, AX/MC/V.
- Mamma Teresa Ristorante, 300 Somerset Street West; (613) 236-3023. Ottawa landmark. Standard Italian cuisine. Central. Moderately priced.
L/D, $$$, AX/V/MC.
- Maple Lawn Café, 529 Richmond Road; (613) 722-5118. Heritage building. Elegant garden setting in summer. Food is beautifully presented and served. Closed for lunch on Saturday. Brunch served Sunday from Easter to end of October. Closed Sunday and Monday in winter.
L/D, $$$, AX/MC/V.
- Opus Bistro, 1331 Wellington Street; (613) 722-9549. Bistro-style. Nicely presented food. Good seafood. French in flavour. Small. Simple decor. Closed on Sunday and Monday. Book ahead if possible.
D, $$, MC/V.
- Le Tartuffe, 133 rue Notre Dame, Hull; (819) 776-6424. Really nice, non-standard French/Alsace food. Off beaten track. Closed on Sunday and Monday. Reservations if possible.
L/D, $$$, AX/MC/V.
- Il Vagabondo, 186 Barrette Street, Vanier; (613) 749-4877. Lovely little restaurant. Odd combination of Italian and other things. Creative chef. Lunch Tuesday to Friday.
L/D, $$, AX/MC/V.

# NIGHT LIFE

This section provides information about what to do in Ottawa after dark. Refer to the Night Life, p. 96 for more details of the events and establishments listed here. In addition to this guide, be sure to check the local newspapers for other events and times.

**Byward Market**

- The Rainbow Bistro. Home of the Blues. Weekend afternoon jamming sessions. 76 Murray St.; (613) 241-5123.
- Zaphod Beeblebrox. Alternative rock music. 27 York St.; (613) 562-1010.

**Sparks Street Mall and Bank Street**

- After Eight Jazz Club. By day a sunny café, by night an intimate candle-lit jazz club. 101 Sparks St.; (613) 237-5200.
- Barrymore's Music Theatre. Formerly a vaudeville theatre. Wide-ranging entertainment from classic rock to reggae. 323 Bank St.; (613) 233-0307.
- The Cave. A cavernous bar. DJ during the week, and often live alternative rock bands on the weekends. 214 Sparks St.; (613) 233-0080.

**The Glebe**

- Irene's Pub. Typical neighbourhood watering hole. Live entertainment on weekends. Celtic, country, folk and rock music. No cover charge. 885 Bank St.; (613) 230-4474.
- Rasputin's. Tiny coffee house which serves drinks. Folk singers. 696 Bronson Ave.; (613) 230-5102.

**Outside Ottawa**

- Black Sheep Inn (Le Mouton Noir). Wakefield, Québec. Eclectic music, from rock to disco, to folk. (819) 459-3228.

# ATTRACTIONS

As Canada's capital city, Ottawa is home to a tremendous number of attractions. The area around Ottawa — Lanark County, Manotick, Burritts Rapids, Merrickville and the Gatineau Hills — also boasts attractions for visitors. This guide provides a selective list of the major attractions as discussed in the text. For a list of other attractions, consult Ottawa's local newspapers and tourist brochures. The guide *Street Smart* provides details of 60 monuments and sculptures displayed along or close to Confederation Boulevard, and the monthly magazine *Where. Ottawa-Hull* gives information on events and attractions. These guides are available at the Capital Infocentre, 90 Wellington Street, or call (613) 239-5000.

- Byward Market. Just east of Sussex Dr. and north of Rideau St. Since 1840s, the site of farmers' products, specialty shops, gourmet meats. Some of Ottawa's best restaurants are located in the Market. Historic buildings: Clarendon Court on George Street and Tin House Court on Clarence Street.
- Carleton University. Colonel By Drive; (613) 520-7400.
- Casino de Hull. Slot machines, gaming tables, restaurants. Located on Leamy Lake near Hull. East along Highway 148 to Leamy Lake Parkway. (819) 772-2100.
- Central Experimental Farm. Established in 1886. Agricultural research. Attractions include ornamental gardens, fields, Agricultural Museum (see Museums and Galleries), barns, stables, laboratories, greenhouses, Fletcher Wildlife Garden. Across Rideau Canal from Carleton University, at the juncture of NCC Driveway and Prince of Wales Dr.; (613) 991-3044.
- Chateau Laurier. Just east of Parliament Hill. Built in 1912 and named after Prime Minister Sir Wilfrid Laurier (1841-1919). (613) 241-1414.
- Chaudière Falls. Can be viewed from the Chaudière Bridge across to Hull.
- Chinatown. The area centred around Somerset Street, from Bronson Avenue to Preston Street.
- Corel Centre. Palladium Dr. in the west end. An 18,500-seat facility, opened in January 1996. Home of the NHL hockey team, the Ottawa Senators. Hosts a variety of entertainment. Tours are available. Tours (613) 599-0100. Entertainment (613) 599-0123.
- Dow's Lake and Pavilion. Two dams created this lake now popular

for recreation. The Dow's Lake Pavilion includes three restaurants and a terrace. (613) 232-1001.
- Confederation Boulevard. Ottawa's official ceremonial route. The route can be walked in about 90 minutes (without stopping to take in the sights) and takes you past many of Ottawa's landmarks.
- Conference Centre. Its original role was the Ottawa station of the Canadian National Railway. Today it hosts conferences. Across from the Chateau Laurier.
- Gatineau Park. A 20-minute drive from Ottawa. This is a 35,000-hectare park, with trails for hiking, cycling and cross-country skiing. Visitor Centre: 318 Meech Lake Rd., Chelsea, Quebec. (819) 827-2020.
- Hog's Back Falls. Located at the point where the Rideau Canal and the Rideau River separate. A favourite picnic site. Hog's Back Rd. at Colonel By Dr. (613) 239-5000.
- Jacques Cartier Park. In Hull on the Ottawa River between the Alexandra and Macdonald-Cartier Bridges. By the Canadian Museum of Civilization. Picnic site. The small stone house in the park was built by Philemon Wright, the founder of Hull.
- Lansdowne Park and Ottawa Civic Centre. 1015 Bank St. Large recreation complex and home of the Ottawa 67's, Ottawa's Junior A hockey team.
- Maison du Citoyen. 25 Laurier St., Hull. Site of Hull's municipal government. Contains a library, concert hall, art gallery, meeting rooms and restaurant. Tours are available. (819) 595-7175.
- Major's Hill Park. Ottawa's oldest park (1874). Built to commemorate Colonel By's contribution to the Ottawa region, it was originally named Colonel's Hill and renamed after By was succeeded by a Major. Sussex Dr. behind the Chateau Laurier.
- Mooney's Bay Park. Riverside Dr., Ottawa; (613) 564-1094.
- National Arts Centre. 53 Elgin St., Ottawa. A diverse, bilingual performing arts centre. Hosts hundreds of performances every year. (613) 947-7000.
- National Library and National Archives. 395 Wellington St., Ottawa. The National Library (1953) preserves the published heritage of Canada, and the National Archives (1872) contains manuscripts, government records, maps, paintings, prints and electronic information (television, film, radio recordings). Both institutions hold special exhibits. (613) 992-9988 (Library) and (613) 995-5138 (Archives).
- National Peacekeeping Monument. Corner of Sussex Dr. and St. Patrick St. *The Reconciliation* is the world's only monument to peacekeepers. It illustrates peacekeepers overseeing the reconciliation of warring factions. Beyond the monument is the "Sacred Grove".
- National War Memorial. In the centre of Confederation Square, at the junction of Wellington, Sparks and Elgin Streets. Dedicated in 1939. Symbolizes the passing of war into peace.
- Nepean Point. Just behind the National Gallery. Great view. A statue of Samuel de Champlain stands at the top of the hill. An open-air theatre is also located at this site (see Astrolabe Theatre).
- Notre-Dame Basilica. Ottawa's oldest church. Sussex Dr. at St. Patrick St.; (613) 241-7496. Open daily, 8 am to 5 pm for self-guided tours and prayer.
- Ottawa City Hall. 111 Sussex Dr. Tours are available by appointment only. (613) 244-5464.
- Park of the Provinces. Across from the National Library and the National Archives. Wellington St. at Bronson Ave.
- Parliament Hill. "The Hill" is home to the House of Commons, Senate, the Library of Parliament, the Hall of Honour and the Peace Tower and Memorial Chapel. Indoor and outdoor tours are available. Visit the Info-tent, a white tent between the Centre and West blocks, mid-May to 31 August. (613) 239-5000. No charge for tours and programs.
- Prime Minister's Residence, 24 Sussex Dr. Built in 1868 by a wealthy mill owner, and called "Gorfwysa," which in Welsh means

"Place of Peace". It was purchased by the Canadian government in 1943. It is not open to the public.

- Rideau Canal. Construction of this 202 kilometre canal was started in 1826 by Royal Engineer Lt.-Col. John By. The canal was completed in 1832.
- Rideau Hall. 1 Sussex Dr. This is the official residence of the Governor-General of Canada. The grounds of the estate are open daily from 9 am to one hour before sunset. Admission and tours are free. (613) 998-7113, or 1-800-465-6890.
- Rockcliffe Park. Small, exclusive village where many politicians and diplomats live.
- Rockcliffe Park with gardens and picnic area. Rockcliffe Parkway at Princess Ave.
- Royal Canadian Mint. 320 Sussex Dr. This is the national mint, and operates a large gold refinery. Includes boutique for coins and collector products. Guided tours are available. (613) 993-8990, or 1-800-276-7714 (Canada), or 1-800-268-6468 (USA); fax (613) 954-0601; http://www.rcmint.ca
- Sandy Hill. Area between Rideau St. and Highway 417. Heritage buildings are located in this area, as is Université d'Ottawa/University of Ottawa.
- Supreme Court of Canada. Wellington St. Canada's highest court. The lobby and courtroom are open to the public on weekdays from 9 am to 5 pm. Guided tours by reservation only. (613) 995-5361; fax (613) 996-3063.
- Université d'Ottawa/University of Ottawa. Bilingual university founded by the Oblates as St. Joseph's College in the 1840s. Located in Sandy Hill.
- Vincent Massey Park. Picnic area, playing fields, recreational paths. Parking fee charged from May to October. Across the road at Mooney's Bay, there is a marina and beach. Heron Rd., west of Riverside Dr.

## REGIONAL ATTRACTIONS

**Lanark County**

- Balderson Cheese Shop. A cheese factory from 1881 to 1986. Now a shop. Ice-cream, art, gourmet foods. Winner Specialty Food Retailers Award 1992. Village of Balderson. Highway 511. Open daily. (613) 267-4492.
- Code's Felt Mill. Built in 1842 and still manufacturing felt. 53 Harriot St., Perth. (613) 267-2464.
- District Court House and Registry Office. Built in 1872. Perth. (613) 267-2021 (Court House).
- Mill of Kintail Museum and Conservation Area. Museum has a display commemorating Dr. Robert Tait McKenzie. Picnic tables, playground, hiking. Highway 15.
- Victoria Woolen Mill. Historic building. Now a cafe and gallery. Almonte. (613) 256-0268.

**Manotick, Burritts Rapids and Merrickville**

- Arron Merrick Building and Jakes Block, Restored buildings. Merrickville.
- Baldachin Dining Lounge/Harry McLean's Pub. 111 St. Lawrence St., Merrickville. (613) 269-4223.
- Christ Church. Completed in 1832. Burritts Rapids.
- Community Hall. Originally a store built in 1841. Burritts Rapids.
- Gad's Hill Place. Restaurant with a Dickens theme. St. Lawrence St., Merrickville. (613) 269-2976.
- Goose and Gridiron. English-style pub in historic building. 317 St. Lawrence St., Merrickville. (613) 269-2094.

**Gatineau Hills**

- Wakefield Mill. A grist mill dating from 1838, then a museum. Now closed. Wakefield.
- Pink Lake. Unique eco-system in ancient glacial lake. Gatineau Park.

# FESTIVALS AND EVENTS

## WINTER

- Christmas Lights Across Canada. Early December to early January. Christmas lights, concerts and activities. Parliament Hill and Confederation Blvd; (613) 239-

5000 or 1-800-465-1867.

- "Deck the Halls". Late December to early January. Open house viewing in the Centre Block of Parliament. Parliament Hill. 5-9 pm. 1-800-465-1867.
- Winterlude. February. Celebrates Canada's northern way of life. Skating, concerts, fireworks, snow and ice sculpture competitions, and sporting events. National Capital Region; (613) 239-5000 or 1-800-465-1867.

## SPRING–SUMMER

**May**

- Canadian Tulip Festival. Activities include annual Flotilla, concerts, fireworks and the National Capital Marathon. Downtown Ottawa, especially Major's Hill Park, and the Tulip Route (a 15 kilometre road lined with tulip beds which follows the Rideau Canal). (613) 567-5757; fax (613) 567-6216; http://tulipfestival.ca
- National Capital Race Weekend. This is the annual Duck Race for Tiny Hearts. Approximately 100,000 plastic ducks race down the Rideau Canal to raise money for charity. Festival Plaza. (613) 234-2221; fax (613) 234-5880; email: ncm@synapse.net
- National Capital Air Show. Includes air show, rides, demonstrations. Macdonald-Cartier International Airport. Shuttle buses leave from downtown sites. (613) 526-1030; fax (613) 728-5547; web site http://ncas.ottawa.com

**June**

- Carnival of Cultures. Celebration and exploration of the cultures that make up Canada. Festival Plaza. (613) 692-5243 or (613) 742-6952.
- Children's Festival de la jeunesse. Plays, music. Canadian Museum of Nature. (613) 728-5863; fax (613) 728-5547; web site: www.childfest.ca
- Festival Franco-Ontarien. Presents francophone culture over several days, culminating with St.-Jean Baptiste Day celebrations on June 24. Music, comedy.
- Italian Week. Celebrates the food, music and dance of Italy. Preston Street. (613) 726-0920 or (613) 224-4388; fax (613) 727-6205. Manotick Fringe Festival.
- Alternative theatre. Mill Square, Village of Manotick. (613) 692-0548; fax (613) 692-5481.
- Musical Ride. Equestrian performances by the Royal Canadian Mounted Police; Canadian Police College. (613) 993-3751.
- Ottawa Fringe Festival. Last week of June. Theatre performances. Arts Court, 2 Daly Ave., Ottawa. (613) 232-6162; fax (613) 569-7660.

**June-July**

- Changing the Guard. June-August. Daily parade (10:00 am) of the Ceremonial Guard from Cartier Square Drill Hall to Parliament Hill. (613) 239-5000, or (613) 993-1811 or 1-800-465-1867.
- Festival Canada. Mid-June to mid-July. Opera, recitals, concerts, jazz, theatre, cabaret and workshops. National Arts Centre, Parliament Hill. (613) 996-5051; fax (613) 943-1400.
- Cultures Canada. Concerts, activities from the end of June to mid-July. Astrolabe Theatre. (613) 239-5000 or 1-800-465-1867.
- Hull's Twilight Concerts series. Concerts held June and July. Downtown Hull. (819) 595-7400; fax (819) 595-7425.
- National Capital Dragon Boat Race Festival. Celebrate Canada's Oriental heritage. Rideau Canoe Club, Mooney's Bay. (613) 238-7711; fax (613) 238-1078.

**July**

- Canada Day. July 1 — Canada's birthday. Concerts, fireworks. Parliament Hill and Major's Hill Park in Ottawa and Jacques Cartier Park in Hull. (613) 239-5000 or 1-800-465-1867.
- H.O.P.E. Beach Volleyball Tournament. 1,000 teams compete. Mooney's Bay Beach. (613) 237-1433; fax (613) 237-1601; web site: HOPE.magi.com/HOPE
- Ottawa Citizen Bluesfest. A new event, but attracts thousands of fans to hear the blues in Major's Hill Park. (613) 233-8798; fax (613) 567-8467.

Park. (613) 233-8798; fax (613) 567-8467.
- Ottawa International Jazz Festival. Music from avant gard to rhythm and blues. Confederation Park. (613) 594-3580; fax (613) 594-5519; web site: http://jazz.ottawa.com

**July-August**
- Ottawa Chamber Music Festival. End of July to the beginning of August. Since 1994. Local and national ensembles. Downtown Ottawa. (613) 234-8008; fax (613) 565-4338; web site: http://www.interlog.com/~ei/ocmf/
- Portuguese Festival. Celebrates the Portuguese community in Ottawa.

**August**
- Central Canada Exhibition. Entertainment, rides. Lansdowne Park. (613) 237-7222; fax (613) 230-1748; web site: http://www.the-ex.com
- CKCU/Sparks Street Ottawa International Busker Festival. Early August. Performers from across Canada. (613) 520-2898.
- CKCU Ottawa Folk Festival. Music, dance, entertainment. Britannia Park. (613) 520-2772; fax (613) 520-4060; website http://ottawafolk.org
- Fete Caribe. Celebration of Ottawa's Caribbean community.

### FALL

**September**
- Gatineau Hot Air Balloon Festival. Labour Day Weekend. One of the largest balloon events in North America. Gatineau. (819) 243-2330.

**October**
- Ottawa International Animation Festival. Every second year.

**November**
- European Union Film Festival. End of November. Two weeks of films at the National Library of Canada. (613) 992-9988.
- Lebanorama. Food, music, dance of Lebanon. Festival Plaza. (613) 742-6952; fax (613) 742-6953.

## MUSEUMS AND GALLERIES

We have tried to make this list as comprehensive as possible, including public galleries and museums. Consult the numbers provided or the Ottawa Yellow Pages for further information.

### ART GALLERIES

- Art Mode Gallery. 531 Sussex Dr. (Byward Market), Ottawa; (613) 241-1511; Hours: weekdays 10-6, Sat 10-5, Sun 11-4.
- Atrium Gallery, 101 Centrepointe Dr. (Nepean Civic Square), Nepean, (613) 727-6652. Hours: Mon-Fri 8:30-9, Sat 9-5, Sun 1-5.
- Calligrammes Gallery, 21 Murray St., Ottawa; (613) 241-4732. Hours: Wed-Fri 11-6, Sat 10-6, Sun 12-5.
- Carleton University Art Gallery. St. Patrick's Bldg., Carleton University; (613) 788-2120. Hours: Sept-May, Tues-Fri noon-7, Sat-Sun noon-5; June-Aug, Tues-Sun noon-6. No charge.
- Carmel Art Gallery Co. Ltd., 196 Bank St., Ottawa; (613) 232-4330. Hours: Mon-Sat 9-6.
- Darshan Gallery, 113 Murray St., Second Floor, Ottawa; (613) 241-7020. Hours: Mon-Sat 10-6, Fri 10-9. Sun noon-5.
- Echo Diffusart (Gallery), 55 Byward Market, Ottawa; (613) 241-7500. Hours: Nov-Easter daily 9:30-5:30, closed Monday; Easter-Oct daily 9:30-5:30.
- Galerie d'Art Jean-Claude Bergeron, 150 St. Patrick St., Ottawa; (613) 562-7836. Hours: Fri-Sun noon-5:30.
- Galerie D'Art Vincent. Chateau Laurier (1 Rideau St.), Ottawa; (613) 241-1144. Hours: Mon-Fri 9-6, Sat 9-5, Sun by appt.
- Inuit Art Showcase, 531 Sussex Dr., Ottawa; (613) 241-1511. Hours: Mon 10-4, Tues-Fri 10-6, Sat 10-5, Sun 11-4.
- The Jack Pine Gallery, 1292 Wellington St., Ottawa; (613) 724-7757. Hours: Tues-Sat 10-5.
- Karsh/Masson Gallery. Ottawa City Hall, 111 Sussex Dr., Ottawa; (613)

244-4430. Hours: daily 9-9.

- Koyman Gallery. Rideau Centre, Second floor, Ottawa; (613) 230-1847. Hours: Mon-Fri 9:30-9, Sat 9:30-6, Sun noon-5.
- National Gallery of Canada. 380 Sussex Dr. (Corner of Sussex Dr. and St. Patrick St.), Ottawa; (613) 990-1985. Hours: May-Oct, daily 10-6, Thurs 10-8; Nov-Apr, Wed-Sun 10-5, Thurs 10-8. Free admission to permanent collection, charges apply to special exhibits.
- The Ottawa Art Gallery, Arts Court, 2 Daly Ave., Ottawa; (613) 233-8699; fax (613) 569-7660. Hours: Tues-Fri 10-5, Thurs 10-8, Sat-Sun noon-5.
- Perspective Art Gallery, 2285 St. Laurent Blvd., Bldg C, Unit 5, Ottawa; (613) 247-1088. Hours: Mon-Sat 1-5, closed Sun.
- Robertson Galleries, 162 Laurier Ave. W., Ottawa; (613) 235-2459. Hours: open only by appt.
- Rothwell Gallery, 1718 Montreal Rd., Ottawa; (613) 745-6410. Hours: Tues-Thurs 10-6, Fri 10-7, Sat 10-4. Closed Sun and Mon.
- Saw Gallery, 67 Nicholas St. (Basement of Arts Court bulding), Ottawa; (613) 236-6181. Hours: Tues-Sat 11-6.
- Wallack Galleries, 203 Bank St., Ottawa; (613) 235-4339. Hours: Mon-Fri 9-5:30, Sat 9-5, closed Sun and Mon.

## MUSEUMS

- Agricultural Museum. Building 88, Central Experimental Farm. Across the Rideau Canal from Carleton University (juncture of National Capital Commission Driveway and Prince of Wales Drive). (613) 991-3044. Hours: Apr-Nov. 9-5 every day. Closed Dec-Mar. Admission.
- Billings Estate Museum. 2100 Cabot St.; (613) 247-4830. Hours: May-Oct, Sun-Thurs noon-5. Open by appt. only after Thanksgiving weekend. Admission.
- Bytown Museum. Just west of the Chateau Laurier; (613) 234-4570. Hours: Mon-Sat. 10-5, Sun 1-5; Oct-Nov, Mon-Fri 10-5, Dec-Apr open by appt. Admission.
- Canadian Museum of Civilization. 100 Laurier Street, Hull; (819) 776-7000 or 1-800-555-5621; fax (819) 776-8300; tours (819) 776-7014; http://www.cmcc.muse.digital.ca; Hours: To April 30, Tues-Sun 9-5; May-June every day 9-6, Thurs until 9; July-Aug, every day, 9-6, Thurs and Fri until 9; Sept-Dec. Tues-Sun 9-5. Admission. Free admission Sunday am 9-12.
- Canadian Museum of Contemporary Photography. 1 Rideau Canal; (613) 990-8257; fax (613) 990-6542; web site: http://cmcp.gallery.ca or http://mcpc.beaux-arts.ca. Hours: May-Labour Day, Mon, Tues, Fri, Sat, Sun 11-5, Wed 4-8, Thurs 11-8. Labour Day-April, Wed, Fri, Sat, Sun 11-5, Thurs 11-8, closed Mon, Tues. Free admission.
- Canadian Museum of Nature. Corner of Metcalfe and McLeod Streets; (613) 566-4700 or 1-800-263-4433; fax (613) 364-4021; clucas@mus-nature.ca . Hours: May-Sept daily 9:30-5, Thurs 9:30-8; Oct-April daily 10-5, Thurs 10-8; Half-price admission Thurs until 5 pm, free admission Thurs after 5 pm. Free Admission Canada Day, July 1.
- Canadian Ski Museum. 457A Sussex Drive. (613) 722-3584.
- Canadian War Museum. 330 Sussex Dr. Sister museum of the Canadian Museum of Civilization; (819) 776-8600, tours (819) 776-8627; fax (819) 776-8623; http://www.cmcc.muse.digital.ca. Hours: open same hours as the Canadian Museum of Civilization. Admission.
- Children's Museum. Inside the Canadian Museum of Civilization; (819) 776-7001. Hours: Jan-Apr, Tues to Sun, 9-5, (closed Monday); May-June, daily 9-5. Admission.
- Currency Museum, Bank of Canada, 245 Sparks St., Ottawa; (613) 782-8914. Hours: Tues to Sat 10:30-5; Sun 1-5. (Open Mon from May 1 to Labour Day). Admission. Free admission on Tues.
- Laurier House. 335 Laurier Ave. E. Ottawa; (613) 992-8142. Hours: Winter Tues-Sat 10-5, Sun 2-5; Summer Tues-Sat 9-5, Sun 2-5. Closed Mon. Admission.
- Logan Hall. Geological Survey of Canada. 601 Booth St., Ottawa;

(613) 995-4261. Hours: weekdays, 8-4, closed weekends and holidays. Free admission.

- National Aviation Museum. Aviation Parkway, (Rockcliffe Airport), Ottawa; (613) 993-2010, 1-800-463-2038; fax (613) 990-3655; kinsella@fox.nstn.ca. Hours: May-Labour Day daily 9-5, Thurs until 9; Labour Day-April, daily 10-5. Admission. Free admission Thurs 5-9.
- National Museum of Science and Technology. 1867 St. Laurent Blvd. Ottawa; (613) 991-3044. Hours: May-early Sept, daily 9-5, Thurs 9-9; mid-Sept-Apr, Tues-Sun 9-5, Thurs 9-9. Free admission on Thurs 5-9 pm.
- National Postal Museum. Inside the Canadian Museum of Civilization, 100 Laurier St., Hull; (819) 776-7000, 1-800-555-5651. Same hours as Canadian Museum of Civilization. Admission.

### REGIONAL MUSEUMS AND GALLERIES

- Heritage House Museum, Old Slys Rd., Smith Falls; (613) 283-8560. Hours: Mon-Fri 8:30-4:30, Sat-Sun 11-4:30. Admission.
- Mackenzie King Estate. In Gatineau Park. Includes three residences: Kingswood, Moorside and the Farm (now the official residence of the Speaker of the House of Commons). Visitor Information Centre (819) 827-2020. Hours: May-June, Mon-Wed 11-5; June-Oct, daily 11-5; closed winter. Admission.
- Mississippi Valley Textile Museum. 3 Rosamond St., E. Almonte; (613) 256-3754. Hours: mid-May to mid-Oct Wed-Sun 11-4:30. Admission.
- Perth Museum. 11 Gore St. E., Perth; (613) 267-1947. Hours: Mon-Fri 10-5, Sat 11-4. Closed Sundays. Admission.
- Railway Museum. Williams St., Smith Falls; (613) 283-5696. Summer hours: Wed-Sun 10-4. Admission.
- Rideau Canal Museum. 34 Beckwith St. S., Smith Falls; (613) 284-0505. Hours: Summer/Fall: 11-4:30 daily. Admission.
- Mill of Kintail Museum. Ramsey Township. Concession Rd. #8, near Almonte; (613) 256-3610. Summer: Wed-Sun 10:30-4:30.

## THEATRES AND CINEMAS

### LIVE THEATRE

- Arts Court. 2 Daly Ave., Ottawa; (613) 233-8699 (gallery) or (613) 564-7240 (theatre programming).
- Astrolabe Theatre. Outdoor theatre on Nepean Point behind the National Gallery. Summertime venue for concerts produced by the National Capital Commission; (613) 239-5000 or 1-800-465-1867.
- Cumberland Town Hall Theatre. 255 Centrum Blvd., Orleans; (613) 830-6204.
- Dramamuse. In-house theatre company at the Canadian Museum of Civilization; (819) 776-7000 or 1-800-555-5621.
- Great Canadian Theatre Company, 910 Gladstone Ave., Ottawa K1R 6Y4; (613) 236-5196; fax (613) 232-2075; email: aw982@freenet.carleton.ca
- Twilight Concert series of summer weekend performances to highlight Canada's cultural mosaic. Canadian Museum of Civilization; (819) 776-7000, 1-800-555-5621.
- Le Groupe Dance Lab, 2-2 Daly Ave., Ottawa K1N 6E2; (613) 235-1492; fax (613) 235-1651; bj581@freenet.carleton.ca.
- Odyssey Theatre. 2 Daly Ave., Ottawa K1N 6E2; (613) 232-8407; fax (613) 564-4428.
- Opera Lyra Ottawa, 110-2 Daly Ave., Ottawa K1N 6E2; (613) 233-9200; fax (613) 233-5431.
- Ottawa Little Theatre, 400 King Edward Ave., Ottawa K1N 7M7; (613) 233-8948; fax (613) 233-8027.
- Rascals, Roots and Rads. A summer series offered by the National Gallery, 380 Sussex Dr. Children's entertainers, folk music, and new artists; (613) 990-1985.
- Salamander Theatre for Young Audiences. 2 Daly Ave., Ottawa; (613) 569-5629.
- "See and Hear the World." During the fall and winter. Annual

showcase of performing artists from across the world. Canadian Museum of Civilization. 100 Laurier St., Hull; (819) 776-7000 or 1-800-555-5621.
- Theatre la Catapult, 2 Daly Ave., Ottawa; (613) 233-0851.

## CINEMAS

This is a listing of cinemas in the Ottawa area. For further listings, check the Ottawa telephone directory.
- Bytowne Cinema, 325 Rideau, 789-3456.
- Canadian Film Institute, 2 Daly Ave., 232-6727.
- Cine-Campus, 101 St. Jean Bosco, 773-1888.
- Somerset Cineplex Odeon, 386 Somerset W., 2369528.
- World Exchange Cineplex Odeon, 111 Albert St., East Ottawa, 233-0209.
- St. Laurent Cinemas, St. Laurent Shopping Centre, 746-8822.
- Vanier Cineplex Odeon, 150 Montreal Rd., Vanier, West Ottawa, 749-4145.
- Westgate Cinemas, Westgate Shopping Centre, 725-2229.
- Famous Players Inc., 50 Rideau, 234-3712.
- Mayfair Theatre, 1074 Bank St., 730-3403.
- Westend Family Cinema, 710 Broadview Ave, 772-8218.

## DINNER THEATRE

- Eddie May Murder Mysteries, 881 Bellevue Ave., Ottawa: (613) 729-8832; http://ventures.ca/murder.mystery

# RECREATION

## AMUSEMENT PARKS

- The Midway Family Fun Centre. 2277 Gladwin Crescent, Ottawa; (613) 526-0343.

## SPECTATOR SPORTS

**Baseball**
- Ottawa Lynx Baseball Club. AAA farm team of the Montreal Expos. 300 Coventry Rd., Ottawa K1K 4P5; (613) 749-9947, or 1-800-663-0985; fax (613) 747-0003; lynx@magi.com OR http://www.magi.com/lynx/. April-September. Admission charge.

**Hockey**
- Ottawa Senators Hockey Club. NHL action at the Corel Centre. 1000 Palladium Dr., Kanata, Ontario K2V 1A4; (613) 599-0250, or 1-800-444-7367. September to April.

**Horse Racing**
- Rideau Carleton Raceway, 4837 Albion Rd., Gloucester, Ontario K1X 1A3; (613) 822-2211; fax (613) 822-1586. Live harness racing Wednesday, Friday and Saturday nights, and Sunday afternoons. Open May to November.

## ACTIVITIES

**Bird Watching**
- Arboretum at the Experimental Farm. Beside Dow's Lake
- Britannia Filtration Plant. Take Carling west to Britannia Road. Turn right and head north to the yacht club, then turn right at Cassels Street.
- Mer Bleu. In the Ottawa greenbelt.
- Ottawa Field Naturalists Club maintains a bird status hotline (613) 722-3050 for details of bird sightings around Ottawa.

**Canoeing, Kayaking, Windsurfing and Swimming**
- Britannia Bay is the best place for windsurfing in Ottawa. On the Ottawa River, just west of downtown.
- Carleton University Pool. Colonel By Drive. (613) 520-5631.
- Dow's Lake Pavilion, 1001 Queen Elizabeth Dr., Ottawa K1S 5K7; (613) 232-1001; fax (613) 232-1245. Pedal boats, canoes, bicycle and in-line skate rentals. Open year-round.
- Gatineau Park. There are three big lakes in the park which are great for water sports.
- Ottawa River. It's difficult to get to the shore, but once on the river,

you get a great view of Ottawa.
- Rideau Canal. You can rent canoes at Dow's Lake marina.
- Rideau River. Canoes can enter the river at any of the parks along its banks, but avoid the waterfall at Hog's Back Park and the rapids at Vincent Massey Park.
- University of Ottawa Pool. 125 University Drive. (613) 562-5789.
- YM-YWCA, 180 Argyle St., (613) 788-5000.

**Cycling**
- Gatineau Park. Challenging trials for mountain biking and paved roads with steep hills for touring. 15 minutes by bike from downtown. (819) 827-2020.
- Ottawa. There is a network of 130 kilometres of recreational cycling/walking paths.
- Every Sunday morning from end of May until after Labour Day, three roads are closed to cars: Ottawa River Parkway from the Portage Bridge to Carling Avenue, the Rockcliffe Driveway from the Aviation Museum to St. Joseph Boulevard, and Colonel By Drive from the Laurier Avenue bridge to Hog's Back.

**Cross-country Skiing**
- Camp Fortune. Challenging terrain and wide variety of trails for intermediate and advanced skiers.
- Central Experimental Farm. Across the Rideau Canal from Carleton University, (juncture of NCC Driveway and Prince of Wales Dr.). (613) 991-3044.
- Gatineau Park. 190 kilometres of groomed trails, marked by their level of difficulty. (819) 827-2020.
- Greenbelt. Maps are available at Capital Information Centre, 90 Wellington St.
- Lac Philippe. Good track-set skiing at the beginner level. In Gatineau Park. Take Highway 5, then Highway 366 west. Turn left at the Lac Phillipe sign. User fees for access to beaches in summer and cross-country ski trails in winter.
- Mer Bleu Conservation Area. In Ottawa's greenbelt. Southeast edge of Ottawa. Follow Innes Road to Anderson Road, then south to Dolman Ridge Road and then follow signs.
- Mooney's Bay. Has easy track-set trails. Riverside Drive, Ottawa. (613) 564-1094.
- Ottawa River. Ski on the river.
- Rideau Canal. Ski on the canal.

**Downhill Skiing and Snowboarding**
- Edelweiss Valley Ski Resort, RR#2, Wakefield, Quebec J0X 3G0; (819) 459-2328; fax (819) 459-3481. 18 runs. Open November to April. About 30 minutes from Ottawa.
- Mont Ste-Marie. About an hour north of Ottawa. Night skiing, ski instruction, discount packages.
- Mount Packenham. 45 minutes west of Ottawa. Instruction, good place for beginners and children.
- Ski Fortune. Box L0 (Gatineau Park), Old Chelsea, Quebec, J0X 1N0; (819) 827-1717; fax (819) 827-3893. 15 minutes from Ottawa. Lessons.
- Vorlage. Wakefield, about 25 minutes north of Ottawa. A good family ski hill.

**Golfing (Public courses only)**
- Canadian Golf and Country Club, RR#4, Ashton, Ontario K0A 1B0; (613) 780-3565; fax (613) 253-3292. 27-hole, semi-private. April to October.
- Highlands Golf Club, Highway 15 at McWatty Rd., Pakenham, Ontario K0A 2X0; (613) 624-5550; fax (613) 752-2031. Championship course. March to November.
- Manderley on the Green, RR#3, North Gower, Ontario K0A 2T0; (613) 489-2092; fax (613) 489-2046. Call to set tee off times (489-2066).
- Mont Cascades Golf Club, 915 ch. Mont Cascades, Cantley, Quebec J8V 3B2; (819) 459-2980; fax (819) 459-3562. Located in Gatineau Hills. Open April to October.
- National Golf Course Owners' Association, Box 11027, Station H, Nepean Ontario K2H 7T8; (613) 826-1046, or 1-800-660-0091; fax (613) 826-1046. Information for golf courses in Ottawa area.

**Hiking**
- Gatineau Park. Numerous maintained trails. Some are

universally accessible. Information: (819) 827-2020.
- Ottawa's Greenbelt. This is a rural area surrounding Ottawa's core. Almost 100 kilometres of hiking, skiing and nature trials.
- Pink Lake. Boardwalk around the lake. Gatineau Park.
- Stony Swamp Conservation Area. Not really a swamp, encompasses a variety of habitats. 38 kilometres of trails. Moodie Drive and Knoxdale Road, within the Greenbelt.

**Rafting**
- Equinox Adventures, Box 161, Grand Calumet Island, Quebec J0X 1J0; 1-800-785-8855. May to September.
- Esprit Rafting, Box 463, Pembroke, Ontario K8A 6X7; (819) 683-3241 or 1-800-596-RAFT (7238); fax (819) 683-3641; esprit@iosphere.net. Open April to October.
- OWL Rafting, Box 29, Forester's Falls, Ontario K0J 1V0; (613) 238-7238, or 1-800-461-7238; fax (613) 234-4097; owlmkc@fox.nstn.ca. Open May to September.
- RiverRun Paddling Centre, Box 179, Beachburg Ontario K0J 1C0; (613) 646-2501 or 1-800-267-8504; fax (613) 646-2958; riverrun@icacomp.com. Open May to September.
- Wilderness Tours, Box 89, Beachburg, Ontario K0J 1C0; (613) 646-2291 or 1-800-267-9166; fax (613) 646-2996. Open May to August.

**In-line Skating**
- Recreational paths around Ottawa are popular for in-line skating.

**Skating**
- Rideau Canal. An eight-kilometre-long groomed outdoor skating surface. In the evening the ice is lit up and there are warming shacks for putting on your skates. There are also fast-food stalls along the canal. Ice conditions: (613) 239-5234.

# SHOPPING

**Antiques and Flea markets**
- Antique District. Cross the bridge beside the stadium at Lansdowne Park to enter the antique district. Numerous small shops.
- Ottawa Antique Market. About 40 dealers have stalls. 1179-A Bank St.; (613) 730-6000.
- Stittsville Fleamarket. Located in Stittsville, just west of Ottawa. About 250 vendors. (613) 836-5617.

**Books**
- The Bookery of Ottawa. Specializes in children's books. 541 Sussex Dr.; (613) 241-1428.
- Books Canada. Books about Canada or by Canadians. 71 Sparks St.; (613) 236-0629.
- Chapters. Huge bookstore. Includes Starbucks Café. 47 Rideau St.; (613) 241-0073.
- Food for Thought Books. Specializes in cookbooks from around the world. 103 Clarence St., Ottawa; (613) 562-4599.
- Nicholas Hoare. Book store, specializing in literary books. 419 Sussex Dr.; (613) 562-2665.
- Renouf Books. Specializes in government (federal, provincial, international) publications. 71-1/2 Sparks St.; (613) 238-8985; fax (613) 238-6041; http://www.renoufbooks.com.

**Children's Games/Toys**
- Mrs. Tiggy Winkle's. Children's toys and games. 809 Bank St.; (613) 234-3836; Rideau Centre: (613) 230-8081.

**Clothing**
- Eaton's. Canadian department store. 1 Mackenzie King Bridge; (613) 560-5311.
- Holt Renfrew. Canada's most exclusive department store. 240 Sparks St., Ottawa, K1P 6B5; (613) 238-2200; fax (613) 238-6223.
- Justine's. Women's clothes. 541 Sussex Dr.; (613) 562-4000.
- Kaliyana Artwear. Women's clothes. 515 Sussex St.; (613) 562-3676.
- Norma Peterson Fashions. Clothes

for women by a Canadian designer. 167 Sparks St.; (613) 230-8455.
- Marks & Spencer. English chainstore, clothes, British foodstuff. 194 Sparks St.; (613) 238-8761.
- Puerta del Sol Sunwear. Swim wear. 335 Cumberland St.; (613) 789-4372.
- Richard Robinson's Maison de Haute Couture. Local designer of haute couture. 447 Sussex Dr.; (613) 241-5233.

**Crafts/Canadiana/Art**
- Art Mode Gallery. Predominantly Canadian art works and reproductions. 531 Sussex Dr., Ottawa K1N 6Z6; (613) 241-1511; fax (613) 241-6030; artmode@magi.com
- Canada's Four Corners. Indian and Inuit art and crafts. 93 Sparks St., Ottawa K1P 5B5; (613) 233-2322; fax (613) 233-6678.
- Galerie lynda greenberg. All-Canadian crafts and art. 13 Murray St., Ottawa K1N 9M5; (613) 241-2767.
- Giraffe. The African Store. Tribal masks, African arts and crafts. 111 Clarence St.; (613) 562-0284.
- O'Shea's Market Ireland. Celtic clothes and gifts. 91 Sparks St.; (613) 235-5141.
- Quichua Crafts. Wool sweaters from Ecuador. 799 Bank St.; (613) 567-7767.
- Snapdragon Fine Crafts. All-Canadian craft shop. 791 Bank St.; (613) 233-1296.
- Snow Goose Handicrafts. Indian and Inuit art and crafts. 83 Sparks St., Ottawa K1P 5A5; (613) 232-2213

**Gifts**
- The Country Clover Co. Traditional pine furniture and gifts. 55 William St.; (613) 241-3899.
- Cows Ottawa. Cow paraphanelia. 43 Clarence St., (in Times Square Bldg). (613) 789-2697.
- Dilemme. Flying angels from Bali. 785 Bank St.; (613) 233-0445.
- Nocean. Gift shop. 159 Sparks St.; (613) 233-6700.
- Oh Yes Ottawa. Canadian gifts. Rideau Centre, Level 3; (613) 569-7520; fax (613) 569-7519.
- Ottawa Souvenirs & Gifts. Canadian gifts. 50 Rideau St.; (613) 233-0468.
- Rubynak. Gift shop. 101 Sparks St.; (613) 230-7656.
- True South Trading. Nose rings from Thailand. 827 Bank St.; (613) 233-2026.

**Jewelry/Collectibles**
- East Wind. Chinese figurines. 794 Bank St.; (613) 567-0382.
- Kulu Trading. Clothing, Jewellery and merchandise from the Far East. 6 York St.; (613) 562-3815.
- Lilliput. Miniatures and dollhouses. 9 Murray; (613) 241-1183.
- McIntosh & Watts Ltd. English china by Wedgewood and Royal Crown Derby. Crystal, silver, miniatures. 193 Sparks St.; (613) 236-9644.
- Striking Galeria Museo de Oro. Jewellery, especially gold. 531-A Sussex Dr.; (613) 562-9398.
- Universal Coins and Collectibles. Coins from around the world. 210 - 47 Clarence St.; (613) 241-1404 or 1-800-668-2646; fax (613) 241-4568.

**General Goods**
- Southern Accent. Houseware imports from Mexico. 86-B Murray; (613) 562-0782.
- The Valley Goods Company. Old-fashioned general store. 41 York St.; (613) 241-3000.
- Thorne & Co. Gargoyles and pots for the garden. 802 Bank St.; (613) 232-6565

# Index

# PHOTO CREDITS

Legend: Top - T; Centre - C; Bottom - B

Photographs by David Barbour, except for those listed below:
Peggy McCalla: maps; 1997 Barnett Newman Foundation/Artists Rights Society (ARS), New York: p. 55T; Art Mode Gallery: p. 86C; Bytown Museum: p. 81C&B; Canadian Museum of Civilization: p. 57T&B; p. 58T&B; p. 59T,C&B; p. 60T,C&B; Canadian Museum of Nature: p. 65T; p. 66T&B; p. 67T,C&B; p. 68T,C&B; Canadian Tourism Commission: cover; p. 38B;p. 43B; p. 113B; p. 116T; Canadian War Museum: p. 82T&B; House of Commons: p. 34T; p. 35B; p. 37T;p. 39B; 40B; p. 41T; Houston, Diane: p. 45B; Johnson, Steve: p. 92B; Laframboise, Luc: p. 89T; Malak Photographers Limited: p. 77T,C&B; p. 78T; Maple Lawn Cafe: p. 93B; 94T; Merrithew, Jim: p. 109T; p. 110T; p. 112T; p. 112C; p. 114T; McElligott, W.P.: p. 80B; p. 81T; National Capital Commission: p. 18T; 42B; p. 104T&B; p. 105T;p. 106C; p. 107T; p. 108T&B; National Gallery of Canada: p. 13T; p. 83; p. 30B; p. 31; p. 52T&B; p. 53T, C&B; p. 54T,C&B; p. 55T&B; p. 56T&B; National Library and National Archives of Canada: p. 80T; National Museum of Aviation: p. 78B; Oh Yes Ottawa: p. 87C; Ottawa Tourism: p. 18BR; 151B; Snow Goose: p. 84B; Ville de Hull: p. 119T; p. 121B; p. 122T; Whiten, Colette: p. 54C.

**Canadian Cataloguing in Publication Data**
Ottawa
(Colourguide series)
Includes index.
ISBN 0-88780-396-2
1. Ottawa (Ont.) — Guidebooks. I. Martin, Carol. II. Burns, Kevin. III. Barbour, David. IV. Series
FC3096.18.083 1997 917.13'84044 C97-950011-7
F1059.5.09087 1997